DORSET FLIGHT

The Complete History

RODNEY LEGG

Dorset Publishing Company
National School North Street Wincanton Somerset BA9 9AT

To **Michelle and Steve Lusher**
in their wedding year

Copyright
First published MMI, copyright Rodney Legg © 2001. All rights reserved. No part of this publication may be reproduced, stored in a retrieval system, or transmitted in any form by any means, electronic, computerised, recorded, photographed, photocopied or otherwise, without prior permission in writing from the author and publisher.

Printing credits
Typeset by Julia Crabb with design and layout by Julie Green. Set in Verona 12 on 14pt. Printed by F W B Printing at Bennetts Mead, Southgate Road, Wincanton, Somerset BA9 9EB. Telephone 01-963-33755.

Publishing details
Published by Dorset Publishing Company at Wincanton Press, National School, North Street, Wincanton, Somerset BA9 9AT. Telephone 01-963-32583.

Distribution
Trade distribution and library sales by Halsgrove from Lower Moor Way, Tiverton, Devon EX16 6SS. Telephone 01-884-243-242. E-mail: sales@halsgrove.com

Updatings
Information for further editions will be welcomed by the author, Rodney Legg, at Wincanton Press, National School, North Street, Wincanton, Somerset BA9 9AT.

International standard book number
ISBN 0 948699 71 X

Preface

For me the wonder of childhood was in the sky. Aircraft of all types, from pre-war biplanes to the latest airliners and fighters came over my home in Moordown, Bournemouth, which was between two operational airfields. The Airspeed Ambassador was being built at Christchurch and there was a constant roar of aeroengines being tested at Hurn. One day we heard that the huge Bristol Brabazon was approaching on what, sadly, was to be a crucial dis-proving flight from Filton. It turned above the Stour meadows as we stood on what was still waste ground on the corner of Malvern Road and Homeside Road with an open view northwards across the valley. Overhead for the next decade were military Vampires and Sea Vixens and the lumbering Bristol freighter — with bulbous bow door like that of the Horsa glider — car-carrying from Hurn Aerodrome to the Channel Islands.

One of my early escapes from Easter Road was to the Farnborough Air Show where I sat at the controls of a captured auto-giro from a German U-boat. The closest I've come to that almost totally exposed position in the air, over sea, rocks and cliffs at breathtaking proximity, was navigating a Bell helicopter which had its doors removed so that an Independent Television News cameraman could hang out in the hope of filming botulism-infected seagulls dying on Steep Holm island in the Bristol Channel. Otherwise, with the single exception of being a passenger on a wartime Dakota as it flew over the D-Day beaches during the fiftieth anniversary celebrations for the Battle of Normandy, my relatively few flying hours have been as routine as they come, which after 11 September 2001 is the only sort of aviation I wish to experience.

The thrilling moments of the grounded kind, with 12-year-old contemporary Norman Chislett in 1959, included clambering on to the flight-deck of one of the last flying-boats in Poole Harbour, City of Liverpool, as she lay like a beached whale on the shore at Hamworthy.

As an historian, most of my flying anecdotes and records have been collected from the comfort and security of the ground. They span aviation's first century and include personal interviews with Great War fighter pilot Yvone Kirkpatrick and Westland's test-pilot Harald Penrose whose greatest Dorset and world first was to fly higher than the highest point on Earth — over Poole Bay — in order to prove that an aeroplane could conquer Everest. My ultimate hero, who I never met but now realise retired and died in a ramshackle cottage across the hill from mine, was Louis Arbon Strange of Worth Matravers. No other fighter pilot saw combat in the Great War for the full duration from the first-wave arrivals of the Royal Flying Corps in August 1914 through to front-line operations on Armistice Day in 1918. Then he pioneered civilian flying before returning to the Royal Air Force in the Second World War, to bring home a Hurricane from the fall of France, and went on to mastermind the training of paratroops. A taste of these and other highlights are to be found in what I have listed as "Dorset firsts" — an amazing catalogue of county feats and records — which have been the inspiration for this research.

My first failed job interview was with Flight Refuelling Limited in Wimborne, which was probably for the best as it resulted in my going to the Atomic Energy Establishment on Winfrith Heath for six months, followed by leave from Dorset as a reporter in Basildon New Town for four years. The subsequent three decades back in residence and producing county and regional magazines has seen me taking every opportunity to interview survivors of the Battle of Britain including returnees to RAF Warmwell. Little of the front-line aerodrome survives on the ground which has since been literally torn asunder for huge sand and gravel pits and is now being recycled into the new village of Crossways. Fortunately its wartime watering hole has still offers a warm welcome and is where this introduction is being written.

Rodney Legg,
at the Frampton Arms, Moreton
17 ix MMI

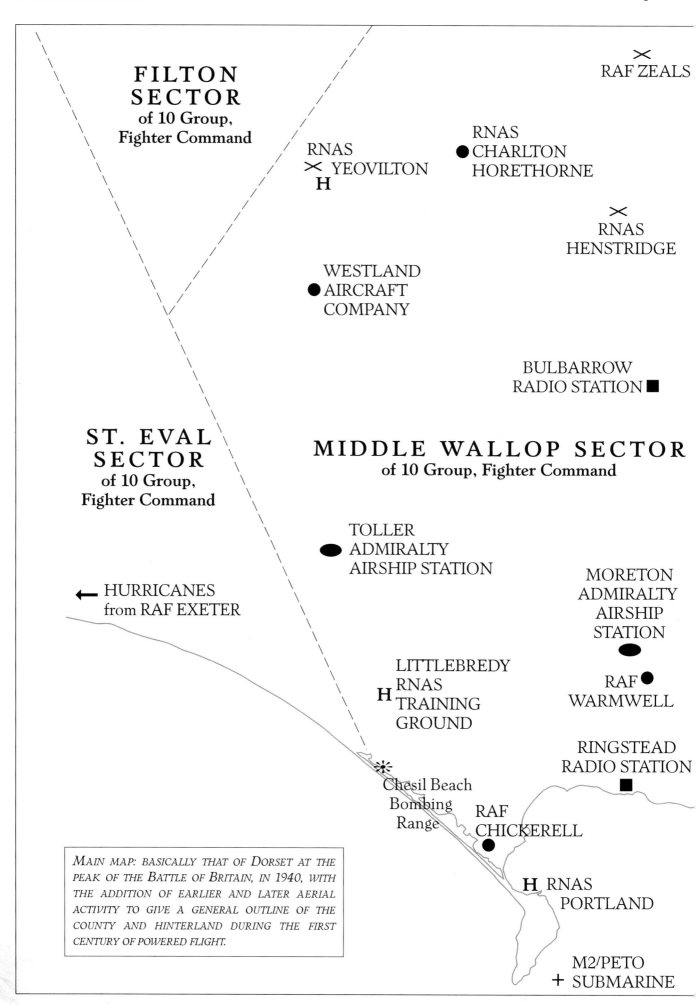

FILTON
SECTOR
of 10 Group,
Fighter Command

× RAF ZEALS

RNAS
× YEOVILTON
H

RNAS
● CHARLTON
HORETHORNE

× RNAS
HENSTRIDGE

WESTLAND
● AIRCRAFT
COMPANY

BULBARROW
RADIO STATION ■

ST. EVAL
SECTOR
of 10 Group,
Fighter Command

MIDDLE WALLOP SECTOR
of 10 Group, Fighter Command

TOLLER
● ADMIRALTY
AIRSHIP STATION

MORETON
ADMIRALTY
AIRSHIP
STATION

← HURRICANES
from RAF EXETER

LITTLEBREDY
RNAS
H TRAINING
GROUND

RAF ●
WARMWELL

RINGSTEAD
RADIO STATION
■

☀
Chesil Beach
Bombing
Range

RAF
CHICKERELL
●

H RNAS
PORTLAND

M2/PETO
+ SUBMARINE

MAIN MAP: BASICALLY THAT OF DORSET AT THE PEAK OF THE BATTLE OF BRITAIN, IN 1940, WITH THE ADDITION OF EARLIER AND LATER AERIAL ACTIVITY TO GIVE A GENERAL OUTLINE OF THE COUNTY AND HINTERLAND DURING THE FIRST CENTURY OF POWERED FLIGHT.

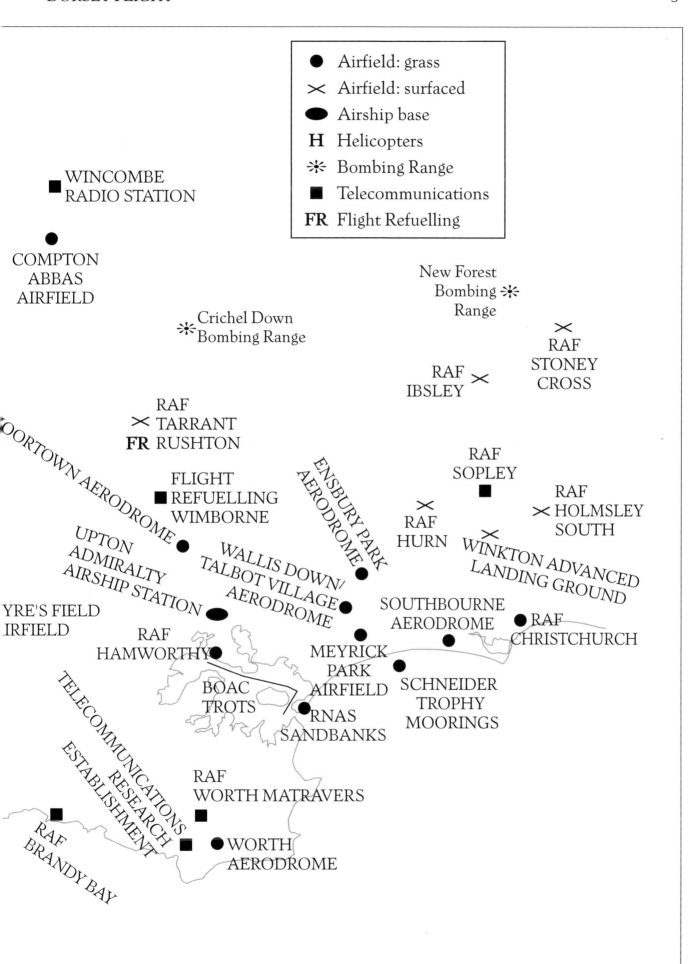

Airfield: grass
Airfield: surfaced
Airship base
H Helicopters
Bombing Range
Telecommunications
FR Flight Refuelling

WINCOMBE
RADIO STATION

COMPTON
ABBAS
AIRFIELD

Crichel Down
Bombing Range

New Forest
Bombing
Range

RAF
STONEY
CROSS

RAF
IBSLEY

RAF
TARRANT
FR RUSHTON

RAF
SOPLEY

RAF
HOLMSLEY
SOUTH

OORTOWN AERODROME

FLIGHT
REFUELLING
WIMBORNE

ENSBURY PARK
AERODROME

RAF
HURN

WINKTON ADVANCED
LANDING GROUND

UPTON
ADMIRALTY
AIRSHIP STATION

WALLIS DOWN/
TALBOT VILLAGE
AERODROME

SOUTHBOURNE
AERODROME

RAF
CHRISTCHURCH

YRE'S FIELD
IRFIELD

RAF
HAMWORTHY

MEYRICK
PARK
AIRFIELD

SCHNEIDER
TROPHY
MOORINGS

BOAC
TROTS

RNAS
SANDBANKS

TELECOMMUNICATIONS
RESEARCH
ESTABLISHMENT

RAF
WORTH MATRAVERS

RAF
BRANDY BAY

WORTH
AERODROME

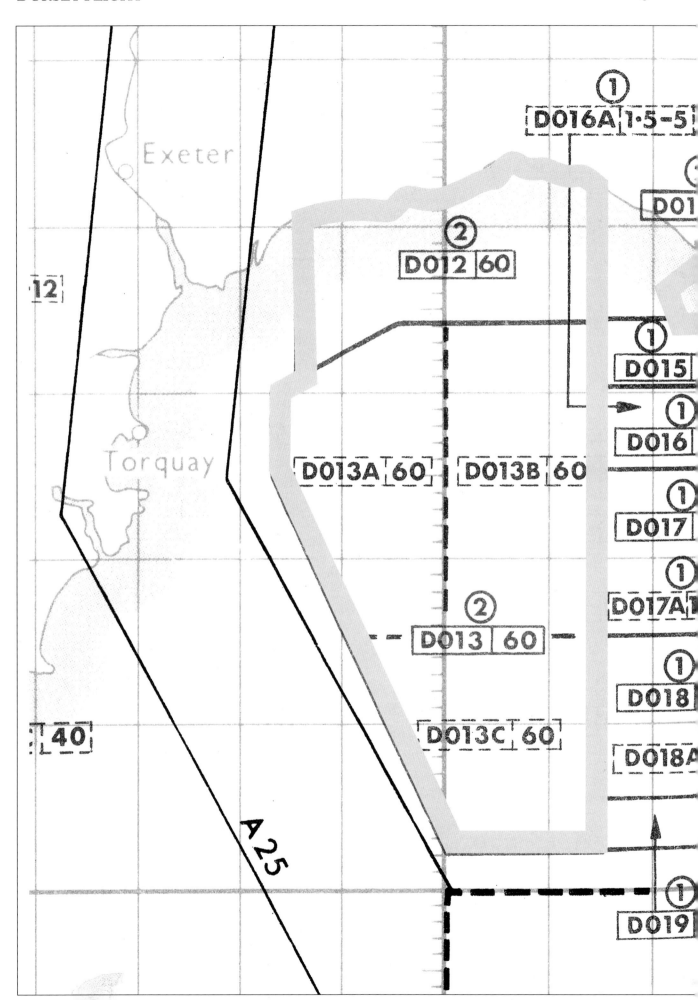

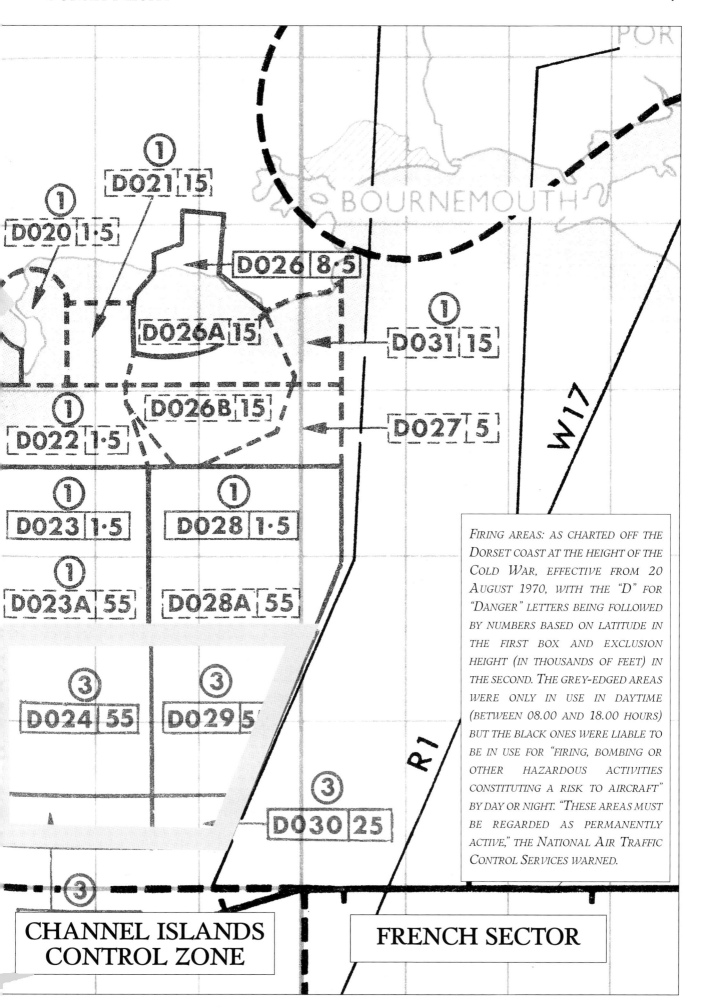

① DO21 15

① DO20 1·5

DO26 8·5

DO26A 15

BOURNEMOUTH

① DO31 15

DO26B 15

① DO22 1·5

DO27 5

W17

① DO23 1·5

① DO28 1·5

① DO23A 55

DO28A 55

③ DO24 55

③ DO29 5

③ DO30 25

R1

FIRING AREAS: AS CHARTED OFF THE DORSET COAST AT THE HEIGHT OF THE COLD WAR, EFFECTIVE FROM 20 AUGUST 1970, WITH THE "D" FOR "DANGER" LETTERS BEING FOLLOWED BY NUMBERS BASED ON LATITUDE IN THE FIRST BOX AND EXCLUSION HEIGHT (IN THOUSANDS OF FEET) IN THE SECOND. THE GREY-EDGED AREAS WERE ONLY IN USE IN DAYTIME (BETWEEN 08.00 AND 18.00 HOURS) BUT THE BLACK ONES WERE LIABLE TO BE IN USE FOR "FIRING, BOMBING OR OTHER HAZARDOUS ACTIVITIES CONSTITUTING A RISK TO AIRCRAFT" BY DAY OR NIGHT. "THESE AREAS MUST BE REGARDED AS PERMANENTLY ACTIVE," THE NATIONAL AIR TRAFFIC CONTROL SERVICES WARNED.

③

CHANNEL ISLANDS CONTROL ZONE

FRENCH SECTOR

A-Z format

with self-indexing entries

AVIATION HISTORIAN: MOTHER GLADYS LEGG AND AUTHOR RODNEY LEGG ON A U-BOAT AUTOGIRO AT THE ROYAL AIRCRAFT ESTABLISHMENT, FARNBOROUGH, SHOWING THE WISDOM OF THE OLD ADAGE ABOUT CATCHING THEM YOUNG.

A

Abbotsbury crashes — New Zealand Squadron Leader Terence Lovell-Gregg fell to his death at Abbotsbury Swannery from a Hurricane of 87 Squadron from RAF Exeter [15 August 1940]. He had led his men against impossible odds, head-on at 18,000 feet into a vast "Beehive" of German aircraft that were attacking Portland.

Opposite, on the pebbles of the Chesil Beach, Pilot Officer Maxwell had better luck when he crash-landed Hurricane L1764 on the day the Luftwaffe blitzed Sherborne [30 September 1940].

ADDLS — Aerodrome Dummy Deck Landing System, practised on a pad at Henstridge Royal Naval Air Station that was laid out like the deck of an aircraft-carrier, with arrester wires for authenticity [1943-52]. The tarmac survives, with runways in line with its landing axis, and grass at the side representing the sea.

AE — code letters of 402 (Royal Canadian Air Force / Winnipeg Bear) Squadron, flying "Hurri-bombers" and then Spitfires from RAF Warmwell [1941-42 and 1945].

Aerodromes — see entries for Anti-Terrorist Airport; Bournemouth (Hurn) Airport; Bournemouth International Airport; Bovington Relief Landing Ground; Chickerell Aerodrome; Compton Abbas Aerodrome; HMS Dipper; Emergency Dispersal Point; Ensbury Park Aerodrome and Racecourse; Eyres Field; RAF Hamworthy; Henstridge Royal Naval Air Station; Hurn Aerodrome; Meyrick Park Airfield; Moortown Aerodrome; HMS Osprey; RAF Poole; Portland Royal Naval Air Station; Powerstock Admiralty Air Station; Sandbanks Royal Naval Air Station; Station 416; Station 454; Talbot Village Aerodrome; Tarrant Rushton Aerodrome; Toller Admiralty Air Station; Trots; Upton Admiralty Airship Station; Wallis Down Aerodrome; Warmwell Aerodrome; Winfrith Heath Decoy Aerodrome; Winkton Advanced Landing Ground; Woodsford Aerodrome; Worth Aerodrome; and Zeals Aerodrome.

AFS — No. 210 Advanced Flying School of Training Command was formed at RAF Tarrant Rushton, bringing Meteor and Vampire jet trainers to join the tankers and trials aircraft of Flight Refuelling Limited [November 1952].

An Airspeed Oxford provided piston-engine experience and the school went on to amass a total of 36 aircraft.

It lost a Meteor, with its pilot, over Oxfordshire, but there was only one crash at the base itself, from which the trainee flyer was able to walk away, when a Vampire crumpled on take-off [June 1953].

Some 150 flights were being achieved on an average day and a total of 16,500 flying hours would be clocked up by the school before its closure [March 1954].

Agazarian — Armenian / French Spitfire flyer **Pilot Officer Noel le Chevalier Agazarian** [killed 1941] of 609 Squadron from RAF Warmwell had an impressive tally of victories. These were a Messerschmitt Bf.110 [11 August 1940]; a shared Bf.110 [25 August 1940]; a shared Heinkel He.111 [25 September 1940]; and a Bf.109 [26 September 1940].

Next day's success, 25 miles south of Portland Bill, was Bf.110 (S9+GK) belonging to Erprobungsgruppe 210, an experimental proving unit from Cherbourg that was taking part in an abortive raid on the Parnall Aircraft Company at Yate, near Chipping Sodbury [27 September 1940].

His last decisive day with the Dorset-based squadron, off Thorney Island, Hampshire, accounted for a Bf.110 and Dornier Do.17, shared with Pilot Officer Nowierski [2 December 1940].

He was then posted to the Middle East and lost his life when 274 Squadron was intercepted by Bf.109s over the Western Desert at Gambut [16 May 1941]. He is buried in Knightsbridge War Cemetery, Acroma, Libya.

One of the Spitfires he flew from Warmwell, R6915, survives suspended over the main hall in the Imperial War Museum, Lambeth Road, London SE1. It was also flown over Dorset by Flight-Lieutenant John Dundas.

Air Defence Research and Development Establishment — at Somerford, Christchurch, first made national news with reports that it had developed a "death ray" [August 1939]. This was probably a cover story for the development of radar and other systems. Perfecting ideas passed on to them by the Telecommunications Research Establishment at Worth Matravers they built the mobile Type 15 ground-to-air radar antenna which was put into a field at Sopley [25 December 1940] and would enable 604 Squadron at RAF Middle Wallop to score their first radar-controlled interception that ended in a kill [4 March 1941].

AI (Air Interception) radar — developed by scientists at the Telecommunications Research Establishment, at Worth Matravers and Langton Matravers [1940]. It was fitted in the Perspex nose-cones of Bristol Beaufighter night-fighters and first proven operationally from RAF Middle Wallop [1942].

Air Safari — moved with its engineering facilities into Hangar 104 at Hurn Airport [1961], under the management of David Haselum [born 1924], from Crawley. He had a works staff of 120 and was responsible for maintenance of the Air Safaris fleet of eight Viking and nine Hermes transports. Their total wage bill was around £1,500 a week.

Principal engineer in the workshops was Anthony Brooke, former chief engineer of Borneo Airways and Malayan Airways for some 12 years, with Ronald Barton being the engineer in charge of the hangar. Among the licensed engineers was Douglas Arthur Randall, of Markham Avenue, Kinson, who was born at Springbourne, Bournemouth, and had been at Hurn since leaving the RAF [1946]. The chief inspector was C. A. Tivvites who had also served in the RAF [1921-46].

Air Traffic Control Evaluation Unit — moved from London Airport to Bournemouth (Hurn) Airport [1963] and used the busy South Coast aerodrome to test new radar systems. Operated separately from the airfield's own air traffic system.

AIRSPEED AMBASSADOR: G-AGUA, THE PROTOTYPE OF THE TWIN-ENGINED AIRLINER, SEEN BESIDE THE WORKS AT SOMERFORD, CHRISTCHURCH, WHERE IT WAS MADE, IN MARCH 1948. PRODUCTION WOULD BEGIN IN WHAT BECAME THE AIRSPEED DIVISION OF DE HAVILLAND AIRCRAFT LIMITED IN 1951. NOTE THE TWO MOSQUITO FIGHTER-BOMBERS, WITH RAF ROUNDELS, IN THE BACKGROUND.

AMBASSADOR G-AGUA: TAKE-OFF FROM CHRISTCHURCH AERODROME, ADJOINING THE AIRSPEED WORKS AT SOMERFORD, IN JULY 1947.

Air Whaling Limited — established by helicopter test pilot Alan Bristow for Antarctic whaling expeditions and based at Henstridge Aerodrome [1953-54].

Airspeed (1934) Limited — aviation company, makers of the Envoy and the Oxford, which established a shadow-factory at Somerford, beside Christchurch Aerodrome [January 1941]. A total of 550 twin-engined Oxfords would be made there, mainly for use as trainers. Production then concentrated on the making of Horsa gliders for the airborne divisions [1943-44] and conversions of Supermarine Spitfires into Seafires, with folding wing modifications, plus the pilot's canopy having all-round vision, for use on Royal Navy aircraft-carriers.

Ownership of Airspeed [1934] Limited was acquired by the de Havilland Aircraft Company Limited [1940] and it would be renamed Airspeed Limited [25 January 1944]. Though it retained its separate identity it made parts for the famous de Havilland Mosquito.

Airspeed's principal post-war hope lay in plans for the twin-engined Ambassador airliner which it had already sold, ahead of production, to British European Airways. Flight tests were ominous and the company was merged into its parent de Havilland Aircraft Company Limited [1951]. The Ambassador subsequently saw the skies, with British European Airways, in their "Elizabethan" class, honouring the new Queen [1952]. Twenty "Elizabethan" Ambassadors comprised the BEA fleet.

They would fly a combined distance of 31 million miles, carrying 2,450,000 passengers, by the time of the last scheduled flight [30 July 1958]. This was the aircraft of one of the longest remembered of all air crashes, in which the Manchester United soccer team was virtually wiped out on take-off from Munich after victory in Belgrade, though that was caused by slush-drag rather than a mechanical fault [7 February 1958]. The Ambassador was soon to be upstaged by the more advanced turboprop Vickers Viscount.

In a way it had been both before and behind its time, having origins in Hessell Tiltman's A514 design — also named Ambassador — from the pre-war revival of Airspeed (1934) Limited with £220,000 of Swan Hunter capital. The airlines declined what Harald Penrose described as "an elegant mock-up" and then came the clouds of war.

Airspeed Division — see entry for de Havilland.

Airways House — at 4 High Street, Poole, being the offices of the British Overseas Airways Corporation [1940-46].

Airwork Services — provided target-towing flights for the Fleet Air Arm, from Bournemouth (Hurn) Airport [1952]. Deployed the same types of aircraft as were currently on aircraft-carriers, plus the superbly versatile Mosquito. Operated in association with the Fleet Requirements Unit, giving active retirements to a succession of famous ex-RAF fighters, such as the Gloster Meteor and Hawker Hunter, and a virtual squadron of Canberra bombers painted in yellow and black stripes. After two decades the survivors left for the Royal Naval Air Station at Yeovilton [1972].

Akroyd — Spitfire flyer **Pilot Officer Harold John Akroyd** [1913-40] of 152 Squadron from RAF Warmwell claimed a Junkers Ju.87 in a fierce dog-fight from which he was lucky to return to RAF Warmwell, having had the rudder of R6910 jam over Portland [15 August 1940]. That luck ran out during one of the most hectic days of the Battle of Britain, when Spitfire N3039 was crippled over west Dorset and burst into flames on crashing at Shatcombe Farm, Wynford Eagle [7 October 1940].

Though pulled from the wreckage he was suffering extensive burns. He was taken to the Dorset County Hospital, Dorchester, where he died the following day, and is buried in the RAF plot at Warmwell churchyard.

Alcock — the legendary **Pilot Alcock**, of Imperial Airways took flying-boats to India. As soon as he was in a warm airstream he used to drop his shorts and fly naked. His autobiography had the obvious title — *I Flew With No Trousers*.

Alington — RAF intelligence officer **Napier George Henry Sturt, 3rd Baron Alington** [1896-1940] of Crichel House, Moor Crichel, died in Egypt [17 September 1940]. He had no heir, so the Alington barony died with him. His memorials are in Witchampton Church and on the war memorial there.

Allen — Spitfire flyer **Pilot Officer John Woodward Allen** of 152 Squadron from RAF Warmwell plummeted vertically into the ground at Field Grove, near Travellers' Rest, Durweston [29 November 1940]. He may have fainted because of loss of oxygen. No enemy aircraft was involved. As he was killed before he could complete a single operational sortie, Allen was not among those posthumously awarded the Battle of Britain clasp.

Allied Expeditionary Air Force — control of 38 Group Airborne Forces and its aerodromes at RAF Hurn and RAF Tarrant Rushton, was transferred to the air-wing of the Allied Expeditionary Force [1 February 1944] for the imminent invasion of Europe. AEAF was commanded from Stanmore, Middlesex, and Norfolk House, St James's Square, which was the headquarters of the Air Officer Commanding-in-Chief, Air Chief Marshal Sir Trafford Leigh-Mallory.

Altair — Catalina flying-boat, formerly British Overseas Airways FM, which left Poole Harbour for Trincomalee, Ceylon [17 April 1943] where she was handed over to RAF South-East Asia Command.

Alton Pancras crash — at Austral Farm, of a Hurricane of 56 Squadron from RAF Boscombe Down, which had been battling against the formation of Messerschmitt Bf. 110 fighter-bombers of Zerstörergeschwader 26 that were attacking the Westland Aircraft factory at Yeovil [16.00 hours, 7 October 1940]. Pilot Officer Dennis Nichols parachuted clear but was taken to Dorchester Hospital after landing badly.

Ambassador — post-war airliner, ordered by British European Airways, and manufactured by Airspeed Limited at Christchurch [1951]. See entry for Airspeed [1934] Limited.

Anti-Aircraft Artillery — batteries issued with heavy 3.7-inch AA guns, and then the ubiquitous Bofors 40-mm gun, defended the Bournemouth and Poole conurbation and the ports of Weymouth and Portland during the Second World War. Guns were also mounted around military establishments and aerodromes.

Several American "triple A" battalions, of Anti-Aircraft Artillery, passed through Dorset [1943-44] and were deployed to protect Blandford Camp and Tarrant Rushton Aerodrome. The 184th Auxiliary Anti-Aircraft Gun Battalion provided protection for the beach landing assault exercise area at Studland [April 1944]. It had 25 officers and 716 enlisted men.

Anti-Aircraft Co-Operation Unit — its H-Flight was posted from Gosport to Christchurch Aerodrome to work with the Air Defence Experimental Establishment in countermeasures against German bombers [1 November 1940].

Anti-Terrorist Airport — Bournemouth International Airport, at Hurn, was designated Britain's standby airfield for the diversion and reception of hijacked flights [1985]. An area towards the far perimeter was allocated for the isolation of such emergency arrivals, and a team briefed for carrying out negotiations with gunmen or bombers.

Preparations were also made for the control and manipulation of the inevitable media attention. Major anti-terrorist exercises followed [1988] with elite forces, spearheaded by an SAS detachment from Hereford, practising storming techniques on a parked airliner.

Contigency plans were devised for the management of such an incident, under the national command of government officials, with Dorset Police providing man-power on the ground.

AP — squadron code of 130 (Punjab) Squadron, briefly flying Spitfires from RAF Warmwell [30 November — 5 December 1941].

Appleby — Spitfire flyer **Pilot Officer Michael Appleby** flew with 609 Squadron from RAF Warmwell. He put a Messerschmitt Bf.109 into the sea, off the Isle of Purbeck, after an interception with Green Section at 23,000 feet over Swanage [30 September 1940]. He was posted to the Central Flying School, Upavon, as an instructor [November 1940] and would survive the war.

Argentina — an ex-BOAC Mark V Sunderland flying-boat from Poole, converted into a Sandringham-2 for carrying 45 passengers and sold to the Argentine airline Dodero. Flown from Poole Harbour to Buenos Aires by a BOAC crew [17 November-25 November 1945].

Arne crashes — of a Messerschmitt Bf.110 (3U+IM) belonging to Zerstörergeschwader 26, the Geschwader named Horst Wessel after the Nazi subject of a militant anti-Semitic song which became a national anthem [27 September1940]. Crewmen Arthur Niebuhr and Klaus Deissen were killed as it exploded above Salter's Wood, Middlebere. The kill was claimed by a Spitfire of 152 Squadron from RAF Warmwell. They had been taking part in an abortive raid on the Parnall Aircraft Company at Yate, near Chipping Sodbury.

Some of Purbeck's most dramatic dog-fights of the Second World War occurred during a busy afternoon in the Battle of Britain, when the Luftwaffe attacked the Westland Aircraft Company at Yeovil [7 October 1940]. A Messerschmitt Bf.110 (3U+BT) belonging to the 9th Staffel of Kampfgruppe 26 came low across the Frome meadows and flew into the gorse-clad slope of Hyde-Hill, south of Stoborough [16.00 hours]. The pilot, Leutnant Kurt Sidow, and his navigator, Gefreiter Josef Repik, died in the fireball.

Heinkel He.111 bomber G1+ES belonging to the 8th Staffel of the 3rd Gruppe, Kampfgeschwader 55, was brought down off Patchin's Point [12 May 1941]. It had just destroyed BOAC flying-boat *Maia* and was hit in the process by machine-gun fire from ships in Poole Harbour and Bofors anti-aircraft shells from the mainland. Two of the crew were killed but the other pair survived.

Arnhem airlift — nearly a hundred gliders, towed by their Halifax tug-planes, left RAF Tarrant Rushton [17 September 1944] to join the armada of 300 Allied craft that were to land behind enemy lines in the Netherlands. Operation Market Garden was airborne and the Tarrant Rushton planes towed the British 1st Airborne Division towards the farthest dropping zone, around Oosterbeek, eight miles west of the great bridge over the Neder Rijn — the Lower Rhine at Arnhem — which would become "the bridge too far".

Ashmore crash — Tiger Moth G-APRX, visiting Compton Abbas Airfield from Thruxton, stalled on a morning take-off and crashed into the trees of West Wood, behind Gore Farm [circa 1965]. The pilot was unhurt and his passenger, Ron Powell, survived with a relatively minor head wound.

Askerswell crash — farmer Hugh Elder [1961-93] of Stancombe Farm was killed when a Stolp Starduster II biplane crashed on take-off from his own private airstrip [3 October 1993]. The pilot, Lieutenant Richard Boswell — a Royal Navy helicopter instructor — survived the crash but was treated in Weymouth District Hospital for head injuries.

Atkinson — Hurricane flyer **Pilot Officer Harold Derrick Atkinson** [1918-40], in R4099 of 213 Squadron from RAF Exeter, shot down a Heinkel He.111 bomber into Lyme Bay [14 August 1940]. He was slightly hurt by return fire and received medical attention for shell splinters in the arm.

During the following week he claimed two Messerschmitt Bf.109s and celebrated his 22nd birthday [19 August 1940]. Then his luck ran out, off Portland, and he was shot down in P3200 [17.30 hours, 25 August 1940]. His body was recovered and is buried at Market Weighton, Yorkshire.

AZ — code letters of 234 (Madras Presidency) Squadron, flying Spitfires from RAF Warmwell [1941].

ASHMORE CRASH: TIGER MOTH G-APRX IN THE TREES OF WEST WOOD, HAVING FAILED ON TAKE-OFF FROM COMPTON ABBAS AIRFIELD.

B

BA — squadron code of 277 Squadron, flying Air-Sea Rescue missions off the Dorset coast, with Spitfires and Walrus amphibians [1943-44].

Baillon — Spitfire flyer **Pilot Officer Paul Abbott Baillon** of 609 Squadron from RAF Warmwell was reported missing in action after dog-fights with Messerschmitt Bf.109s of Jagdgeschwader 2, off the Isle of Wight [28 November 1940]. He had only joined the squadron the previous month.

Balloon *Gerard A. Heineken* — the world's largest hot-air balloon lifted off from Creech Barrow Hill, Church Knowle [evening of 25 July 1975], in an attempt at the international distance and duration flight record which ended half an hour later two parishes away at Coles Farm, Langton Matravers. The unique two-tier basket of the 140-feet balloon snagged four power cables, 25 feet above a field, and plunged the village into darkness.

"It's a miracle we're alive," said Army balloonist Major Christopher Davey. "It was twilight and we couldn't see the cables until too late. Three cables broke and the other one wrapped itself around our flagwires. Then the basket swung like a pendulum until we were able to break free."

The fabric of the balloon was hardly damaged and pilot Don Cameron was talking of a second attempt within minutes of the unscheduled landing. Also in the basket was French balloonist Comte Jean de Costa Beauregard. Half a million cubic feet of hot air had lifted the balloon for its passage across three Purbeck parishes. They were attempting to beat the 334 miles record, in a 16 hour flight, set in the United States [1974]. People converged on Langton Matravers from miles around and police closed the roads to prevent any more from trying to see the huge but collapsed balloon.

Major Davey, whose £1 million insurance had also escaped a close call, issued an apology to the villagers: "We, the crew of hot-air Balloon *Gerard Heineken*, would like to make a full apology to the people of Langton Matravers for the inconvenience and damage caused to them and their property as a result of our forced landing at the start of our cross-Channel voyage. We particularly regret damaging the high power tension cables that blacked out the area — and which probably saved us from careering over the cliffs".

Balloons — see entries for Balloon *Gerard Heineken*, *Double Eagle II*, and *Saladin*. Also Loders crash; Moreton Admiralty Airship Station; Toller Admiralty Airship Station; Hatton Turner; Upton Admiralty Airship Station; Zero Airships.

Banks — Hurricane flyer **Sergeant-Pilot William Henry Banks** [1916-80], having sustained damage in combat in P3774 of 504 Squadron from RAF Filton, made a successful forced-landing in a west Dorset field [30 September 1940]. He was unhurt and the fighter repairable.

William Banks stayed in the RAF after the war and retired as Squadron Leader in 1958.

Barker — Spitfire flyer **Sergeant-Pilot John Barker** [1917-40] of 152 Squadron from RAF Warmwell was killed in action during the Battle of Britain, apparently by return fire from a Dornier Do.17 bomber he engaged off the Isle of Wight [4 September 1940]. He baled out but was killed. His body was washed ashore in France and buried in Étaples Military Cemetery.

Barran — Spitfire flyer **Flying Officer Philip Henry "Pip" Barran** [1909-40] of 609 Squadron from RAF Warmwell lost his life in a Battle of Britain dog-fight, as the Luftwaffe attacked Channel shipping. He baled out from L1069 and was picked up from the sea, five miles off Portland Bill, but

CYRIL BEALE: THE WORLD'S FIRST FLYING FATHER CHRISTMAS IN HENRI SALMET'S TWO-SEATER BLERIOT MONOPLANE, AT SOUTHBOURNE AERODROME, BOURNEMOUTH, IN DECEMBER 1912.

was badly wounded and burnt, dying before he could be brought ashore [11 July 1940]. He is buried in his home town, in Leeds Cemetery. His family owned a colliery and brickworks.

Baynes — aircraft designer and inventor **Leslie Everett Jeffery "Baron" Baynes** [1902-89] is buried in Swanage Cemetery, Washpond Lane, Godlingston. He built novel little flying machines such as an auxiliary sailplane with a Carden engine which, together with its propeller, could be retracted into the fuselage, as displayed to the Royal Aeronautical Society meeting at Fairey's Heathrow aerodrome [5 May 1935].

He was pioneering ultra-lights, such as the Scud II with diamond-section fuselage and tapering wing, as the two-seater, twin-engined Bee. The latter, only 29 feet 10 inches in length, was being constructed by Carden-Baynes Aircraft Ltd at Heston. The twin 40hp Carden-engined Baynes Bee was taken up by Hubert Broad on its maiden flight [April 1937]. It and similar frivolities would be squeezed from the sky by the gathering clouds of war.

During the conflict he devised the conversion of the American-built Boston bomber into a Havoc night-fighter that carried the Turbinlite airborne searchlight. Bitterness marred his post-war career. Baynes was positive that his ideas had been stolen, by the Americans and others, and blamed the Ministry of Supply for blocking a paper he was to have presented to the Royal Aeronautical Society [1949]. They called in his plans for a 1,000 mph variable-wing fighter and classified them top secret. For fun he devised a sail-plane with a retractable propeller and engine, which could turn itself into a glider [1955], but he felt it should have been his destiny to make the British equivalent of the F-111. He regarded it as a waste of national talent that he was running an antique shop in Corfe Castle.

The Baynes Bee, plus a finely sculpted head, are carved on his Purbeck marble gravestone at Godlingston.

Beagley — Coastal Command **Flying Officer Derek Mordaunt Beagley** [1924-45] was killed on 11 February 1945. He is buried in Radipole churchyard, Weymouth.

Beale — Bournemouth department store owner **Cyril Beale**, dressed as Santa Claus, was taken up as the passenger from Southbourne Aerodrome in Henri Salmet's two-seater Bleriot monoplane

[December 1912]. Their low-level circuit over the crowded town centre Square and Lower Gardens gave the world its first flying Father Christmas (apart from the original, of course).

Beaminster crash — of a Dornier Do.17 bomber, shot down at night over South Buckham Farm [February 1943]. Its destruction was credited to Wing Commander Rupert Francis Henry Clerke, flying a Beaufighter of 125 (Newfoundland) Squadron from RAF Fairwood Common, in South Wales. The farmer, however, recalled a Canadian pilot arriving in triumph at the crash site to claim the kill. Not only was Clerke "very British" but he had received an Eton and Cambridge education.

Beaumont — Spitfire flyer **Pilot Officer Walter Beaumont** [1914-40] of 152 Squadron from RAF Warmwell successfully crash-landed at Spyway Farm, Langton Matravers, after a Battle of Britain dog-fight over the English Channel [8 August 1940]. A week later he claimed his squadron's first battle double set of kills, with two Messerschmitt Bf. 109s over the Isle of Wight [16 August 1940]. He shot down a Messerschmitt Bf.109 which fell at Tatton Farm, north of Chickerell, on the day that three German aircraft crashed in that parish [25 August 1940].

It was regarded as tempting fate that he drove out in "shirtsleeves and sweat" to the scorched scene of his triumph. He baled out as Spitfire R6831 was shot down, into the sea, eight miles off Portland [27 August 1940]. Posted "Missing in Action" in Spitfire R7016 [23 September 1940], having apparently been shot down over the sea. His body was not recovered. He was posthumously awarded the Distinguished Flying Cross.

Bedford — chief test pilot **Alfred William "Bill" Bedford** [born 1920] achieved the first vertical landing by a fixed wing aircraft on an aircraft-carrier when he brought his Hawker Siddeley P1127 Kestrel, prototype of the Harrier, down on HMS *Ark Royal* as she sailed at 5-knots to the east of The Shambles, Portland Bill [8 February 1963].

Benbow — air hero **Captain Edwin Louis Benbow MC** [1895-1918] of the Royal Flying Corps and the newly created Royal Air Force was shot down near Ypres on 30 May 1918. Born at La Mortola, Abbotsbury, he is buried in the British cemetry at Duhallow, and has a plaque back home in Abbotsbury parish church.

Berlin Airlift — three Lancasters and nine Lancastrian tankers of Flight Refuelling Limited, based at Tarrant Rushton, flew a total of 6,975,021 gallons of petroleum products into the beleaguered western sector of Berlin when Josef Stalin closed its land links with West Germany [27 July 1948 — 10 August 1949]. The round the clock operation totalled 11,827 hours of flying time for Flight Refuelling, but at a cost. Returning Lancaster G-AHJW flew into a hill at Conholt Park, Andover, killing Captain Cyril "Pop" Taylor and six of his crew [22 November 1948], and Lancastrian G-AKDP force-landed in the Russian zone [10 May 1949].

The 652 staff at Tarrant Rushton were particularly proud to hear that at 4.15 sorties per "Aircraft Day" theirs was the "Peak Utilisation Factor" for any aerial contribution; American, British or French.

Bulk fuel deliveries were almost as essential as those of food in ensuring the success of Operation Plainfare (originally called Operation Carter Paterson, until it was realised that linkage with a removals company was a propaganda faux pas). The outcome was decisive and lasting. Post-war patterns of occupation would remain intact, to the inch and the letter, until the collapse of communism.

Bermuda Sky Queen — Boeing B-314 Clipper flying boat that took off from Poole Harbour on her final flight [12 October 1947], via Foynes, Limerick [13 October 1947], outward bound across the Atlantic. She made 1,400 miles and was then forced by heavy winds to abandon the flight off

LORDSHIP'S HUMILIATION: LORD VENTRY'S AIRSHIP BOURNEMOUTH DWARFED BY THE IMMENSITY OF SHED 2 AT CARDINGTON, AND THEN TAKEN OUT FOR A LOW-LEVEL MAIDEN FLIGHT THAT ENDED ENTANGLED WITH THE GYMNASIUM ROOF ON 19 JULY 1951.

Newfoundland, ditching beside an American weather ship. All 69 passengers and crew were safely taken off and the flying-boat was abandoned to her fate, sinking in the Atlantic Ocean.

Blake — Spitfire flyer **Squadron Leader "Mindy" Blake** of 234 Squadron at RAF Warmwell accounted for two Messerschmitt Bf.109s as his fighters escorted Blenheims of 21 Squadron that were bombing Cherbourg docks [10 July 1941]. Blake was then reported missing in action but later sighted by Sergeant Pilot Fox, alive and well and cheerfully paddling his dinghy in the general direction of the Isle of Wight, to be picked-up by a rescue launch.

Blandford crashes — because Blandford Forum is a tightly contained urban parish, crashes near it were generally in adjacent parishes, such as Pimperne and Durweston. Several, however, cannot be located with any precision. These include the loss of a Short Stirling bomber [16 February 1942], identified as R9306 of 90 Squadron.

Blind-Landing Detachment — moved to the recently opened RAF Hurn from the Royal Aircraft Establishment, Farnborough, and was merged into the Air Ministry's newly formed Telecommunications Flying Unit [August 1941].

BN — code letters of 297 (Army Co-operation) Squadron, flying Mustangs from RAF Hurn [1942].

BN (Blind Navigation) radar — pioneered by the Telecommunications Research Establishment at Worth Matravers and Langton Matravers, and first tested in a Blenheim bomber of the Research Section, Telecommunications Flying Unit, from RAF Hurn [November 1942]. Using an AI (Airborne Interception) Mark VII radar set, having tilted its centimetric beam towards the ground, scientists found themselves mapping Bournemouth and could distinguish its streets and houses from the surrounding landscape.

Boitel-Gill — Spitfire flyer **Flight-Lieutenant Derek Boitel-Gill** of 152 Squadron from RAF Warmwell claimed a Junkers Ju.87 "Stuka" over Portesham in the Luftwaffe's Adlertag (Eagle Day) attack [13 August 1940]. "Bottled Gull" would be promoted 152's Squadron Leader and lost his life in a flying accident [August 1941}.

Boudard — French flyer **Denys Boudard**, with Jean Hebert, stole a Luftwaffe Bücker Jungmann biplane from an airfield near Caen and flew to Christchurch Aerodrome [29 April 1942]. They joined the Free French Forces. Boudard was still flourishing in the 1980's.

Bournemouth — the second of the town's Spitfires, paid for by street collections and fund raising events, handed over to 457 Squadron at Baginton, Warwickshire [22 June 1941]. Left with the squadron when it was posted to the Isle of Man [August 1941] but then transferred to a training unit at Grangemouth [October 1941]. Lost in a flying accident [16 March 1942].

Bournemouth — designed by Lord Ventry, the first airship to have flown in Britain since the loss of the R.101 lifted off on her maiden flight from RAF Cardington, Bedfordshire [19 July 1951]. The crew were Captain J. Beckford-Ball, Freddie Twinn and Flight Lieutenant H. Richardson; the latter took Lord Ventry's place because at seventeen stone his lordship disqualified himself from lighter than air travel, blaming his predicament on having given up smoking. The three hung suspended in a gondola for the twenty minute trip. "Stern-heavy" was the verdict on her handling.

Bournemouth Aviation Company — operated from Talbot Village Aerodrome and then Ensbury Park Aerodrome, training military pilots, during the Great War.

Bournemouth Centenary Aviation Meeting — held at the newly laid out Southbourne Aerodrome, and celebrating the first hundred years of Bournemouth [1810-1910] rather than manned flight. Notable for big money prize events attracting pioneer aviators from France, in which Léon Morane flew off with £3,425 of the £8,500 prizes. Remembered for what the newspapers headlined as "THE FIRST FATAL ACCIDENT TO AN AIRMAN IN ENGLAND" with the crash that killed the Honourable Charles Stewart Rolls of Rolls-Royce fame [12 July 1910].

It was the second day of the meeting and Charles Rolls was at the controls of a French-built Wright Flyer. While attempting to land in front of the grandstand, approaching at an altitude of 70 feet, he was caught by a crosswind and found himself too high. He put his nose down sharply which caused the elevator to snap. Rolls broke his neck in the crash.

Bournemouth crashes — Rolls (see entry above) was the first of many. Edmond Audemars stepped clear from the crumpled wreckage of his upside-down Demoiselle monoplane [July 1910]. Henri Salmet was also lucky, in a Bleriot biplane that tangled with a Tuckton tree [summer 1913]. Trainee pilots for the Royal Flying Corps were soon to crash around Bournemouth in some quantity and with inevitable fatalities.

Bournemouth Aviation Company operated from Talbot Village Aerodrome, where the casualties included Second-Lieutenant Edward Rebbeck, son of an ex mayor and heir to an estate agency [24 April 1916]. The death toll continued after their move to Ensbury Park Aerodrome. Major John Lockock was killed when his Bristol Fighter hit a tree on the corner of Christchurch Road with Annerley Road, near the Lansdowne [16.00 hours, 22 July 1918].

More spectacularly, watched by hundreds, a Westland Widgeon collided with a Blackburn Bluebird beside the stands at Ensbury Park Racecourse, killing test pilot Major Laurence Openshaw [6 June 1927].

Bournemouth's first air crash of the Second World War was at the height of the Battle of Britain [15 August 1940] when New Zealand Pilot Officer Cecil Hight, in Spitfire R6988 of 234 Squadron from RAF Middle Wallop, was shot down by a German rear-gunner. Hight baled out but was fatally wounded. His stomach had been ripped open by machine-gun bullets and he lost consciousness before he could pull the rip cord. He fell into the garden of Mr and Mrs Hoare's house in Leven Avenue, west of Meyrick Park. The fighter left a large crater, and one of the wings landed on a hedge in Walsford Road. Mr Hoare would lose his life a little later when a German bomb fell on his house. Hight is buried at Boscombe Cemetry and has a memorial tablet unveiled by the New Zealand Ambassador in St Peter's Church [7 April 1943]. The town would name Pilot Hight Road in his memory.

Another Spitfire of 234 Squadron from RAF Middle Wallop, badly damaged in the dog-fights over Bournemouth, made a successful forced-landing in fields beside the town [15 August 1940].

An unidentified aeroplane fell into the sea off Hengistbury Head after machine gun fire had been heard. No one baled out [1 October 1940].

A Messerschmitt Bf.110 fighter-bomber crashed on the edge of the town and was claimed by Flight-Lieutenant John Dundas of 609 Squadron from RAF Warmwell [15 October 1940].

Hurricane V6792, belonging to 238 Squadron from RAF Chilbolton, on the Hampshire Downs, was shot down by Messerschmitt Bf109's over Bournemouth [5 November 1940]. Pilot Officer Brian Considine would bale out over Sturminster Marshall, and his fighter crashed at Crab Farm, Shapwick.

Anti-aircraft gunners took the credit for the German aircraft that crashed into the sea off Hengistbury Head [1 December 1940].

Fairey Battle fighter-bomber K9230 of the Special Duty Flight from Christchurch Aerodrome, ditched near the same spot [28 April 1941]. Second Lieutenant Andrew Page of the Lancashire Fusiliers swam to the aid of the pilot but despite heroic efforts, which won him the George Medal, he could not prevent the entangled parachute from drowning him.

Bournemouth hangars: these five being those of Barnes and Boyle (left), Moore and Brabazon, Ogilvie, Dickson and Audemars, at Southbourne Aerodrome in July 1910.

BLÉRIOT MONOPLANE: BESIDE THE BARNES AND BOYLE HANGAR (RIGHT), WITH ALAN R. BOYLE'S AVIS MACHINE BEHIND, ALONG TO THE SHED ADVERTISING W. L. A. ENGINES, AT BOURNEMOUTH CENTENARY AVIATION MEETING IN JULY 1910.

No contest: Armstrong Drexel's Bleriot monoplane being totally ignored (left) but Claude Grahame-White's Farman biplane attracts a photo-call as he prepares to take passengers at Southbourne Aerodrome, with the Morane hangar in the background in July 1910.

MOTORISED CONCOURSE: THE AIRBORNE SET CAME TO SOUTHBOURNE AERODROME WITH THE BEST COLLECTION OF TOP-CLASS MOTOR CARS IN THE COUNTRY, TO A BACKDROP OF MARQUEE HANGARS WHICH START WITH THOSE OF ROLLS (LEFT) AND GRAHAME-WHITE, IN JULY 1910. NOTE THE AUTOMOBILE ASSOCIATION SIGN BEHIND THE CAR ON THE FAR RIGHT.

PILLION PASSENGER: "TRAVELLING DE LUXE THAT IS HARDLY LUXURIOUS," THE ORIGINAL CAPTION OF JULY 1910 READS AS IT GOES ON TO SAY THAT MRS ASTLEY'S POSITION BEHIND CLAUDE GRAHAME-WHITE "MIGHT BECOME TRYING ON A LONG AIR-VOYAGE, SAY, FROM LONDON TO MANCHESTER".

TRAVELLING DE LUXE THAT IS HARDLY LUXURIOUS: THE DIFFICULTIES OF GETTING A PASSENGER ON BOARD AN AEROPLANE.

BOURNEMOUTH FLYING: MAKING HEADLINES IN THE MANCHESTER GUARDIAN, WITH "MR GRAHAME-WHITE IN COURSE OF A FLIGHT WITH A LADY PASSENGER".

THE MANCHESTER GUARDIAN, FRIDAY, JULY 15, 1910.

FLYING AT BOURNEMOUTH.

Mr. Grahame-White in course of a flight with a lady passenger.

LUCKY LADY: "NOT DETERRED BY THE ACCIDENT TO MR ROLLS," MRS ASTLEY GIVES A HUGE SMILE AS SHE PREPARES TO RISK HER HAT IN THE SKY, BEHIND CLAUDE GRAHAME-WHITE, AT SOUTHBOURNE AERODROME IN JULY 1910.

BOURNEMOUTH PILOT: WILLIAM MCARDLE, A MOTOR CAR DEALER IN HOLDENHURST ROAD, HAD THE SHORTEST DISTANCE TO TRAVEL IN ORDER TO ATTEND THE BOURNEMOUTH CENTENARY AVIATION MEETING AND IS SEEN IN FRONT OF THE HANGAR OF DREXEL AND JONES IN JULY 1910.

COLOURFUL CHARACTER: SELF-STYLED "COLONEL" SAMUEL FRANKLIN CODY, AN AMERICAN WHO LATER NATURALISED AS A BRITISH CITIZEN, MADE THE COUNTRY'S FIRST OFFICIALLY RECOGNISED POWERED FLIGHT — IN BRITISH ARMY AEROPLANE NO. 1, AT FARNBOROUGH, ON 16 OCTOBER 1908 — AND WAS ALSO AT SOUTHBOURNE AERODROME IN JULY 1910.

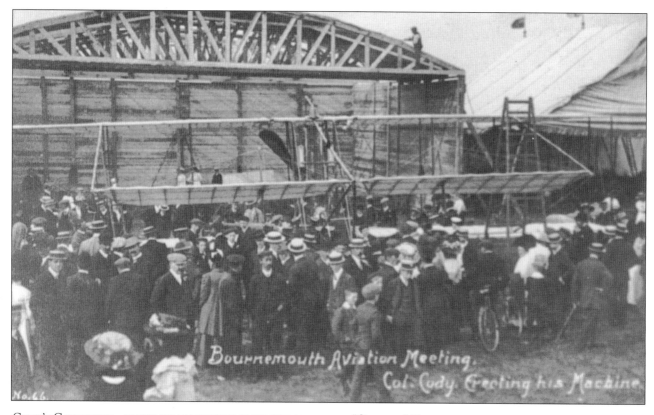

CODY'S CATHEDRAL: AS THE GIANT OF ITS TIME WAS KNOWN, WITH "COLONEL" CODY PIECING IT TOGETHER WHILE WORKMEN COMPLETE THE ERECTION OF TENTED HANGARS AT SOUTHBOURNE AERODROME IN JULY 1910.

AIRBORNE AGAIN: UNDAUNTED BY THE LOSS OF HIS DEMOISELLE MONOPLANE, AND HAVING TAKEN THE WISE PRECAUTION OF BRINGING A SECOND AEROPLANE, EDMOND AUDEMARS WAS BACK IN THE SKY ABOVE SOUTHBOURNE IN INFURIATED GRASSHOPPER.

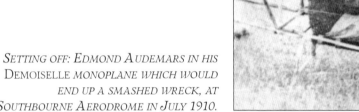

SETTING OFF: EDMOND AUDEMARS IN HIS DEMOISELLE MONOPLANE WHICH WOULD END UP A SMASHED WRECK, AT SOUTHBOURNE AERODROME IN JULY 1910.

SEA FLIGHT TO THE NEEDLES.

Morane, the winner of the sea flight.

Morane in the air.

HE CHIEF EVENT AT THE BOURNEMOUTH AVIATION MEETING YESTERDAY WAS THE FLIGHT TO THE NEEDLES AND

NEEDLES EXPEDITION: A REMINDER OF HOW A ROUND TRIP OF 20 MILES COULD STILL MAKE NEWS, WITH LÉON MORANE'S LIGHT-WEIGHT MONOPLANE WINNING THE SEA FLIGHT FROM BOURNEMOUTH TO THE ISLE OF WIGHT. THE FRENCHMAN HELD THE CURRENT WORLD AIR SPEED RECORD OF 66.18 MILES PER HOUR, HAVING BROKEN THROUGH THE 100 KILOMETRES PER HOUR BARRIER A FEW DAYS EARLIER, ON 10 JULY 1910.

PROPELLER PUSHING: GEORGE A. BARNES PREPARES HIS HUMBER FOR FLIGHT AT THE BOURNEMOUTH CENTENARY AVIATION MEETING IN JULY 1910.

War Weapons Week fund-raising efforts were marred when one of three Hurricanes of 32 Squadron from RAF Ibsley, giving a flying display across the centre of Bournemouth, failed to pull out of a victory roll [17.55 hours, 21 February 1941]. It crashed on the rear of houses at 36 and 38 St. Clement's Road, killing the 22-year old Czech pilot, but not injuring an old resident in the buildings, who was pulled from the rubble by firemen.

Two of the attacking Focke-Wulf FW.190s that devastated Bournemouth town centre in an air-raid at lunchtime on a Sunday would be shot down over the town [23 May 1943]. One, which crashed in Poole Bay, was claimed by Lance-Bombadier John Howard and Lance-Bombadier Norman Lawrence of the 87th Light Anti-Aircraft Regiment, Royal Artillery, who were firing triple Lewis guns from the flat roof of Beales department store which was already burning beneath them as the result of a direct hit. They would be awarded the British Empire Medal for bravery by King George VI [1 November 1943]. The second FW.190, credited to a Spitfire, but also claimed by Bofors gunners above the Pier, crashed into St Ives Hotel, 34 Grove Road [23 May 1943]. The pilot, Unteroffizier F.K.Schmidt, died in the fireball but his unreleased bomb failed to detonate. Fire gutted the building and two people were also killed in the next hotel along the road, between the Lansdowne and East Cliff.

A four-engined Halifax glider tug-plane, from RAF Hurn, crashed beside Bournemouth Pier during a period of intensive training flights in the run-up to D-Day [26 January 1944].

Nine people were killed when fully-fuelled Halifax bomber JP137, carrying medical supplies and ammunition from RAF Hurn in a flight by 1658 Conversion Unit that should have taken it to a base in North Africa, crashed on the Bournemouth suburb of Moordown [22 March 1944]. It had left shortly after midnight and failed to gain sufficient height. The accident could have been much worse as the aircraft happened to hit one of the few pieces of open ground in the densely populated area, below Meadow Court flats east of Wimborne Road, though two civilians were killed by the widely strewn wreckage. Sergeant Pilot Dennis Evans also died in the explosion, as did the six members of his crew.

A Bournemouth Flying Club single-engined Piper PA28, being flown by hotelier Terry Brand plunged from 2,000 feet, into the sea four miles south of Boscombe Pier [6 November 1997}. Student pilot Terry Brand, who drowned in the aircraft, had just completed his first solo flight, but disregarded instructions from air traffic controllers to prepare for landing at Hurn. Instead, he went off on an additional unauthorised flight which ended with his suicide dive into the water. "Please give my apologies to everyone," he radioed moments before.

Bournemouth (Hurn) Airport — interim name of Hurn Aerodrome [1952], before it became known as Bournemouth International Airport [1989].

Bournemouth International Airport — formerly known as Hurn Aerodrome which opened as RAF Hurn [1941-44]. Renamed from Bournemouth (Hurn) Airport [1989].

Bournemouth II Crest — Mark Va Spitfire financed by public donations and war-weapons events in the town, handed over to 54 Squadron at Hornchurch, Essex [21 March 1941]. It would have a good war, being handed on to a variety of units including the 82nd Fighter Group of the USAAF, and ended up in the post-war French Air Force.

Bovington Relief Landing Ground — satellite station to Portland Royal Naval Air Station, for its helicopters, being the site of the untimely death of the Commandant of the Royal Armoured Corps Centre in a crash [14 May 1969]. Established on the edge of a tank training area (Ordnance Survey map reference SY 843 904).

Bowen — Hurricane pilot **Flight-Lieutenant Charles Earl Bowen** [1916-40], flying with 607 Squadron from RAF Tangmere, was shot down and killed in combat with Messerschmitt Bf.110s between Swanage and the Isle of Wight [11.20 hours, 1 October 1940]. He was from Chelsea and had joined the RAF in 1936.

Bowhay — Canadian flyer **Pilot Officer Bowhay** of 418 (City of Edmonton) Squadron was killed when a Mosquito fighter-bomber crashed at Alder Road, Poole [23 July 1944].

BOURNEMOUTH CRASH: ENTRANT NUMBER "18" WAS THE HONOURABLE CHARLES STEWART ROLLS WHO LAY DEAD IN THE WRECKAGE OF HIS WRIGHT FLYER BIPLANE AT THE BOURNEMOUTH CENTENARY AVIATION MEETING AS STEWARDS AND SPECTATORS FORMED A CIRCLE TO KEEP BACK PHOTOGRAPHERS ON 12 JULY 1910.

FATAL FIRST: PIONEER AVIATOR ROLLS HAD ACHIEVED A STRING OF AERONAUTICAL RECORDS BUT WITH HIS CRASH AT SOUTHBOURNE AERODROME ON 12 JULY 1910 HE CAPPED THEM ALL, BY BECOMING THE FIRST AIRMAN TO DIE IN BRITAIN FROM AN ACCIDENT DURING POWERED FLIGHT.

BR — code letters of 184 Squadron flying Mark Ib Typhoons from RAF Warmwell [1944-45].

Bradford Peverell crash — Sergeant Pilot Sidney Wakeling of 87 Squadron from RAF Exeter was killed when Hurricane V7250 crashed in flames at New Barn, south of the village, during a Battle of Britain dog-fight [25 August 1940].

Brand — Bournemouth hotelier **Terry Brand** [1952-97] was the student pilot who ended his first solo flight by deliberately diving a Piper PA28 from 2,000 feet to plunge into the sea off Boscombe Pier [6 November 1997]. No problem had been reported but Brand was disregarding landing instructions by going off on an unauthorised course. "Please give my apologies to everyone," were his last words.

The inquest recorded a suicide verdict. The coroner, Nigel Neville-Jones, had read a death note in which Brand quoted a Buddhist poem: "Freedom, as free as a bird, takes my breath away, the divine wind blows." The letter explained: "My sole intention from learning to fly was to move on in one dramatic moment. My actions are premeditated and calculated.

"I'm not sad, I'm not depressed, nor should those who are close to me be so. It is the right thing for me to do. It is my destiny, my right, my karma."

Brandy Bay — **RAF Brandy Bay** was a Purbeck coastal radar station, established on the ridge above Egliston Gwyle [1941-43] on the 450-feet contour (Ordnance Survey map reference SY 900 801), with Tyneham House being requisitioned for administrative and staff quarters.

Brazil — an ex-BOAC Mark V Sunderland flying-boat from Poole, converted into a Sandringham-3 for carrying 21 passengers and sold to the Argentine airline Dodero [November 1945].

Brennan — the five sons of **Mr and Mrs R.J. Brennan** of Worgret Bakery, near Wareham, claimed something of a record by enlisting in the RAF [1940-41]. They were Samuel, Eric, Peter, Archibald and Edwin, and their ages ranged from 20 to 33. The other two Brennan children were girls.

Bridport crash — at West Bay, in a forced-landing on the beach with the pilot thinking he was over France, of a Heinkel He.111 of Kampfgruppe 100, the elite two per cent of German pathfinder bombers operating from Vannes, Brittany [6 November 1940]. It carried the identification code "6N+AH" and would prove to be the most significant and revealing of all enemy aircraft captured in the Second World War, yielding to Air Ministry boffins at the Royal Aircraft Establishment, Farnborough, and the Telecommunications Research Establishment, Worth Matravers, a priceless haul of aerials and related radio equipment. This apparatus would correct a false assumption about

BOURNEMOUTH CRASH: EDMOND AUDEMARS WAS ABLE TO WALK CLEAR FROM HIS DEMOISELLE MONOPLANE AFTER THIS CRASH IN JULY 1910 AND HAD TAKEN THE SENSIBLE PRECAUTION OF BRINGING A SECOND AEROPLANE TO THE MEETING AT SOUTHBOURNE AERODROME.

UNIDENTIFIED WRECKAGE: ANOTHER SMASHED MONOPLANE WHICH ENDED ITS FLYING CAREER UPSIDE-DOWN IN A BOURNEMOUTH FIELD.

AERIAL BOURNEMOUTH: WEST CLIFF PROMENADE, PIER APPROACH, BATH ROAD, EAST CLIFF PROMENADE AND UNDERCLIFF DRIV
"TAKEN FROM THE BOURNEMOUTH AVIATION CO. LTD'S AVRO PASSENGER BI-PLANE AT 2,000 FEET ... BY MR EDGE OF FLIGHT".

om The Bournemouth
nger Biplane At 2000ft.
hoto By Mr Edge Of Flight.

From The Bournemouth
ssenger Biplane At 2000ft.
Photo By Mr. Edge Of Flight.

G-AGBZ BRISTOL: A BOEING CLIPPER FLYING-BOAT OF BRITISH AIRWAYS, MOORED OFF BROWNSEA ISLAND IN 1946.

the frequency of the radio direction beam, and enable effective British countermeasures, in time to save the vital Rolls-Royce aero engine plant at Derby [8 May 1941].

Bristol — Boeing Clipper flying-boat G-AGBZ which was part of the long-haul fleet of British Airways operating from Poole Harbour during and after the Second World War. Her notable flight, however, was from Stranraer, when she took Prime Minister Winston Churchill to America for a decisive meeting with President Franklin D. Roosevelt [17 June 1942].

Bristow — test-pilot **Alan Bristow** [born 1923], a Fleet Air Arm pilot [1943-46] who then tested prototypes for Westland Aircraft Limited [1946-49], operated Air Whaling Limited from Henstridge Aerodrome [1953-54]. His four Westland S-55 helicopters were then sold to the South Georgia Company, for whale spotting in the Falkland Islands Dependency, but returned each summer for their annual overhaul until their final migration to the Antarctic [October 1957]. Bristow Helicopters Limited became the aviator's main business [1954-68] and then British United Airways Limited [1967-70]. His record-breaking contribution to world aviation, when serving with 771 Naval Air Squadron, was to bring down his Fleet Air Arm Sikorski R4B Hoverfly on to the makeshift floorboarded flight-deck of trials ship K253, the frigate HMS *Helmsdale*, off Portland [6 September 1946]. It was the first helicopter landing on a naval escort-vessel at sea. Bristow would become chairman of the Bristow Helicopter Group [1967].

The Brit — named Spitfire bought for the RAF by the people of west Dorset and named after Bridport's river. Handed over to 308 Squadron [10 May 1941]. Transferred to 403 Squadron [28 May 1941] and then to a training unit near Chester, being lost at the end of the year in a flying accident [21 December 1941].

British Aerospace plc — as British Aircraft Corporation became, would inherit the 500-series and then make a 475-series of the 1-11 airliner at Bournemouth (Hurn) Airport. With the completion of the last of this line the factory closed, just a month later [June 1984]. Hopes of maintenance work were insufficient to keep it open.

British Aircraft Corporation — absorbed the Vickers Armstrongs' works at Hurn which had produced the Vickers Viscount and the less successful Vickers Vanguard. Its mainstay became the new BAC.1-11 which was made at Hurn and took off from there on its maiden flight [20 August 1963]. The airliner would go into a 500-series, with the 475-series following.

British Aircraft Corporation was transformed into Bristol British Aerospace plc, as the government privatised its planemaking interests [1984].

British Airways — short operating name of British Overseas Airways Corporation (see its entry), on advertisements, aircraft and uniforms, when BOAC was operating flying-boats from Poole Harbour [1940-48].

British European Airways — flew passenger services from Bournemouth (Hurn) Airport, principally to Jersey [1961-66]. Operated Vickers Viscounts, appropriately as every other one had been made at Hurn.

British Island Airways — operated from Bournemouth (Hurn) Airport, principally to the Channel Islands [1970s].

British Overseas Airways Corporation — formed by amalgamating Imperial Airways and British Airlines [August 1939], under the chairmanship of Lord Reith, the founder of the BBC. Its sea-based fleet of Short C-class "Empire" flying-boats were moved, with their supporting facilities, from Hythe, on Southampton Water, to Salterns Pier and its club rooms requisitioned from Poole Harbour Yacht Club, at Lilliput, Poole. These became the Marine Terminal.

Water runways, called "Trots", were marked by lines of tyres and extended from the Wareham Channel, between Hamworthy and the Arne peninsula, to Brownsea Roads anchorage between the island and Sandbanks.

SPLASH DOWN: AN "EMPIRE" FLYING-BOAT OF BRITISH AIRWAYS, WHICH HAS LANDED ON A "TROT" (WATER RUNWAY) IN POOLE HARBOUR ON ARRIVAL FROM CALCUTTA, IS LED BY THE DUTY OPERATIONS OFFICER IN HIS LAUNCH, AS SHE TAXIS TO HER MOORING BUOY. THEY ARE OFF LILLIPUT, HEADING WESTWARDS, AND TWO OTHER FLYING-BOATS CAN BE GLIMPSED IN THE BACKGROUND (CENTRE LEFT) OFF SALTERNS PIER.

BOAC re-established the Transatlantic air link, from Poole Harbour, in "Empire" flying-boat *Clare* [4-5 August 1940].

Harold Balfour MP, the Under-Secretary at the Air Ministry, was among the VIPs on *Clare*'s second outward flight from Poole [14 August 1940]. He returned having purchased three long-range Boeing 314 "Clipper" flying-boats [18 August 1940] for delivery to British Overseas Airways in 1941.

In fact the first big American arrival at Poole would be *Guba* (G-AGBJ), a Consolidated Catalina, which gracefully dropped into Poole Harbour [1 February 1941]. She brought a new sound to Dorset skies, being the Twin Wasp engines of Pratt and Whitney which were louder than the familiar Bristol Pegasus 9-cylinder radial engines of the Short "Empire" flying-boats.

The "Clippers" seemed to dwarf the "Empire" boats and appeared to take an age to take-off from the "Trots". Poole people were accustomed to seeing the "Empire" flying-boats rising from the water in 20 seconds. A "Clipper" would take an almost worrying 60 seconds. Explained an onlooker from Southampton: "This is understandable as she is 100 per cent heavier than the 'Empire' boat but has only 50 per cent more power for take-off. The principle is sound enough as water is cheaper than motors if you can get enough of it."

"Empire" flying-boat *Clio* was withdrawn to short Brothers' Belfast works for a military refit [12 March 1941]. She was equipped with radar, armour plating, bomb-racks, and four machine guns in each of the two Boulton-Paul turrets in the dorsal and the tail. On being fitted out for service use she was handed over to 201 Squadron of Coastal Command to patrol the Iceland Gap from northern Scotland.

Clare would move on to the new Empire route to Africa [1941] but become a casualty shortly after setting out from Poole for Bathurst, West Africa [14 September 1942]. She was carrying 13 passengers and six crew. They radioed after take-off to report engine trouble and followed this with a second emergency call, 30 minutes later, to say she was on fire. Nothing more was heard or found.

The corporation's "land" flights — those from the ground rather than the water — were also transferred to Dorset/Hampshire, from Lyneham, Wiltshire, to RAF Hurn [1943-44]. The first of its land-planes to land there was a Mark 1 Lancaster, G-AGJI, which was the first civilian-flown Lancaster in the British Isles. It was kitted out as a transporter rather than a bomber and was without gun-turrets though it retained wartime camouflage.

POOLE WELCOME: JOCKEY, MUSIC HALL CELEBRITY AND FILM-STAR GEORGE FORMBY WITH WIFE BERYL INGHAM, IN WARTIME ENTERTAINMENTS NATIONAL SERVICE ASSOCIATION UNIFORMS, BEING GREETED BY SEAWOMAN MOLLIE SKINNER OF BRITISH AIRWAYS ON RETURNING TO BRITAIN IN A FLYING-BOAT FROM A CONCERT TOUR FOR TROOPS OVERSEAS.

Following tests with a Development Flight unit the first of what would become post-war civilian Lancasters, to be known as the Lancastrian, were then ordered [September 1944].

Avro York transport MW103, an RAF aircraft loaned for civilian use, was next to use Hurn and took off for Cairo, via Morocco and the southern Mediterranean [22 April 1944].

BOAC flying-boats repatriated prisoners-of-war from Japanese camps, with the first touching down to sensational press interest in the men's stories of degrading and inhuman treatment [18 September 1945].

Former Halifax bombers, in conversions known as Haltons, were operating the BOAC land-plane route from Hurn to the Gold Coast and Lagos, Nigeria.

FLAG FLYING: G-AGBZ BRISTOL, *A* BOEING CLIPPER *FLYING-BOAT OF BRITISH AIRWAYS, ON A MOORING IN POOLE HARBOUR AS A LAUNCH COMES ALONGSIDE WITH WARTIME TRAVELLERS BOUND FOR NEW YORK IN 1945.*

British United Airways — operated from Bournemouth (Hurn) Airport [1960s]

Broadwindsor crash — Westland Lysander R9015 of 16 Squadron dived into the ground, out of low cloud in the hills above the village [16 December 1940].

Brownsea Island Major Strategic Night Decoy — deception pyrotechnics, at the western end of the largest island in Poole Harbour, drew 150 tons of bombs intended for the new RAF Hamworthy [25 May 1942]. In all this "Starfish" apparatus would claim a total of 1,000 tons of high explosive that would otherwise have dropped on the Bournemouth conurbation.

Brumby — Hurricane flyer **Sergeant-Pilot Norman Brumby** [1918-40], in combat with 607 Squadron from RAF Tangmere, was shot down and killed by Messerschmitt Bf.110s between Swanage and the Isle of Wight [11.20 hours, I October 1940]. His body was recovered and returned to his hometown of Hull, where he is buried in the Northern Cemetry. He had volunteered for the RAF Reserve in 1938 and was called-up a year later.

Bruneval Raid — organized and practised for in Dorset by Combined Operations, under Acting Admiral Louis Mountbatten at Anderson Manor and Poole, this audacious air-sea commando operation brought back a German Würzburg radar apparatus from the French coast between Le Havre and Fécamp [27 February 1942].

The raiding party jumped from 12 Whitley bombers and landed on top of the 400-feet cliff in deep snow. They took their objective with complete surprise and dismantled the equipment for removal by landing craft from the beach below. Its components were taken for scientific examination to the Telecommunications Research Establishment at Worth Matravers.

Würzburg operated from a parabolic aerial at 53 centimetres frequency (between 558 and 560 MHz) and had a range of about 40 kilometres.

Buchanan — Spitfire flyer **Pilot Officer James Richebourg Buchanan** [1915-40] of 609 Squadron from RAF Warmwell was shot down over Weymouth Bay in a Battle of Britain dog-fight [27 July 1940]. He crashed into the sea in Spitfire N3023 and his body was not recovered.

Burton Bradstock crashes — a Hurricane of 238 Squadron from RAF Middle Wallop was shot down in a Battle of Britain dog-fight and crashed at Bredy Farm, a mile east of the village [13 August 1940]. Sergeant Pilot Ronald Little escaped unhurt.

Both the machine and pilot survived when Sergeant Pilot Ernest Snowdon crash-landed Hurricane N2646 of 213 Squadron, from RAF Exeter, at Burton Bradstock during another action-packed day [25 August 1940].

A Martinet from the Armament Practice Camp at Warmwell Aerodrome developed engine problems over the Chesil Beach Bombing Range [12 March 1945]. The pilot crash-landed at Burton Mere, on the coast between Swyre and Burton Bradstock, but was trapped in the wreckage. Two pensioner heroes, Burton villagers Miss Harriette Evelyn Bendy (aged 68) and Levi Rogers (aged 65) ignored the flames which were about to engulf the aircraft. They untangled the pilot's feet and pulled the shocked airman to safety as his aeroplane became an inferno.

Bush — Hurricane flyer **Sergeant-Pilot Basil Martin Bush**, in combat with 504 Squadron from RAF Filton, was shot down and force-landed south of Yeovil [16.55 hours, 30 September 1940]. He was unhurt but P3021 was written-off.

Basil Bush would become a flare-dropping Mosquito pilot, with 128 Squadron for 8 (Pathfinder) Group, Bomber Command, and survived the war.

Butterfield — Hurricane flyer **Sergeant-Pilot Samuel Leslie Butterfield** [1913-40] was shot down and killed off Portland while flying with 213 Squadron from RAF Exeter [10.23 hours, 11 August 1940]. His body would be washed up in France and is buried in B Cemetery at Boulogne. He was born in Leeds and had fought over France, from Merville and Biggin Hill, in support of the British Expeditionary Force. He had a number of Messerschmitts to his credit and had survived baling out of a burning Hurricane off Dunkirk, for which he was awarded the Distinguished Flying Medal.

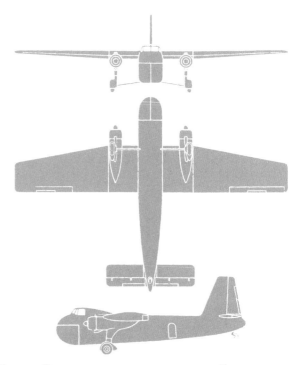

BOEING CLIPPER: BOUGHT BY BOAC FOR THE POOLE FLYING-BOAT FLEET.

BRISTOL FREIGHTER: FAMILIAR SIGHT OVER BOURNEMOUTH DURING THE 1950S, OPERATING FROM HURN AERODROME.

C

Cabot — Poole-based Short "Empire" flying-boat G-AFCU seconded from BOAC to 119 Squadron at Invergordon and sunk by the Germans in Bodø fjord, Norway [4-5 May 1940]. She had been the first of the Short S30 flying-boats to be converted and improved to the "Empire" specification from Imperial Airways [1938-39]. "Hydromatic" de Havilland constant-speed propellors had been fitted. Flight refuelling gear was installed for intended peacetime Trans-Atlantic crossings, to enable a carrying weight of 53,000 pounds, compared with the usual take-off weight of 46,000 pounds. In practice flights over Southampton Water, Geoffrey Tyson flew Harrow bomber G-AFRL which had been modified as a tanker, and Lankester Parker was *Cabot*'s pilot [24 May 1939].

FLIGHT REFUELLING: "EMPIRE" FLYING-BOAT CABOT LINKED TO HARROW TANKER G-AFRL IN THE PRACTICE FLIGHT ABOVE SOUTHAMPTON WATER ON 24 MAY 1939.

Cambrian Airways — operated from Bournemouth (Hurn) Airport [1960s].

POLITICAL POSITION: THIS WAS THE PICTURE THAT WAS INTENDED TO MAKE THE POINT, BY SHOWING FLYING-BOAT CABOT OVER A LINER HEADING FOR SOUTHAMPTON, TO IMPLY THAT THE FUTURE BELONGS TO AIR TRAVEL.

THOUSAND GALLONS: REFUELLING PETROL IN FLIGHT WAS TO TAKE PLACE ABOVE FOYNES AND BOTWOOD, NEWFOUNDLAND, TO ENABLE FLYING-BOATS TO INAUGURATE BRITAIN'S TRANS-ATLANTIC AIR SERVICES BUT INSTEAD CABOT WOULD BE CALLED TO WAR. THIS PARTICULARLY CLEAR SHOT, SENT WORLDWIDE BY PLANET NEWS, ALSO SHOWS CALSHOT CASTLE SEAPLANE STATION (MIDDLE DISTANCE).

Candy — wartime air cadet **Richard Stafford Candy**, from Shillingstone, was lost at sea off West Africa [30 October 1942].

Caribou — Poole-based Short "Empire" flying-boat seconded from BOAC to 119 Squadron at Invergordon and sunk by the Germans in Bodø fjord, Norway [4-5 May 1940]. She had taken part in successful pre-war flight refuelling rehearsals at Hamble on Southampton Water [3 July 1939].

Cattistock crash — a £7 million Sea Harrier of 899 Squadron, on a training flight from the Royal Naval Air Station at Yeovilton, went out of control above the village [09.34 hours, 21 January 1983].

It narrowly missed homes in West End and Beech Tree Close and crashed into a hedge one field away from the bungalows.

No-one was hurt. The pilot, 28-year-old Flight Lieutenant Kevin Fox, had ejected safely.

Asked about village reactions, a huntsman at the nearby kennels told television reporters: "There may be some complaints from old women of both sexes but there are many military families in the area and most of us realise that these things are bound to happen from time to time."

Mrs Sheila Smith of Ramsay Cottage watched the Harrier "flutter to the ground like a leaf". She met the pilot as he was about to be taken from Lankham Bottom, by helicopter, to the hospital at Yeovilton air base: "I told him that he had not hit anything and he was very pleased to know that."

Earth and fragments of wreckage were thrown onto the tiled roof of Fred Wainwright's bungalow. He came out of his garage as there was a second bang and the fighter hit the hedge: "We had a quick look down there to see if there was anyone trapped but you just couldn't get near. It was one sheet of flame, an inferno with black smoke rising from the wreckage."

Police had to break into one of the bungalows to reassure pensioner Mrs Evelyn Ardagh who had been so frightened by the explosions that she locked the doors and refused to come out. "It certainly knocked the stuffing out of me," she said after receiving treatment for shock.

Cawse — wartime flyer **Pilot Officer Frederick Norman Cawse** [1915-1940] of 238 Squadron from RAF Middle Wallop was shot down in Hurricane P3222 off Weymouth by a Messerschmitt Bf.109 [11 August 1940]. His body was washed up on the other side of the Channel and he is buried in the community cemetery at Cayeux-sur-Mer.

Chaldon Herring crashes — of Messerschmitt Bf.110 (3M+KM) belonging to the 1st Staffel of II Gruppe, Zerstörergeschwader 2, in one of Dorset's busiest days of the Battle of Britain [25 August 1940]. It became a fireball at East Chaldon and the two crewmen died in the explosion. The kill was claimed by Squadron Leader H. S. "George" Darley, and American volunteer "Red" Tobin in Spitfires of 609 Squadron from RAF Warmwell.

152 Squadron from Warmwell lost Spitfire R6607 at the northern extremity of the parish, beside Tadnoll Mill, when Sergeant Pilot Edmund Shepperd plunged into the ground [18 October 1940]. No other aeroplane was involved and there was no obvious reason for the accident.

Channel Airways — operated from Bournemouth (Hurn) Airport to Jersey and Guernsey [from 1966]. Its principal aircraft was the Trident.

Cheselbourne crashes — of Spitfire X4107, with Pilot Officer Mick Miller of 609 Squadron from RAF Warmwell, after his fatal collision with a Messerschmitt Bf.110 (3U+FT) at 24,000 feet above Bellamy's Farm, Piddletrenthide [27 September 1940]. Most of the wreckage fell to the east of Doles Ash Farm, on the Cheselbourne side of the parish boundary.

A Lockheed P-38 Lightning of the 474th Fighter Group of the United States Army Air Force, flying from Warmwell Aerodrome, crashed near Cheselbourne [21 May 1944]. Lieutenant Kimball was killed in the accident.

Chesil Beach Bombing Range — established along the Fleet lagoon [1937] and extended as the Lyme Bay Bombing Range [August 1939] with a notable wartime role that included the initial testing of the Dambuster bombs [December 1942-March 1943].

Chesil Beach crashes — other than those listed elsewhere, under the specific parish entries for Abbotsbury, Chickerell, Fleet, and Langton Herring. Most misadventures were to users of the Chesil Beach Bombing Range and often those that fell on the beach itself and the adjacent mainland were listed and recorded as range rather than parish casualties.

Fairey Battle K7594 of 226 Squadron spun out of control into the Chesil Beach [11 December 1937].

Hawker Fury K8223 of 9 Flying Training School hit a drogue, caught fire, and crashed into the sea off the pebble bank [25 May 1938].

Hawker Fury K8271, also belonging to 9 Flying Training School, came down into the pebbles [10 December 1938].

Hawker Audax K4396 of 6 Flying Training School crashed on failing to pull out of a dive [13 March 1939].

Boulton-Paul Overstrand K8173 of 10 Bombing and Gunnery School at RAF Warmwell crashed into the sea off the Chesil Beach [22 April 1940].

Blenheim L9405, a Mark V bomber, ditched in Lyme Bay, off the Chesil Beach [29 November 1941].

Chickerell Aerodrome — now built upon, at the eastern edge of the parish between the B3157 at Marquis Farm and West Haven Hospital, Westham, Weymouth (Ordnance Survey map reference SY 657 793). It was a grass airstrip with a main runway of 2,400 feet and a hangar in the south-east corner. Established as Royal Naval Air Station Portland in 1918 with No.513 Flight operating DH6s against U-boats in the English Channel.

These de Havilland aircraft and their crews were reformed into 241 Squadron of the Royal Air Force in August 1918, being attached to 75 Wing of 10 Group. They were disbanded on 23 January 1919. Short-term civilian use followed, with Handley Page Air Transport flying ex-military 0-400s from Cricklewood, but giving Weymouth an air service was an idea ahead of its time.

Between the wars the aerodrome, which doubled as playing fields, was visited by Sir Alan Cobham's Flying Circus. The military lease of the land resumed in October 1936, through the Air Ministry, on behalf of Bomber Command. It was commissioned as the Forward Landing Aerodrome for the Chesil Beach Bombing Range, to act as a satellite airfield to Warmwell Aerodrome (known as Woodsford Aerodrome from its opening in May 1937 until renaming on 1 July 1938). The main reason for requisitioning Chickerell was so that aircraft in landing difficulties had an emergency landing strip within a mile of the east end of the range. As well as hosting the fire engine and ambulance it also accommodated range personnel.

K. S. West's researches have shown that Pilot Officer A. E. de Pencier, killed on 13 March 1939, was one of its emergencies. Martinet aircraft from No.771 FRU Squadron based at Royal Naval Air Station Gosport were at Chickerell from September 1945 until August 1955, a period when the Chesil Beach was used for practice runs by bombers and Sunderland flying-boats. The aerodrome was derequisitioned in 1959.

Chickerell crashes — a Lysander of 613 Squadron, on a training flight during the "Phoney War", crashed in the village [23 April 1940].

A Messerschmitt Bf.109, crashed into the Chesil Beach during one of the busiest days of the Battle of Britain [25 August 1940]. The pilot, Hauptmann Maculan, apparently fell out and drowned.

The same dog-fights accounted for a Bf.110 at Tatton House, west of Buckland Ripers, killing both crew. Then a Bf.109 belly-landed in an adjoining field at Tatton Farm. Its pilot, Gefreiter Josef Broker of Jagdgeschwader 53, escaped with wounds as the fighter was engulfed in flames.

Spitfires from RAF Warmwell claimed the kills; the first was credited to Squadron Leader H. S. "George" Darley of 609 Squadron, and the third to Pilot Officer W. Beaumont of 152 Squadron.

Losses on the Chesil Beach Bombing Range, other than those that can be identified with a particular parish, are listed in the entry for Chesil Beach crashes.

Child Okeford crash — of Spitfire N3231 from RAF Warmwell at Netmead in the common land meadows west of the village, beside the River Stour [16.00 hours, 7 October 1940]. It was shot down in one of the dog-fights following the attack on the Westland Aircraft Company factory at Yeovil, and Pilot Officer Michael Staples of 609 Squadron baled out at 21,000 feet with what he described as "a big hole" in his leg. He landed without further damage and was taken to Blandford Cottage Hospital.

Chilfrome crash — Hawker Typhoon R8663 of 257 Squadron crashed in a wartime forced-landing at Chilfrome [15 December 1942].

Christchurch Aero Club — formed in the late 1930s and re-formed post-war [1950], it became the last users of Christchurch Aerodrome, after the withdrawal of de Havilland to Chester [1962]. Flew a selection of Tiger Moths and Austers, plus a few Airspeed Oxfords that had been pensioned off by the RAF's Air Service Training arm. These were particularly appropriate, being returnees to the airfield where some of them had been constructed.

Other aircraft included Rapides, Colt and Tripacer trainers. Gradually they disappeared as housing estates encroached but a photograph in Leslie Dawson's *Wings over Dorset* shows G. E. H. Gould's rebuilt Auster J1-N being fuelled at the Christchurch Aero Club pumps in 1972 — eight years after the airfield had been officially closed [1964].

PEACETIME PASSING: EVOCATIVE REMAINS OF AVRO 504K G-EBVL, WITH WHICH BUD FISHER BEGAN FLYING AT CHRISTCHURCH IN 1931, LYING DERELICT BESIDE THE AERODROME IN THE LAST MONTH OF PEACE, IN AUGUST 1939.

Christchurch Aerodrome — RAF Christchurch, a grass airfield of five runways at 20 feet above sea level on a gravel plain at Somerford, to the east of the town (SZ 185 930), established on an existing leisure-flying field created by stunt-flyer Bud Fisher [1931] and chosen for the use of the Air Defence Research Establishment [1935]. The Special Duty Flight, attached to the Telecommunications Research Establishment, came to Christchurch when the scientists moved from Dundee to Worth Matravers [5 May 1940]. They were protected by three Hurricane fighters, L1552, L1562 and L1592. Became a major manufacturing base with the establishment of a shadow-factory for Airspeed (1934) Limited [January 1941].

Airfield pundit code "XC".

As it expanded, Christchurch Aerodrome attracted inevitable attention from the Luftwaffe, though the first wave of bombs exploded harmlessly or not at all [10 May 1941]. The next raid hit nearby civilian buildings [12 May 1941].

The Airspeed factory at Christchurch Aerodrome converted 160 standard Supermarine Spitfires into Seafires, for use by the Fleet Air Arm on Royal Navy aircraft-carriers [1943-45].

As preparations for the invasion of Europe gathered pace, RAF Christchurch became Station 416, Advance Landing Group Christchurch, of the 9th United States Army Air Force [7 March 1944]. Nearly a thousand officers and men of the 405th Fighter Bomber Group arrived by train from the liner *Mauretania*, which had docked at Liverpool.

The 405th comprised 509, 510 and 511 Squadrons of the USAAF, equipped with Republic P-47 Thunderbolt fighter-bombers.

For the people of Christchurch the noise, excitement and danger from bomb-laden crash-landings would soon become a memory, as the entire 405th Fighter Bomber Group were ordered to follow the war across the Channel and took off for Airstrip 8, at Picauville, in the Allied-occupied Cherbourg peninsula [11 July 1944].

CHRISTCHURCH LIVERY: RED FUSELAGE AND SILVER WINGS AND TAIL, BEING THE UNIFORM OF CHRISTCHURCH AERO CLUB, IN THE SPRING OF 1939.

HEAVY LANDING: AIRSPEED AMBASSADOR PRODUCTION PROTOTYPE G-ALFR HAVING SCRAPED TO A HALT ON CHRISTCHURCH AERODROME, ON 13 NOVEMBER 1950.

Christchurch crashes — Royal Navy Seafire MB315, arriving at Christchurch Aerodrome from Donibristle, Scotland, overshot the runway and crashed into a bungalow, "Musoka" in Caroline Avenue, at Stanpit [25 June 1943]. The pilot, Sub-Lieutenant Peter Lamb, was taken to hospital with head injuries but survived to continue his career, though he had to grow his hair long to cover the scars. "Not my best landing," he wrote in his log.

An American P-47 Thunderbolt from Christchurch Aerodrome crashed in the playground at Highcliffe School [19.30 hours, 30 April 1944]. The pilot had baled out, landing unhurt in the nearby recreation ground, and the school was empty at the time of the accident.

An RAF Wellington bomber crashed near Christchurch Aerodrome, on the north side of the railway line [13.00 hours, 25 May 1944].

The worst air-crash of the war, for Christchurch and the rest of the conurbation and Dorset itself, occurred when Foxwood Avenue, Mudeford, was devastated by three P-47 Thunderbolt fighter-bombers of the 509th Squadron of the 405th Fighter Bomber Group. In the first mishap on take-off from Christchurch Advance Landing Ground, Lieutenant Vincent R. James survived and no one was hurt on the ground [06.45 hours, 29 June 1944].

Then at 14.00 hours the same pilot tried again to lift off. Once more he failed to gain proper height and this time overshot the runway into a bungalow. His fuel tanks and bombs exploded, bringing down another Thunderbolt that was coming in to land. Its pilot was unhurt.

Sixteen were killed and 18 injured in the accident and the subsequent explosion as a bomb went off among rescue workers. Mortally wounded, 20-year-old Lieutenant James would die in the arms of nurse Irene Stevenson, in Boscombe Hospital.

The next Thunderbolt mishap was less dramatic. A P-47 landed short of the runway and came down in a perimeter field, from where it bounced on to the Lymington road [17.00 hours, 2 July 1944]. It came to rest upside down. There was no fire, no civilian involvement, and the pilot escaped.

A lucky escape was had by men of the 306th Bombardment Group of the United States Army Air Force, arriving for recuperation at the seaside, when B-17 Flying Fortress 866 overshot the western boundary of the notoriously short Christchurch Aerodrome [15 July 1945]. It ploughed into scrubland, ripping out the near-side port engine, but came to a halt without exploding. No one was hurt.

TWIN ENGINES: LEFT DETACHED ON THE GRASS AT CHRISTCHURCH AFTER AIRSPEED AMBASSADOR G-ALFR HAD TURNED ITSELF INTO A GLIDER ON 13 NOVEMBER 1950.

The production prototype Airspeed Ambassador, G-ALFR made in the factory beside the aerodrome, came down heavily during a flight trial and lost both engines before it flopped to a halt [13 November 1950].

One post-war afternoon, just three days before the US Air Force bombed North Korea, a Fairey Barracuda of 750 Naval Air Squadron — one of four from the Observer Air Training School at Royal Naval Air Station St Merryn, Cornwall, that were taking part in Exercise Castanets — crashed into Christchurch Bay, off Highcliffe [20 June 1952]. It had suffered engine failure.

The pilot, Lieutenant Albert Standbridge, and his passengers, Midshipmen Thomas Penfold and Francis Kirk were able to escape in rubber dinghies. The three were picked up by a Sea Otter within twenty minutes. Rather than risking a take-off it then taxied to the shore at Christchurch from where the men were taken to Boscombe Hospital for a brief check-up.

More than a decade later the engine and the mid-section of the fuselage were winched from the water and taken to the Military Engineering Experimental Establishment [4 June 1968].

Two British Army Sioux helicopters of the Blue Eagles crashed at Christchurch after a mid-air collision [23 August 1969].

Christie — Spitfire flyer **Sergeant Pilot John McBean Christie** [[1918-40] of 152 Squadron from RAF Warmwell was shot down in K9882 by Messerschmitt Bf.109s off Swanage [26 September 1940]. He had been attempting to intercept the formation of some 60 Heinkel He.111 bombers that wrecked the Supermarine Works at Woolston, Southampton. His body was recovered from the sea and sent home, to Arkleston Cemetery, Renfrew.

Church Knowle crashes — a Messerschmitt Bf.110 crashed into Creech Barrow Hill during a day of Battle of Britain dog-fights [25 August 1940]. The crew parachuted into captivity.

It is also possible that the volcano-shaped mass of Creech Barrow Hill, swelling out of the Purbeck heaths, also claimed Short Stirling R9306 of 90 Squadron [16 February 1943]. The bomber flew into the ground in Dorset but conflicting locations have been given. Blandford has been recorded but Creech Barrow would seem much more likely.

Churchill — wartime **Prime Minister Winston Churchill** [1874-1965] was flown in a twin-engined de Havilland Flamingo transport aircraft from Warmwell Aerodrome to Paris for secret discussions on the Fall of France [31 May 1940]. He was escorted by nine Hurricanes of 601 (County of London) Squadron, who saw him safely home the following day.

Later in the war, shortly after its opening, RAF Hurn was provided with a VIP hangar for the Prime Minister's personal Liberator and other special aircraft [July 1942].

City of Liverpool — one of the two Sunderland flying-boat hulks abandoned in Poole Harbour when British Overseas Airway Corporation departed for Southampton Water [1948]: *Solway* was the other.

City of Liverpool would be highest up the shore when the two fuselages were finally stranded at Lower Hamworthy, like beached whales [1958-59]. She had been built as Short's S.1927, became RAF serial number NJ205, and ended her flying days as a Mark 2 Solent conversion, civilian call-sign G-AKNS.

City of Swanage — Short S.8 Calcutta flying-boat G-AATZ, which was bought by Imperial Airways [May 1930] and given its elevated name (Swanage is no city!) on being assigned to Air Pilots Training Limited. It was used to train pilots, generally for 25 hours, in the practicalities of seamanship, such as taxying, manoeuvring, turning, attaching drogues, and of course mooring. It operated off Hamble and would be scrapped there [1939].

CITY STATUS: SWANAGE ELEVATED TO CITY OF SWANAGE ON SHORT CALCUTTA FLYING-BOAT G-AATZ USED FOR PILOT TRAINING ON SOUTHAMPTON WATER IN THE 1930s.

Censored photograph: British Overseas Airways Corporation tenders, top brass, and "Empire" flying-boat Clare on her return to Poole Harbour from re-establishing the trans-Atlantic air route in August 1940. The Royal Air Mail penant and red ensign are stiff in the westerly wind into which she has just landed but the interesting thing about the photograph released by Photographic New Agencies, from Old Mitre Court, Fleet Street, is that the censor has deleted what would have been our glimpse of the Poole coast (left) to keep the location secret.

Baltimore bound: Clipper flying-boat of Pan American Airways moored off the west end of Brownsea Island, preparing for next Trans-Atlantic flight from Poole Harbour, in 1945.

PIONEER AVIATOR: ALAN COBHAM PIONEERED AIR ROUTES AROUND THE GLOBE AND WENT ON TO PERFECT FLIGHT REFUELLING TECHNIQUES.

AUSTRALIAN RETURN: ALAN COBHAM BRINGS HOME DE HAVILLAND DH50 G-EBFO, DESCENDING OVER WESTMINSTER BRIDGE TO LAND IN THE THAMES BESIDE THE HOUSES OF PARLIAMENT ON 1 OCTOBER 1926.

Clare — British Overseas Airways Corporation's Short "Empire" flying-boat, which resumed the transatlantic air service between Britain and the United States, from Poole Harbour [4-5 August 1940]. Seats were at a premium, being reserved for VIPs on war service. Air Ministry Under-Secretary Harold Balfour would go on *Clare*'s second wartime crossing — to buy three Boeing 314 "Clipper" flying-boats [14 August 1940].

Clio — Poole-based British Overseas Airways Corporation Short "Empire" flying-boat, flown to Belfast for a military refit to equip her with four machine guns in each of two Boulton-Paul turrets, in the dorsal and tail, plus armour plating, bomb-racks on the wings, and radar. She became Coastal Command aircraft AX659 and was posted to 201 Squadron in northern Scotland [12 March 1941], covering the Iceland Gap, until being lost [22 August 1941].

Clyde — British Overseas Airways Corporation Short "Empire" flying-boat, which flew Colonel René de Larminat from Poole Harbour to Léopoldville in the Belgian Congo, to organise the repossession of French Equatorial Africa [5 August 1940].

Cobham — pioneer aviator **Sir Alan Cobham** [1894-1973], the first to make return flights to Cape Town and Australia, developed the flight refuelling techniques that would extend the horizons for long-distance flying. His post-war Flight Refuelling Limited was based at Tarrant Rushton Aerodrome and has its offices at Wimborne. Sir Alan retired to Falaise, a 1913-built mansion at 13 West Overcliff Drive, Bournemouth.

Alan Cobham, initially a veterinary sergeant in the Royal Field Artillery, flew in the Royal Flying Corps [1917] and after the Great War gave thousands of people their first experience of the sky with joy-rides in an Avro 504K. Then with the creation of the de Havilland Aircraft Company in 1921 he became a test pilot. He also flew 8,000 miles in three months on charter flights across Europe and North Africa.

Long-distance flying became his forte. Using a four-seater de Havilland passenger aeroplane, the DH-50, he became the first to fly over the Himalayas. On 16 November 1925 he took the adventure further, with the first "Air Route Survey" flight for Imperial Airways from Croydon Aerodrome to Capetown, which was reached on 26 February 1926. They were back in England on 13 March 1926, having covered 16,000 miles with Cobham being solo at the controls for more than ninety hours. Despite the prolonged stop-offs, necessary to sort out the arrangements of commercial landings, they were still able to beat a liner back to Britain by a day.

This first return crossing of the entire African continent earned Alan Cobham a string of accolades. These included the Air Force Cross, the Britannia Trophy, Royal Aero Club Gold Medal, Royal Institute of Transport Aviation Gold Medal, and the Royal Institute of Aeronautical Engineers' Simms Gold Medal.

Then on 30 June 1926 he lifted off the River Medway in a DH-50 fitted with floats and headed for Australia. The flight would have been a total success but for the trauma of what happened when the plane flew over what then and now is the most dangerous area of the globe. The engineer, Arthur Elliott, was killed by a Bedouin bullet as they crossed the Iraqi desert between Baghdad and Basra. The subsequent triumph of landing in Sydney was capped by a London homecoming at 14.05 hours on 1 October 1926 that took place in spectacular style. Cobham had landed in the Thames between Westminster Bridge and Vauxhall Bridge. He was then rowed to the steps of the Houses of Parliament and was greeted at the top by Sir Samuel Hoare, the Secretary of State for Air.

LAST LEG: ALAN COBHAM STRIDES UP THE STEPS TO A PARLIAMENTARY WELCOME ON 1 OCTOBER 1926, WHICH WOULD BE CAPPED BY A KNIGHTHOOD.

FLYING CIRCUS: SIR ALAN COBHAM BROUGHT HIS NATIONAL AVIATION DAYS AROUND BRITAIN IN THE 1930S, WITH AUTOGIRO G-ABUC LOOKING DISTINCTY FUTURISTIC IN COMPARISON WITH THE MAIN PLAYERS.

Within a week he had conquered the second bastion of the British establishment and walked out of Buckingham Palace as Sir Alan Cobham, Knight of the Order of the British Empire.

The next spin was 23,000 miles around Africa in a Short Singapore flying boat. These exploits would be popularised by his three books, *My Flight to the Cape, Australia and Back*, and *20,000 Miles in a Flying Boat*.

In the early 1930s he toured Britain with the stunt planes of "Sir Alan Cobham's Air Display" which took the breath away with wing-walks on an Avro 504K and had queues lining up for a flight in his own de Havilland 61, called *Youth of Britain*, a process which was delayed by the fact that they all wanted the pilot's autograph as a memento. Geoffrey Tyson, the country's best stunt pilot, would show how he could pick up a lady's handkerchief from the ground with a spike attached to the left-hand wing-tip of his Tiger Moth.

The barnstorming days gave way in 1935 to the first experiments with in-flight refuelling, aimed to keep open the air route to India in the event of the gathering storm becoming a full-blown

WING WALKING: G-EBYW OF AVIATION TOURS LIMITED FROM CROYDON, TAKING PART IN COBHAM'S FLYING CIRCUS.

BREATHTAKING MOMENT: G-ACEZ LOWERS A WING-TIP AND SKIMS THE GRASS, TO PICK-UP A HANDKERCHIEF FROM THE GROUND IN AN INCREDIBLE DEMONSTRATION OF FLYING SKILL.

TWENTIES STYLE: SIR ALAN AND LADY GLADYS COBHAM PICNIC BENEATH A WING.

FLIGHT REFUELLED: SIR ALAN COBHAM (RIGHT) IN 1947, WITH HIS PILOT AIR VICE-MARSHAL DONALD BENNETT, WARTIME AIR OFFICER COMMANDING OF PATHFINDER MOSQUITOES IN RAF BOMBER COMMAND BELOW THEIR LANCASTRIAN WITH AN ANSON IN THE BACKGROUND.

war. A Harrow bomber registration G-AFRL was converted into a fuel tanker and successfully fed Short S30 flying-boats of Imperial Airways in trials above Southampton Water. The hose-link grab attachments were fitted to flying-boats *Cabot, Caledonia, Cambria* and *Caribou*.

In the war the system would be used with Wellington bombers as tankers to connect with Hurricanes and Spitfires that were being flown across the entire length of the southern Mediterranean to bases in Egypt. The subsequent post-war story of Cobham's company, Flight Refuelling Limited, is told under its entry and that for Tarrant Rushton Aerodrome.

As for Sir Alan, he went into semi-retirement at Falaise on Bournemouth's West Cliff in the early 1950s. From 1956-67 he was chairman of the Bournemouth Symphony Orchestra which came many times to play on his outsized garden lawn. Lady Gladys died in 1961 and Sir Alan moved to Suffolk in 1970. They are buried in Tarrant Rushton churchyard.

Cobham's Flying Circus — the dates of its Dorset visits are given in the entry for National Aviation Displays.

Cobham plc — Sir Alan Cobham's company, Flight Refuelling Limited, as it was renamed in its founder's honour [1994].

GLIDER TOWING: AN AUSTER TOWING A BLANIK GLIDER, EASTWARDS ALONG THE GRASS OF COMPTON ABBAS AIRFIELD, IN THE 1960S.

Cock — Australian Hurricane flyer **Pilot Officer John Reynolds Cock** [1918-88], in combat with 87 Squadron from RAF Exeter, baled out of V7233 on being shot down off Portland Bill [11.00 hours, 11 August 1940]. Though wounded he swam ashore.

He would also survive a mid-air collision [24 October 1940] and left the RAF as Squadron Leader [1948]. From Renmark, South Australia, he returned to Britain for the occasion of the recovery of wreckage of V7233, by Portland divers [30 August 1983].

Compton Abbas Airfield — grass leisure aerodrome on top of the Cranborne Chase escarpment, at 810-feet above sea level, on the east side of Spread Eagle Hill (Ordnance Survey map reference SY 890 186). Westerly take-offs, into the prevailing wind, cross the steep slope of the National Trust's Fontmell Down estate to emerge from the spectacular scenery with instant altitude, high above the Blackmore Vale.

Founded by Shaftesbury Flying Club which won planning permission to use the "land for flying light aircraft and erect a small blister-type hangar" [22 May 1962]. Detailed permission was then given for the hangar, to house an Auster and two Tiger Moths, but plans for a club-house were rejected [16 November 1962].

The club was later given clearance to use a caravan as its flight control office, and to construct a car-park [8 September 1965].

John Thorne and Ralph Jones took over from the club and were allowed to erect additional buildings [9 July 1968]. Six caravans for members of Dorset Flying Club followed [10 September 1969] and P.W. Lewis was given consent for his own portable hangar. It had the feel of a pre-war aerodrome, particularly after the arrival of the Thames Valley Airsports Parachute Club and the creation of the Spread Eagle Display Team [1970]. The club had a veritable squadron of light aircraft and two Austers were busy towing gliders.

The enterprise had lifted off — sparking its own single-issue protest group — and on the ground John Thorne consolidated the structural presence, by obtaining permission for a restaurant, accommodation, and office block [4 March 1971]. Occasional helicopter arrivals included the army on manoeuvres. Bill Boot jumped from a Cessna that had taken off from Compton Abbas, whilst over the Somerset side of the Bristol Channel, and claimed to be the first person to parachute from England into Wales, across the wide waters of the Severn sea.

SEASONAL CHRISTMAS: COMPTON ABBAS NOT QUITE AS ACTIVE AS IT CLAIMED, AS SNOW FELL ABOVE THE 800 FEET CONTOUR OF CRANBORNE CHASE, PHOTOGRAPHED BY RODNEY LEGG ON THE MORNING OF 25 DECEMBER 1995.

Water mains were installed and John Thorne then sold the aerodrome to Earnest Green [1972]. He in turn handed it over to millionaire Alan Curtis of George House (Holdings) Limited [1975]. The new owner brought in mains electricity and was given permission to modify and add to the existing airfield buildings [25 July 1976]. A second hangar and aircraft control tower were then authorised [4 August 1976]. North Dorset District Council's file note of planning permission for the oil fuel and oil facilities includes a reference to a "dope store" which is the aviation term for aircraft paint [27 October 1976].

The airfield's postcard manages to say it all, both visually and with its own caption. "Compton Abbas Airfield has the finest views from any airfield in England" — which is true from the ground as well. "Friendly bar, lovely restaurant, flying training, air charters, engineering, aircraft sales, avionics. An aviation centre that caters for everyone."

A special someone was runaway financier Azil Nadir whose escape to northern Cyprus started by posing as a respectable businessman to hire Clive Hughes to fly him to France.

Compton Abbas crashes — see entries for the adjoining parishes of Asmore, Fontmell Magna and Melbury Abbas.

Considine — Irish citizen **Pilot Officer Brian Considine** [1920-96], flying with 238 Squadron from Tangmere, Sussex and then the newly opened RAF Chilbolton, Hampshire, was one of only eight from the Irish Republic who fought in the Battle of Britain.

He saw action over the English Channel and the Isle of Wight, claiming a Messerschmitt Bf.110 [21 July 1940] and a shared Dornier Do.17 [27 July 1940].

His own downfall, caused by Messerschmitt Bf.109s over Bournemouth, was followed by his baling out, wounded, above Sturminster Marshall [5 November 1940]. Hurricane V6792 crashed at Crab Farm, Shapwick. In retrospect, historians have considered the Battle of Britain to have finished at the end of October. "Unfortunately no one told the Germans," Considine quipped.

He recovered from his injuries and returned to his Squadron, flying via HMS *Victorious* and Malta to Egypt and the Middle East [14 June 1941]. He went on to Aden and then flew Gladiators twice daily over Palestine to monitor the weather. Moves to Malta, Sicily and Cairo led eventually to 48 Squadron in East Anglia — from where he took a glider-towing Dakota in the airborne assault across the Rhine.

As the war in Europe approached its close, the squadron departed for India [15 February 1945] where they carried out supply drops to British troops in Burma.

Post-war, Considine flew airliners for Aer Lingus for four years but then declared himself sick of flying. He went into advertising and insisted on making his annual trips to America by boat.

Constable-Maxwell — Hurricane pilot **Flying Officer Michael Hugh Constable-Maxwell** [born 1917], flying L1764 of 56 Squadron from RAF Boscombe Down, was shot down near Weymouth and force-landed on the pebbles of the Chesil Beach, across the water from Abbotsbury Swannery [17.05 hours, 30 September 1940]. The fighter was written-off by the hostile terrain but the airman walked away from the wreckage.

He would continue to see active service for the remainder of the war, shooting down his last Germans a month after D-Day and later asked to be transferred to the Far East, being ready in Bengal with 84 Squadron, when atomic bombs forced the Japanese surrender. Despite a short intermission as a novice in Ampleforth Abbey he would retire from the RAF with the rank of Wing Commander in 1964.

Cooper-Williams — primary schoolboy **Josiah Cooper-Williams** [1993] was given a single-seat Yugoslav Solo Kraguj fighter for his seventh birthday [March 2000]. His father, a scrap-dealer, found it lying in the grass beside Bournemouth International Airport.

Cordelia — Poole-based British Overseas Airways Corporation Short "Empire" flying-boat, flown to Belfast for a military refit to equip her with four machine guns in each of two Boulton-Paul turrets, in the dorsal and tail, plus armour plating, bomb-racks on the wings, and radar. She became Coastal Command aircraft AX660 and was posted to 119 Squadron for anti-submarine depth charge trials [16 April 1941]. Returned to BOAC's Poole fleet [September 1941] it survived the war, but was scrapped a couple of years later, at Hythe on Southampton Water [6 March 1947].

Corfe Castle crashes — Fairey Swordfish K5985, on a flight along the Channel coast from Gosport, hit trees at Kingston, on the hill to the south of Corfe Castle [18 March 1938].

Messerschmitt Bf.110C (3U+JT) belonging to the 9th Staffel of Zerstörergeschwader 26 made a forced-landing near Corfe Castle after being engaged by the RAF whilst taking part in the German attack on the Westland Aircraft Company at Yeovil [16.00 hours, 7 October 1940]. Gefreiter Bernhardt Demmig, the pilot, survived and was taken prisoner of war, but his Bordfunker, Obergefreiter Josef Bachmann, was killed. They were shot down by Squadron Leader Michael Robinson, in a Spitfire, who had just taken command of 609 Squadron at RAF Warmwell [4 October 1940]. Flying Officer Richard Brooker joined in the kill, in a Hurricane of 56 Squadron from RAF Boscombe Down.

Hurricane P3984 of 238 Squadron from the newly opened RAF Chilbolton, Hampshire, crashed into the roadside quarry immediately north of Castle Hill [10 October 1940]. Pilot Officer Bob Doe parachuted to safety, on Brownsea Island, after breaking through cloud at 16,000 feet into the sights of Messerschmitt Bf.109s. Both locations are now owned by the National Trust.

Spitfire R7142 of 140 Squadron broke up when trying to pull out of a dive and plunged into heathland near Rempstone [16 December 1941].

Hurricane Z3349, a Mark II fighter of 245 Squadron, force-landed on Furzey Island — in the salt-marshes of Poole Harbour [29 March 1942]. Another Hurricane was lost in the waters off neighbouring Green Island [March 1943].

Pilot Officer Duff and seven of his crew were killed in a military Catalina flying-boat of 201 Squadron, which descended on a training flight into thick fog and ploughed into the salt-marshes surrounding Round Island, in the parish of Corfe Castle [04.25 hours, 24 August 1943]. They had missed their home "Trot" off RAF Hamworthy and landed a mile to the south. Ratings from the island's naval camp rescued the other four crewmen.

Two Liberator bombers crashed in the parish of Corfe Castle during the final year of the Second World War. One is said to have flown into a steep hillside above Encombe House, in dense fog [date unknown], and the second fell on Furzey Island in Poole Harbour [July 1944] with the loss of all its American crew.

Cork — the Fleet Air Arm's greatest pilot **Lieutenant-Commander "Dicky" Cork DSO, DFC**, became the Chief Flying Instructor at Henstridge Royal Naval Air Station [1944-45]. He had won his Distinguished Flying Cross while flying with 242 Squadron in the Battle of Britain but would be ordered by an admiral to remove it and replace it with a Distinguished Service Cross after returning to the Royal Navy. King George VI saw him again when Cork was serving on HMS *Victorious*. "You were instructed to put up that medal by your King, and only your King can tell you to take it down," he was told. "You will wear the DFC from now on."

Cork went on to protect the Malta convoys before his interlude on training duties. He resumed the war as Wing Leader of No. 15 Fighter Wing with Corsairs operating from HMS *Illustrious* in the Far East. He extended his score to 13 confirmed "kills" of enemy aircraft, which became the Navy's best, and was killed in a landing accident in Ceylon.

Coryton — high flyer **Air Chief Marshal Sir Alec Coryton** [born 1895] retired to Two Leas at Langton Matravers. He had been Air Officer Commanding of the Bomber Group at the Air Ministry [1942-43] and Air Commodore of the Third Tactical Air Force, in Bengal and Burma, for South East Asia Command [1944-45]. In Purbeck his pride and joy was the restoration [1948-50] of a 1903 De Dion Bouton which was almost a total wreck. The car was bought in Italy by Daniel Hanbury of Castle Malwood, Lyndhurst, who brought it to England in 1910. Hanbury's daughter, Philippa, married Alec Coryton.

Coventry raid — a massed formation of some 150 German aircraft flew across the Channel on a directional radio beam from the Cherbourg peninsula and crossed the coast at Christchurch and New Milton in the "Moonlight Sonata" attack that devastated the city of Coventry [14-15 November 1940]. The other streams crossed the English coast over Dover and the Wash. The landmark of Coventry Cathedral would be targeted by the pathfinders of Kampfgruppe 100.

Covington — Hurricane flyer **Pilot Officer Aubrey Richard Covington** [born 1921] of 238 Squadron from RAF Chilbolton baled out twice over Dorset in a single week. The first occasion was apparently near Sherborne [1 October 1940], after claiming to have accounted for two Messerschmitt Bf.110s.

The second was also as a result of tangling with Bf.110s in dog-fights across the Dorset Downs. Hurricane V6777 crashed at Great Hill, above Meriden Wood, Winterborne Houghton [7 October 1940].

Crashes — chronological county list. See parish entries for details of each. This catalogue is comprehensive but no claims are made for completeness. Updatings and additional information will be welcomed by the author and publisher, for incorporation in future editions.

Balloon *Saladin* at Eype, Symondsbury [10 December 1881].

Charles Rolls in a Wright Flyer at Southbourne, Bournemouth [12 July 1910].

Demoiselle at Bournemouth [July 1910].

Bleriot monoplane near Bournemouth [Summer 1913].

Biplane from Talbot Village, Bournemouth [24 April 1916].

Zero Airship at Loders [summer 1917].

Bristol Fighter at Christchurch Road, Bournemouth [22 July 1918].

Supermarine Sea Lion G-EALP off Bournemouth [10 September 1919].

Blackburn Bluebird at Ensbury Park Racecourse, Bournemouth [6 June 1927].

Westland Widgeon at Ensbury Park Racecourse, Bournemouth [6 June 1927].

Peto seaplane with submarine M2 off Portland [26 January 1932].

Miles Hawk G-ACJD at Crichel Park [August 1934].

Blenheim K7056 at Woodsford (Warmwell) Aerodrome [26 November 1937].

Fairey Battle K7594 on the Chesil Beach [11 December 1937].

Westland Wallace K6057 at Holworth, Owermoigne [14 January 1938].

Westland Wallace K6063 at Langton Herring [10 March 1938].

Fairey Swordfish K5985 at Kingston, Corfe Castle [18 March 1938].

Hawker Audax K3086 at Warmwell Aerodrome [12 April 1938].

Hawker Fury K8223 off the Chesil Beach [25 May 1938].

Hawker Fury K8271 on the Chesil Beach [10 December 1938].

Westland Wallace K6063 at Langton Herring [10 March 1939].

Hawker Audax K4396 beside the Chesil Beach [13 March 1939].

Boulton-Paul Defiant L6982 at Warmwell Aerodrome [2 April 1940].

Hawker Hind K5544 at Warmwell Aerodrome [3 April 1940].

Boulton-Paul Overstrand K8173 off the Chesil Beach [22 April 1940].

Fairey Seal K3480 at Langton Herring [22 April 1940].

Miles Master N7551 at Puddletown [22 April 1940].

Westland Lysander at Chickerell [23 April 1940].

Hawker Hind K6839 at Warmwell Aerodrome [24 April 1940].

Hawker Hind K5382 at Lytchett Matravers [26 April 1940].

Hawker Hind K5425 at Warmwell Aerodrome [27 April 1940].

Fairey Seal K3480 at Warmwell [7 May 1940].

Junkers Ju.87 off Portland [9 July 1940].

Spitfire off Portland [9 July 1940].

Hurricane N2485 off Portland [11 July 1940].

Messerschmitt Bf.110 (2N+EP) at Povington Heath, Tyneham [11 July 1940].

Spitfire L1069 off Portland Bill [11 July 1940].

Spitfire L1095 off Portland [11 July 1940].

Hurricane P3084 off Portland [12 July 1940].

Hurricane at South Down, above Chalbury Lodge, Preston [13 July 1940].

Spitfire on the beach at Studland [18 July 1940].

Spitfire R6634 off Swanage [18 July 1940].

Hurricane P3082 into Lyme Bay [20 July 1940].

Hurricane P3766 into Lyme Bay [20 July 1940].

Spitfire K9880 off Swanage [20 July 1940].

Dornier Do.17 (5F+OM) at Nutford Farm, Pimperne [21 July 1940].

Dornier Do.17 at Fleet [25 July 1940].

Spitfire K9901 off Portland [25 July 1940].

Spitfire N3023 off Weymouth [27 July 1940].

Spitfire K9894 at Bestwall, Wareham [8 August 1940].

Spitfire R6811 at Spyway Farm, Langton Matravers [8 August 1940].

Hurricane L2057 off Portland [11 August 1940].

Hurricane P2978 off Lulworth [11 August 1940].

Hurricane P3222 off Weymouth [11 August 1940].

Hurricane P3585 at Lulworth [11 August 1940].

Hurricane P3598 at Warmwell [11 August 1940].

Hurricane P3783 off Portland [11 August 1940].

Hurricane P3885 off Portland [11 August 1940].

Hurricane R4092 off Portland [11 August 1940].

Hurricane R4094 off the Dorset coast [11 August 1940].

Hurricane V7231 off Portland [11 August 1940].

Hurricane V7233 off Portland [11 August 1940].

Hurricane (number not known) off Portland [11 August 1940].

Junkers Ju.88 (B3+DC) on Portland [11 August 1940].

Messerschmitt Bf.110 near Swanage [11 August 1940].

Messerschmitt Bf.110 off the Dorset coast [11 August 1940].

Spitfire R6614 off Lulworth [11 August 1940].

Heinkel He.111 (1G+AC) at Sturminster Marshall [12 August 1940].

Hurricane at Bredy Farm, Burton Bradstock [13 August 1940].

Hurricane P3177 off Portland [13 August 1940].

Hurricane P3348 off Portland [13 August 1940].

Junkers Ju.87 at Portesham [13 August 1940].

Junkers Ju.87 (or Messerschmitt Bf.110) at Grimstone, Stratton [13 August 1940].

Messerschmitt Bf.109 in Poole Harbour [13 August 1940].

Messerschmitt Bf.109 off the Dorset coast [13 August 1940].

Messerschmitt Bf.109 off Weymouth [13 August 1940].

Messerschmitt Bf.110 (L1+FZ) at Swalland Farm, Kimmeridge [13 August 1940].

Heinkel He.111 in Lyme Bay [14 August 1940].

Hurricane at Abbotsbury [15 August 1940].

Hurricane at Abbotsbury Swannery [15 August 1940].

Hurricane at Symondsbury [15 August 1940].

Hurricane beside Radipole Lake, Weymouth [15 August 1940].

Hurricane P2872 off Portland [15 August 1940].

Hurricane P3215 off Portland [15 August 1940].

Spitfire R6985 off the Dorset coast [15 August 1940].

Spitfire R6988 at Walsford Road, Bournemouth [15 August 1940].

Hurricane N2646 at Burton Bradstock [25 August 1940].

Hurricane N2646 off Portland [25 August 1940].

Hurricane P2766 off Portland [25 August 1940].

Hurricane P3200 off Portland [25 August 1940].

Hurricane V7250 at New Barn, Bradford Peverell [25 August 1940].

Messerschmitt Bf.109 at Tatton Farm, Chickerell [25 August 1940].

Messerschmitt Bf.109 into the Chesil Beach at Chickerell [25 August 1940].

Messerschmitt Bf.110 at Creech Barrow Hill, Church Knowle [25 August 1940].

Messerschmitt Bf.110 at Tatton House, Chickerell [25 August 1940].

Messerschmitt Bf.110 (3M+KM) at East Chaldon, Chaldon Herring [25 August 1940].

Messerschmitt Bf.110 (3M+KH) at Priory Farm, East Holme [25 August 1940].

Spitfire N3226 at Dorchester [25 August 1940].

Spitfire R6810 off Portland [25 August 1940].

Spitfire R6994 off the Dorset coast [25 August 1940].

Spitfire R6831 off Portland [27 August 1940].

Spitfire N3061 off Weymouth [6 September 1940].

Spitfire at Dorchester [7 September 1940].

Miles Magister P6362 at Emmets Hill, Worth Matravers [14 September 1940].

Heinkel He.111 off Portland [15 September 1940].

Spitfire R7016 off the Dorset coast [23 September 1940].

Heinkel He.111 (G1+LR) at Branksome Park, Poole [25 September 1940].

Heinkel He.111 (G1+BH) at Westfield Farm, Studland [25 September 1940].

Spitfire K9882 off Swanage [26 September 1940].

Messerschmitt Bf.110 at Lulworth Camp [27 September 1940].

Messerschmitt Bf.110 (3U+BD) near Tyneham [27 September 1940].

Messerschmitt Bf.110 (3U+DS) at Gaulter Gap, Kimmeridge [27 September 1940].

Messerschmitt Bf.110 (3U+FT) at Doles Ash Farm, Piddletrenthide [27 September 1940].

Messerschmitt Bf.110 (3U+IM) at Salter's Wood, Arne [27 September 1940].

Messerschmitt Bf.110 (S9+DU) at The Beeches, Iwerne Minster [27 September 1940].

Messerschmitt Bf.110 (S9+JH) at Bussey Stool Farm, Tarrant Gunville [27 September 1940].

Spitfire X4107 at Cheselbourne [27 September 1940].

Hurricane at Oborne Road, Sherborne [30 September 1940].

Hurricane L1764 on Chesil Beach, Abbotsbury [30 September 1940].

Hurricane N2434 at Monkton Wyld, Wootton Fitzpaine [30 September 1940].

Hurricane N2472 at Shaftesbury [30 September 1940].

Hurricane N2474 at Shaftesbury [30 September 1940].

Hurricane P2866 at East Knighton, Winfrith Newburgh [30 September 1940].

Hurricane P2987 at Whitcombe [30 September 1940].

Hurricane P3021 South of Yeovil [30 September 1940].

Hurricane P3088 off Portland [30 September 1940].

Hurricane P3414 off Weymouth [30 September 1940].

Hurricane P3655 off Portland [30 September 1940].

Messerschmitt Bf.109 at Sprigg's Farm, Sydling St Nicholas [30 September 1940].

Spitfire L1072 off the Dorset coast [30 September 1940].

Spitfire L1072 off Portland [30 September 1940].

Spitfire L1702 at Shaftesbury [30 September 1940].

Hurricane P3599 in Poole Harbour [1 October 1940].

Unidentified aeroplane off Hengistbury Head, Bournemouth [1 October 1940].

Hurricane V6792 at Crab Farm, Shapwick [5 October 1940].

Hurricane at Austral Farm, Alton Pancras [7 October 1940].

Hurricane V6777 at Meridan Wood, Winterborne Houghton [7 October 1940].

Junkers Ju.88 (9K+5N) at Tapper's Hill, Sydling St Nicholas [7 October 1940].

Messerschmitt Bf.110 at Arish Mell Gap, Lulworth [7 October 1940].

Messerschmitt Bf.110 at Owermoigne [7 October 1940].

Messerschmitt Bf.110 (3U+BT) at Stoborough, Arne [7 October 1940].

Messerschmitt Bf.110 (3U+JP) at Brickhills Field, Kingston Russell [7 October 1940].

Messerschmitt Bf.110 (3U+JT) at Corfe Castle [7 October 1940].

Spitfire N3039 at Shatcombe Farm, Wynford Eagle [7 October 1940].

Spitfire N3231 at Netmead, Child Okeford [7 October 1940].

Spitfire N3238 at Watercombe [7 October 1940].

Spitfire X4472 at Vale Farm, Sutton Waldron [7 October 1940].

Spitfire N3238 at Watercombe [7 October 1940].

Spitfire N3039 at Shatcombe Farm, Wynford Eagle [7 October 1940].

Hurricane P3421 at Worgret, Wareham [10 October 1940].

Hurricane P3984 below Castle Hill, Corfe Castle [10 October 1940].

Messerschmitt Bf.110 at Bournemouth [15 October 1940].

Spitfire R6607 at Tadnoll Mill, Chaldon Herring [18 October 1940].

Heinkel He.111 (6N+AH) at West Bay, Bridport [6 November 1940].

Junkers Ju.88 at Branksome, Poole [14 November 1940].

Spitfire P9427 into Poole Bay [28 November 1940].

Spitfire R6597 near Wareham [28 November 1940].

Spitfire at Field Grove, Durweston [29 November 1940].

Messerschmitt Bf.109 at Woodyhyde Farm, Worth Matravers [30 November 1940].

German aircraft off Hengistbury Head, Bournemouth [1 December 1940].

Westland Lysander R9015 at Broadwindsor [16 December 1940].

Dornier Do.17 off Portland Bill [4 January 1941].

Hurricane V6758 at Warmwell Aerodrome [4 January 1941].

Whitley T4299 at Connegar Farm, Manston [3 April 1941].

Blenheim T2439 at Frampton [4 April 1941].

Heinkel He.111 on the south Dorset Ridgeway [5 April 1941].

Fairey Battle K9230 off Hengisbury Head, Bournemouth [28 April 1941].

Junkers Ju.88 on Winfrith Heath Decoy Aerodrome, Winfrith Newburgh [4 May 1941].

BOAC flying-boat *Maia* in Poole Harbour [12 May 1941].

Heinkel He.111 (G1+ES) at Patchin's Point, Arne [12 May 1941].

Messerschmitt Bf.109E at Worth Matravers [6 June 1941].

Spitfire P8656 at West Knighton, Winfrith Newburgh [14 July 1941].

Blenheim P4832 off Purbeck coast [17 July 1941].

Spitfire P8516 at Owermoigne [4 August 1941].

Whirlwind P6983 at Hurn Aerodrome [6 August 1941].

Spitfire R6639 at Lulworth [10 September 1941].

Lysander L6860 at Stalbridge [7 October 1941].

Wellington X9677 off St Alban's Head, Worth Matravers [10-11 October 1941].

Focke Wulf 190 at Bindon Hill, Lulworth [21 October 1941].

Hurricane Z4993 at Ridgeway Hill, Weymouth [25 October 1941].

Hurricane at RAF Warmwell [11 November 1941].

Blenheim L9405 off the Chesil Beach [29 November 1941].

Spitfire R7142 at Rempstone, Corfe Castle [16 December 1941].

Wellington X9785 at West Milton, Powerstock [16 December 1941].

Wellington beside Fifehead Wood, Fifehead Magdalen [9 January 1942].

Hurricane Z3349 on Furzey Island, Corfe Castle [29 March 1942].

B-17 Flying Fortress at Charity Farm, Lytchett Minster [2 April 1942].

Miles Magister N3980 near Wareham [6 May 1942].

Heinkel He.111 near Shaftesbury [23 May 1942].

BOAC "Empire" flying-boat *Clare*, after take-off from Poole Harbour [14 September 1942].

Westland Whirlwind P7014 at Warmwell Aerodrome [8 October 1942].

Typhoon R7695 at Glanvilles Wootton [24 October 1942].

Typhoon R8823 at Warmwell Aerodrome [27 October 1942].

Typhoon R8663 at Chilfrome [15 December 1942].

Halifax DT684 in Kingston Lacy Park, Pamphill [24 January 1943].

Westland Whirlwind P6991 at Warmwell Aerodrome [9 February 1943].

Short Stirling R9306 either at Blandford or Creech Barrow Hill, Church Knowle [16 February 1943].

Dornier Do.17 near Beaminster [February 1943].

Sunderland T9111 off Hamworthy, in Poole Harbour [21 March 1943].

Hurricane off Green Island, Corfe Castle [March 1943].

Westland Whirlwind P7057 at Warmwell Aerodrome [7 May 1943].

Westland Whirlwind P7059 at Warmwell Aerodrome [22 May 1943].

Seafire MB315 at Caroline Avenue, Christchurch [25 June 1943].

Spitfire EB687 at Hurn Aerodrome [10 July 1943].

Westland Whirlwind P7110 at Warmwell Aerodrome [13 July 1943].

Whitley tug-plane at Hurn Aerodrome [July 1943].

Westland Whirlwind P6981 at Warmwell Aerodrome [1 August 1943].

RAF Catalina flying-boat beside Round Island, Poole Harbour [24 August 1943].

Westland Whirlwind P7096 at Warmwell Aerodrome [10 September 1943].

Four gliders at East Parley, Hurn [sometime in 1943].

Halifax glider tug-plane [26 January 1944].

Typhoon MN129 at West Knighton [12 March 1944].

Hurricane LD972 near Hurn [21 March 1944].

Halifax JP137 at Moordown, Bournemouth [22 March 1944].

P-47 Thunderbolt at Highcliffe School, Christchurch [30 April 1944].

P-38 Lightning at Cheselbourne [25 May 1944].

Wellington at Christchurch [25 May 1944].

P-47 Thunderbolts in multiple crashes at Foxwood Avenue, Mudeford, Christchurch [29 June 1944].

P-47 Thunderbolt in the Lymington road, Christchurch [2 July 1944].

Mosquito at Alder Road, Poole [23 July 1944].

Liberator on Furzey Island, Corfe Castle [July 1944].

Liberator above Encombe House, Corfe Castle [sometime in 1944].

Martinet at Burton Mere, Burton Bradstock [12 March 1945].

B-17 Flying Fortress 866 at Christchurch Aerodrome [15 July 1945].

Tiger Moth M6648 at Thornford [9 November 1945].

BOAC flying-boat *Hailsham* off Brownsea Island, Poole Harbour [4 March 1946].

Prototype Airspeed Ambassador at Hurn Aerodrome [January 1950].

Airspeed Ambassador G-ALFR at Christchurch Aerodrome [13 November 1950].

Fairey Barracuda off Highcliffe, Christchurch [20 June 1952].

Vampire at Tarrant Rushton Aerodrome [June 1953].

Tiger Moth G-APRX at West Wood, Asmore [circa 1965].

Hunter off the Dorset coast [15 July 1968].

Whirlwind helicopter at Portland [9 October 1968].

Meteor at Blandford [13 February 1969].

Helicopter at Bovington Camp [14 May 1969].

Lockhead C-130E Hercules 37789 over the English Channel, off Lulworth [23 May 1969].

Whirlwind helicopter in Portland Harbour [20 June 1969].

Two Sioux helicopters at Christchurch [23 August 1969].

Canberra into Lyme Bay [1 May 1970].

Phantom off the Dorset Coast [13 May 1970].

Wessex helicopter off Portland [20 May 1971].

Sea King helicopter off Portland [13 January 1972].

Wessex helicopter off Portland [16 February 1972].

Balloon *Gerard Heineken* at Coles Farm, Langton Matravers [25 July 1975].

F-111 at Mapperton, Sturminster Marshall [29 April 1980].

Sea Harrier at Cattistock [21 January 1983].

Sea Harrier off Portland [4 October 1989].

Pampa 1 A-63 at Hurn Aerodrome [31 August 1992].

Stolp Starduster II biplane at Stancombe Farm, Askerwell [3 October 1993].

Montgomery- Benson B8M Autogyro at Stag Gate, Sturminster Marshall [11 December 1993].

Robinson R22 helicopter beside Bokerley Ditch, Pentridge [8 June 1994].

Crichel crash: wreckage of Sir Alfred Beit's Miles Hawk G-ACJD after its encounter with a cedar tree in parkland at Crichel Golf Course in August 1934.

Cessna Skyhawk G-BMZV on downland above Longcombe Bottom, Fontmell Magna [21 November 1996].

Piper PA28 off Boscombe Pier, Bournemouth [6 November 1997].

Light aircraft at Hurn Aerodrome [24 December 1999].

Yakovlev Yak-54 at Melbury Abbas [11 August 2001].

Crichel Crash — of Miles Hawk G-ACJD flown by Sir Alfred Beit MP [born 1903], which hit a high cedar tree in Crichel Park after taking off from Crichel Golf Course [August 1934]. Both Sir Alfred and his passenger, Edward Murray, were unharmed though were suffering from shock. The aeroplane was a complete write-off.

Crichel Down Bombing Range — in the parish of Long Crichel, on the chalky foothills of Cranborne Chase, established by the Air Ministry [1939]. Derequisitioned, when civil servants attempted selling the land to a third party — rather than first offering it back to former owner Commander Toby Marten of Crichel House — precipitated the Crichel Down Scandal [1954] which caused the resignation of Conservative Minister of Agriculture Sir Thomas Dugdale. It also nearly ended the political career of Peter Carrington, his Parliamentary Secretary, almost before it had started.

Crook — Spitfire flyer **Pilot Officer David Moore Crook** [1914-44] of 609 Squadron shot down a Junkers Ju.87 "Stuka" off Portland, killing Luftwaffe hero von Dalwigk [9 July 1940]. He claimed a Messerschmitt Bf.110, also over the sea, in another round of Battle of Britain dog-fights [11 August 1940]. A Bf.109 escort fighter, which crashed into the sea, was added to his score on the Luftwaffe's Adlertag (Eagle Day) attack [13 August 1940]. There followed two Bf.109s in a chase across the English Channel, leading Green Section in a line seawards from 23,000 feet over Swanage [30 September 1940]: "I got up to about 500 mph and easily caught mine, gave it a burst and he crashed into the sea. I then chased another and put him in the sea about 25 miles from Cherbourg. It took me a long time to get back to the English coast … pleased to see the white cliffs."

That was in the morning. In the afternoon he had "a very enjoyable few minutes dog-fighting" and chased a Bf.109 to Weymouth, "and then gave him a good burst. He turned over on to his back and spun into cloud streaming glycol and smoke. I could not claim him a definite as I did not see him actually crash but he certainly never got back to France. This was my best day yet."

Awarded the Distinguished Flying Cross [17 October 1940]. His last action with 609 Squadron would be leading it, also in Spitfire X4165, in the commanding officer's absence [8 November 1940]. He became a flying instructor. Lost over the North Sea whilst flying Spitfire EN662 on a high-level photographic reconnaissance [18 December 1944].

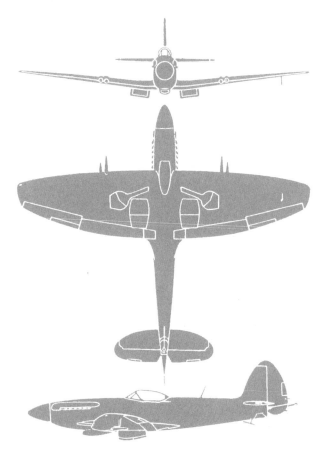

SUPERMARINE SEAFIRE: THE NAVAL VERSION OF THE SPITFIRE WAS AN AIRSPEED CONVERSION AT SOMERFORD, CHRISTCHURCH.

D

D serial number of an ex-RAF aircraft:

D8350 Handley Page 0-400 — see entry for Ensbury Park Aerodrome.

DA — code letters of 210 Squadron, operating Catalina flying-boats from RAF Hamworthy [1943].

Dambuster bombs — aircraft designer Barnes Wallis devised the bouncing bomb at Vickers-Armstrongs' Weybridge works, Surrey, and tested its prototypes on The Fleet lagoon in Dorset [December 1942 — March 1943]. Wooden dummies and steel spheres were dropped from a height of 60 feet from Wellington BJ895/G which operated on test days from RAF Warmwell.

Several failures were followed by the first successful bounce, though this casing then shattered [January 1943] and then a series of thirteen bounces, east of Langton Hive Point, Langton Herring [23 January 1943]. The following day the revolutionary bomb not only zipped across the water but jumped a boom which had been prepared to simulate the wall of a dam.

The sheltered and waveless inshore waters, between the Chesil Beach and the mainland shore, replicated conditions on a lake. The final Dorset tests, with the Wellington approaching at 300 miles per hour, achieved distances of around 4,000 feet [5 February 1943].

Fully-weighted steel versions, some of which remained in The Fleet as mooring buoys into recent times, followed a month later [9 March 1943].

Practice runs for the Lancaster bombers of 617 Squadron were transferred to the totally realistic scenario of actual lakes and dams in the Elan Valley of central Wales, where the mountain obstacles matched the hills of the Ruhr.

Operation Chastise would successfully breach the Mohne and Eder dams [16-17 May 1943] in the most audacious and spectacular aerial action of the Second World War; and at a cost of eight of the 19 participating Lancasters, plus 1,294 victims who were drowned, in the Ruhr, including several hundred Russian prisoners of war.

Dan Air — based its fleet of Hawker-Siddeley 748s at Bournemouth (Hurn) Airport and operated internal passenger flights between British cities [1970s].

Daniel — pre-war NCO pilot **John Daniel** of No.9 Flying Training School was killed when Fury K8271 crashed in a ground attack exercise on the Chesil Beach Bombing Range [December 1938].

Darley — the commander of 609 Squadron at RAF Warmwell throughout the Battle of Britain was **Squadron Leader Horace Stanley "George" Darley** [born 1913]. On one of its busiest days he shot down a Messerschmitt Bf.109 at Chickerell and shared the kill of a Bf.110 over Chaldon Herring [25 August 1940]. His last kill for the squadron was a Dornier Do.17 [25 September 1940].

Posted from Warmwell to become the Station Commander of RAF Exeter [4 October 1940] where he heard that he had been awarded the Distinguished Service Order [22 October 1940]. Progressed to command RAF Kuala Lumpur [11 December 1941] and retreated from the Japanese, via Sumatra, to India. His pre-war flying for the RAF had begun in 1932 and he continued in the service until retirement, as a Group Captain [1959].

Dawson — Bournemouth Flying Club member **David Dawson** [1961-96], from Bere Regis, became the first fatal accident statistic for Compton Abbas Airfield when his Cessna Skyhawk stalled on take-off and plunged into downland above Longcombe Bottom, Fontmell Magna [14.00 hours, 21 November 1996].

Dawson — aviation historian **Leslie Dawson**, who lives at Parkstone, was the first to realise that Dorset's uniquely important aerial story had not been told. He wrote what became the lavishly illustrated *Wings over Dorset: Aviation's story in the South* [1983] that then went to an even better illustrated second edition [1989].

My part in its production was to edit the manuscript and catch his infectious enthusiasm. This inspired me to research and contribute text on the *Saladin* balloon, Rhodes-Moorhouse VC, the Peto submarine-aircraft tragedy, and a virtual diary of both the Telecommunications Research Establishment at Worth Matravers and Battle of Britain memories from across the county. I also found a substantial number of photographs and compiled all the captions.

Leslie Dawson was born in Southgate, London. He first flew as an ATC cadet at Hendon, which is now home to the RAF Museum. On moving to Bournemouth he joined 622 Gliding School at Christchurch Aerodrome.

After instructing at the National Gliding Centre, at Lasham, he was appointed chief gliding instructor of the Gliding School, then at Old Sarum in Wiltshire. He was commissioned into the training branch of the RAFVR.

Instructors from the nearby Empire Test Pilot School at Boscombe Down then taught him powered flight, in a Tiger Moth, and he gained a private pilot's licence. He was selected to fly the gliding sequences for the film *Training for Life*.

DB — squadron code of 411 (RCAF) Squadron, briefly flying Mark IXe Spitfires from RAF Warmwell [15-23 October 1944].

FAMOUS NAME: THE DE HAVILLAND TIGER MOTH, THIS ONE DATING FROM 1932 AND CARRYING ROUNDELS OF THE FLEET AIR ARM AS A MUSEUM SPECIMEN AT YEOVILTON, WAS THE PRINCIPAL TRAINING AIRCRAFT FOR BATTLE OF BRITAIN PILOTS AND REMAINED IN LEISURE USE FOR HALF A CENTURY.

SOMERFORD FACTORY: PRODUCING THE VAMPIRE AS THE AIRSPEED DIVISON OF DE HAVILLAND AIRCRAFT, AT CHRISTCHURCH, WITH MILITARY TRAINER WZ414 TAKING ON KEROSENE AND RECEIVING MAINTENANCE CHECKS.

FACING WEST: CALIBRATION ADJUSTMENTS FOR SEA VIXEN XJ474 BESIDE THE AIRSPEED DIVISION WORKS AT SOMERFORD, WITH CHRISTCHURCH AERODROME GLIMPSED BEHIND.

OVER THE PAGE
PROVING FLIGHT: SEA VIXEN PROTOTYPE XJ474 HEADING SOUTH-WESTWARDS FROM CHRISTCHURCH, ACROSS POOLE BAY, WITH THE SEASIDE PIERS OF BOURNEMOUTH AND BOSCOMBE VISIBLE ON EITHER SIDE OF THE STARBOARD WING.

Deansly — Spitfire pilot **Flying Officer Edward Christopher "Jumbo" Deansly** of 152 Squadron from RAF Warmwell delivered the coup de grace to the Dornier that was the squadron's first kill, but was then shot down in the sea five miles off Portland. He baled out of Spitfire K9901, wounded, but was picked up by a freighter and put ashore at Lyme Regis [25 July 1940].

His next ducking would be into the Channel to the south-east of Poole Bay, twelve miles south of the Needles, when Spitfire K9982 was attacked by a swarm of Messerschmitt Bf.109s [26 September 1940]. This time he was found by an RAF Air-Sea Rescue launch and landed at Swanage.

Transferred to night-fighters at Catterick [23 November 1940], awarded the Distinguished Flying Cross [30 May 1941], he left the RAF at the end of the war as Wing Commander [1945].

de Havilland Aircraft Company Limited — the Hatfield-based firm owned the Airspeed Limited factory beside Christchurch Aerodrome, Somerford, and eventually absorbed its name [July 1951]. It was then known as the Airspeed Division. Aside from the Mosquito, Geoffrey de Havilland's famous creation was the prototype Vampire, six of which, in July 1948, became the first jets to cross the Atlantic Ocean.

As a result, 140 Vampire trainers would be built at Christchurch for the RAF [from 1952], with a further 360 being produced at Chester. The Vampire was already in squadron service, having been the second jet purchased by the RAF, where it was issued to a total of 30 squadrons and units. Numerous marks included night-fighters, ground attack versions, and the Sea Vampire. The third Mark 1 prototype of the latter, LZ511 which was flown by Lieutenant-Commander Eric Brown, landed and took off from HMS *Ocean* in the first-ever aircraft-carrier manoeuvres involving a pure jet aircraft [3 December 1945].

The factory also produced 23 Airspeed Ambassador airliners. British European Airways used them on their newly-named "Elizabethan" class, on the accession of Queen Elizabeth II [1952].

The success of the Vampire was capped by the Venom and Sea Venom. The former was produced in both one and two-seat versions. The original aircraft was powered by de Havilland 4,850-pound Ghost-103 engine and would be produced in quantity, with 375 Mark 1 versions being delivered to the RAF [from June 1951] and 100 being built under licence in Switzerland. Martin-Baker ejection seats were introduced during production. A more powerful Mark 4 Venom had 5,150-pound thrust Ghost-105 engines and under-wing drop tanks. The RAF ordered 150 and export versions were sold to Venezuela (22), Italy (2), Iraq (15). A further 150 were built under licence, in Switzerland, for the Swiss Air Force.

This also had Mark 10 Airborne Interception radar in its two-seater night-fighter Mark 2 version of which 90 were delivered to the RAF [from 1953]. This was followed by 129 of the Mark 3 night-fighter which carried Mark 21 Airborne Interception radar.

The Sea Venom was in British service use for several years [1954-60]. Its debut was with 890 Naval Air Squadron, at RNAS Yeovilton, being formed as the first all-weather jet fighter unit in front-line use with the Fleet Air Arm [March 1954]. Sea Venoms saw combat with 839 Naval Air Squadron from HMS *Eagle* during the Suez crisis [1956]. Production comprised 50 Mark 20 (Ghost-103 engines), 167 Mark 21 (Ghost-104 engines), and 39 Mark-22 (Ghost-105 engines). A refined version, the Mark 53, was produced for the Royal Australian Air Force, with 39 being in operational use [1955-67].

Next came the Sea Vixen, of which 118 were built at Christchurch, being developed from a folding-wing semi-navalised prototype of the DH110 which made its first flight on 20 June 1955. It had two 11,230-pound thrust Rolls-Royce Avon-208 engines and distinctive twin tail booms. The flying weapons system included 28 two-inch rockets, four Firestreak air-to-air missiles, or two 1,000-lb bombs.

Its fully maritime version would be named the Sea Vixen and the first production model followed, making its first flight [20 March 1957]. It was found to be capable of 690 mph, at sea level. with an endurance of 3.2 hours. In anticipation of its heavy airframe, the Royal Naval Air Station at

Yeovilton was closed [November 1956 to December 1957] while contractors Laign laid eight inches of additional concrete across the main runway and also rebuilt the perimeter track. Service trials took place there with 700Y Naval Air Squadron which was then designated an Intensive Flying Trials Unit [November 1958].

Then came operational use with the trials unit re-formed as front-line 892 Naval Air Squadron [1 July 1959]. Four Sea Vixens formed its B-Flight. Red Top air-to-air missiles eventually replaced the Firestreaks.

Aircrew training at RNAS Yeovilton was led by Lieutenant-Commander Peter "Fred" Reynolds, with 766 Naval Air Squadron, who was the first to prove their aerobatic capabilities. The instructors' display team was known as "Fred's Five" [1962]. The attractive lines of these aircraft became familiar over Somerset and Dorset skies as Reynolds increased their number of hours by 40 per cent, claiming a record 575 hours for one aircraft in just one month, and a squadron average of 400 hours.

By this time the Christchurch production line had closed, ending the Airspeed Division, and all aviation work in the town was abandoned in favour of Chester [1962].

Sea Vixens of 890 Naval Air Squadron operated from HMS *Ark Royal* [1964] and 893 and 899 Naval Air Squadrons were on stand-by at Yeovilton. AI-18 Airborne Interception radar was carried. They were to be the last generation of British aircraft-carrier fighters before the advent of the Sea Harrier. The last Sea Vixens in squadron service were flown from Yeovilton by 892 Naval Air Squadron under Lieutenant-Commander Simon Idiens. They became known as "Simon's Circus" for their impeccable formation flying. The first aerobatic performance, after only five weeks practising, thrilled the Biggin Hill Air Fair [1968]. On being withdrawn from squadron service [1972] a few Sea Vixens were converted into pilotless drones for missile target practice over the Aberporth range in west Wales after taking off from RAF Llanbedr.

The last Royal Navy Sea Vixen retained its local connection with its sale to Flight Refuelling Limited at Hurn, on its withdrawal from squadron service [1982].

Sea Vixen XJ580, through an inspired idea by Michael Chaplin, was saved from the scrapyard and sits on a plinth at Somerford as a monument to aircraft construction in Christchurch.

Demetriadi — Hurricane flyer **Pilot Officer Richard Stephen Demetriadi** [1919-40], in R4092 of 601 Squadron from RAF Tangmere, was shot down off Portland [10.24 hours, 11 August 1940]. His body would drift towards France and he is buried in Cayeux-sur-Mer Communal Cemetery.

Richard was the son of commercial diplomat Sir Stephen Demetriadi and the brother-in-law of Pilot Officer William Rhodes-Moorhouse, the son of the first flying VC, who was born at Parnham House, Beaminster.

As a memorial to his son, Sir Stephen bequeathed five acres of Ditchling Beacon, above Brighton, to the National Trust.

de Virac Lart — veteran flyer **Wing Commander Edward Collis de Virac Lart** [1902-41] of Lyme Regis flew in the 1920s with 60 (Bombing) Squadron in India. He served throughout the Battle of Britain but would be lost the following spring when he failed to return to his base [27 March 1941].

Devitt — experienced pilot **Squadron Leader Peter Devitt** [born 1911] who went to Sherborne School and learnt to fly at West Malling at the age of nineteen [1931], brought 152 (Hyderabad) Squadron from Northumberland to RAF Warmwell [12 July 1940].

He had a remarkably lucky war. His closest call was when the return fire from a Heinkel He.111 put shots through his petrol tank. Devitt made a successful forced-landing into the Somerset countryside, at Skew Bridge, Newton St Loe, to the south of Bath [25 September 1940].

Postings followed to the headquarters of No.9 Group [November 1940] and No.14 Group [April 1941]. From there he went to war in the Far East, to No.221 Group in Rangoon, as the Japanese advanced. He commanded the final withdrawal of British forces from Burma, into the state of Assam [8 May 1942].

Promotion followed to Group Captain and Wing Commander. He was to enjoy a long retirement, of upwards of half a century from the end of hostilities.

Dewar — Hurricane pilot **Wing Commander John Scatliff "Johnny" Dewar** [1907-40] was reported missing en route in a coastal flight across Dorset and Hampshire from his home base at RAF Exeter to RAF Tangmere in Sussex [12 September 1940].

His body would be washed up at Kingston Gorse, on Selsey Bill [30 September] and he is buried in St John's churchyard, North Baddesley, near Southampton. Born in Lahore Province, India, of British parents, he would be the highest ranking Royal Air Force officer to be killed in the Battle of Britain.

Dewhurst — cadet **Alex Dewhurst** [born 1965], from Sherborne School, broke the British parascending distance record when, hauled by a Land Rover, he was launched from the top of the chalk escarpment at Batcombe [1980]. He achieved a distance of 3.75 kilometres and landed in the next parish.

Dickie — Hurricane flyer **Pilot Officer William Gordon Dickie** [1916-40], in L2057 of 601 Squadron from RAF Tangmere, was shot down and killed off Portland [10.30 hours, 11 August 1940]. He was from Dundee.

HMS Dipper — the Royal Navy shore-base otherwise known as Henstridge Royal Naval Air Station, which straddled the Dorset-Somerset boundary north of Stalbridge.

Dixon — Hurricane flyer **Sergeant-Pilot Frederick John Powell Dixon** [1919-40] was shot down and killed in the opening phase of the Battle of Britain [08.00 hours, 11 July 1940].

Flying with 501 Squadron from RAF Middle Wallop he was trying to protect a Channel convoy ten miles south-east of Portland Bill.

He baled out from N2485 and the Weymouth lifeboat spent several hours searching for him. He had drowned; his body was recovered off France and his is buried in the extension to Abbeville Communal Cemetery.

Doe — Hurricane flyer **Pilot Officer Bob Doe** of 248 Squadron from RAF Chilbolton, who had recently been awarded the Distinguished Flying Cross, parachuted from P3984 to safety on Brownsea Island after being wounded by a flight of Messerschmitt Bf.109s as he rose out of dense cloud [10 October 1940]. His fighter crashed into a roadside quarry, now a National Trust cafe and car-park, on the north side of Corfe Castle.

His next emergency over Dorset, caused by his engine cooling system icing up as he flew at night over the sea off Portland Bill, ending with a crash-landing into oil drums beside a snow-covered Warmwell Aerodrome [4 January 1941]. Hurricane V6758 was ripped apart but the pilot fared somewhat better, after fragments of glass had been removed from his eye at Bovington Military Hospital.

He continued his career for the duration of the conflict and into post-war jet fighters, retiring as Wing Commander RTF Doe DSO, DFC and bar.

Don — Mosquito photo-reconnaissance **Pilot Squadron Leader Ralph Stidston Don DFC** [1919-1945], the son of Charles and Gertrude Don from Ferndown, served through the Battle of Britain as a Pilot Officer with 501 Squadron at RAF Croydon. He was then flying Hurricanes, until being shot down in combat with Junkers Ju.87s and Messerschmitt Bf.109s, over Dover in P3646 [31 July 1940].

Ralph Don baled out, though injured, as the fighter crashed into Lydden Marsh. He was given command of 142 Squadron [October 1944] which was equipped with Mosquito PR-16s for low-level missions to search out rocket sites and other targets inside enemy territory. He failed to return from one such operation and was reported "Missing in action" [22 January 1945].

Dorchester crashes — a British fighter shot down over the county town by Messerschmitt Bf.109s, during a Battle of Britain dog-fight, has been identified as Spitfire N3226 of 602 Squadron [25 August 1940].

Flying Officer Ralph "Bob" Wolton of 152 Squadron from RAF Warmwell lost control of his Spitfire whilst attempting a sudden dive near Dorchester [7 September 1940]. He baled out at 13,000 feet and narrowly missed plunging into the ground beside his fighter, because his parachute did not open until he was little more than a thousand feet above the ground.

Dorset Firsts — in chronological order.

See entry for *Saladin*, off Eype at Symondsbury, for the first (and regrettably so far only) Member of Parliament to disappear in a balloon [10 December 1881].

See entry for Wallis Down Aerodrome, administratively across the High Road from the Dorset parish of Kinson in the Branksome district of Poole, for Dorset and Bournemouth's first airfield [1909-10].

See entries for Rolls and Bournemouth crashes for the first British death from powered flight [12 July 1910].

See entry for Samson, off Portland, for the world's first flight from a moving ship [3 May 1912].

See entry for Rhodes-Moorhouse, from Beaminster, for the first crossing of the English Channel by a pilot with passengers [4 August 1912].

See entry for Farman, off Bournemouth, for the first float-plane to visit the Dorset-Hampshire coast [1912].

See entry for Beale, from Bournemouth, for the world's first flying Father Christmas [December 1912].

See entry for Hamel, over Meyrick Park, Bournemouth, for the first to achieve 21 loops in a single spiral descent [April 1914].

See entry for Rhodes-Moorhouse, of Parnham House, for the first flyer to win the Victoria Cross [1915].

See entry for Strange, from Worth Matravers, for the only flyer to be among those who first flew to war in France, with the Royal Flying Corps [14 August 1914], and would still be in front-line combat on the day of the Armistice [11 November 1918], plus the remarkable additional feat of returning to France in a Hurricane for the repeat performance in April 1940.

See entry for the Schneider Trophy Contest, off Bournemouth and Studland, for the first time this international sea-plane event visited the British coast [10 September 1919].

See entry for Ensbury Park Aerodrome for Squadron Leader H. J. L. "Bert" Hinkler's Avro Avian G-EBOV which was its star performer [1926] and then made the first solo flight from Great Britain to Australia [7 to 22 February 1927].

See entry for Cobham, who would adopt Tarrant Rushton, for the first flight over the Himalayas, the first return flight from London to Capetown [1925-26], then a flight to Australia and back, plus flying around the entire African continent for the first time in history [1927].

See entry for Peto for the loss of the world's first and only submarine-launched aircraft, with its parent vessel HMS *M2*, off Portland Bill [26 January 1932].

See entry for Penrose, from Nether Compton, who was the first to fly higher than the highest point on Earth when he took the world altitude record by climbing to 35,000 feet above Poole Bay in preparation for a pioneering flight over Mount Everest [26 January 1933].

See entry for Johns for a record-breaking 22,400-feet parachute jump [1937].

See entry for Mantle, mortally wounded in Portland Harbour while firing his anti-aircraft gun against "Stuka" dive-bombers, for the Royal Navy's first Victoria Cross to be won in British territorial waters [4 July 1940].

See entry for Tyneham crashes for the first German flyers to be taken prisoner in the Battle of Britain [11 July 1940].

See entry for *Clare*, a BOAC flying-boat from Poole Harbour, for the first Transatlantic flight of the Second World War [August 1940].

See entry for the Telecommunications Research Establishment, at Worth Matravers and Langton Matravers, for a series of pioneering advances in devising airborne radar apparatus [1940-41].

See entry for Hurn Aerodrome for the first 4-engined land-plane to cross the Atlantic Ocean, being a C-54 Skymaster of Pan American Airways [30 May 1945].

See entry for Flight Refuelling for the first non-stop flight from Britain to Bermuda [28 May 1947].

Also see Flight Refuelling for the world record endurance flight for a jet aircraft, in a Gloster Meteor airborne for 12 hours 3 minutes [7 August 1949].

See entry for Lamb, for a British altitude record of 56,900 feet in a Saunders-Roe SR-53 over Lyme Bay [20 October 1959].

See Flight Refuelling for the non-stop flight of a Vulcan bomber from RAF Scampton to Sydney [1961].

See entry for Bedford, off Portland, for the first vertical landing by a fixed wing aircraft on an aircraft-carrier [8 February 1963].

Return to Flight Refuelling for the furthest and longest bombing raid in history [1 May 1982].

Dorset Gliding Club — operates from Eyres Field, beside Puddletown Road at Gallows Hill, between Bere Regis and Wool.

Dorsetshire Aero Club — formed at Dorchester with the Director of Civil Aviation at the Air Ministry, Air Vice-Marshal Sir Sefton Brancker, being the principal guest [23 August 1926]. He had been brought from Hendon, via Worth Matravers, in the Simmonds Spartan biplane operated by the Isle of Purbeck Light Aeroplane Club.

Double Eagle II — the first hot-air balloon to cross the Atlantic, carrying three Americans from Presque Island, Maine, flew high across central Dorset, following the Stour valley from Marnhull to Poole Harbour, via Bere Regis [10.00 to 11.15 hours, 17 August 1978].

There the balloon still had sufficient height to carry on across the English Channel and into mainland Europe, landing south-east of Paris. It had been a distance of 3,150 miles and a flight of 137 hours 6 minutes.

The crewmen were Ben Abruzzo, Maxie Anderson and Larry Newman.

Douglas — top flyer **William Sholto Douglas** [1893-1969] landed the first commercial flight at Ensbury Park Aerodrome, Kinson, near Bournemouth [1919]. By 1940 he would be Deputy Chief of the Air Staff, then Air Officer Commanding-in-Chief of Fighter Command in the midst of the conflicts of 1940-42, finishing the war as Marshal of the Royal Air Force and retiring in 1948 as first Baron Douglas of Kirtleside.

Dowding — Air Officer Commander-in-Chief at Fighter Command **Air Chief Marshal Sir Hugh Dowding** [1882-1970] visited the Special Duty Flight at Christchurch Aerodrome for a briefing during the Battle of Britain on their top-secret work for the Telecommunications Research Establishment [30 July 1940].

DP — squadron code of 193 (Fellowship of the Bellows) Squadron, flying rocket-firing Typhoons on cross-Channel missions from RAF Hurn [3-11 July 1944].

Dru Drury — Purbeck flyer **Group Captain Edward Stephen Dru Drury** [1910-48] was the son of Corfe Castle's doctor.

Drummond-Hay — young Spitfire flyer **Pilot Officer Peter Drummond-Hay** of 609 Squadron was lost with his fighter, over the sea off Portland, in one of the first Battle of Britain dog-fights [9 July 1940].

DU — squadron code of the Czech 312 Squadron, flying Spitfires on three postings to RAF Warmwell [1942-43].

Dundas — Spitfire flyer **Flying Officer John Charles Dundas** [1916-1940] of 609 Squadron at RAF Warmwell claimed a Messerschmitt Bf.110 but his kill managed to limp back to France [13 July 1940]. His first confirmed kill was another Bf.110, which crashed near Swanage [11 August 1940]. A

MEMORIAL STONE: IN FIELD GROVE, DURWESTON, UNVEILED BY BLANDFORD BRANCH OF THE ROYAL AIR FORCE ASSOCIATION AND DEDICATED BY REV FARQUHARSON ROBERTS IN 1978, COMMEMORATING 19-YEAR-OLD PILOT OFFICER JOHN FREDERICK WOODWARD ALLEN WHOSE SPITFIRE CRASHED HERE IN 1940.

Junkers Ju.87 "Stuka" gunner ruptured Dundas's oil system, stopping the Spitfire's propeller, in the Luftwaffe's Adlertag (Eagle Day) attack [13 August 1940]. He successfully glided the fighter from Portland to a perfect forced-landing at Warmwell Aerodrome.

Similarly the following month he made another emergency landing, with shell splinters in his leg, after the probable kill of one of the Messerschmitt Bf.110 fighter-bombers involved in an attack on the Westland Aircraft factory [7 October 1940]. Belching smoke and white ethylene glycol coolant, the German aircraft was last seen crossing the coast at Weymouth, and presumed to have crashed into the sea. Its parting shot hit Spitfire R6915 and Dundas's leg; the former, which was also flown by Noel Le Chevalier Agazarian would be repaired as it is the fighter that now hangs from the ceiling in the main hall of the Imperial War Museum.

John Dundas was back in the air the next day, promoted Flight-Lieutenant, and awarded the Distinguished Flying Cross [10 October 1940].

His next kill, at 18,000 feet as he swept westwards after soaring alone above Christchurch, was a Bf.110, which crashed on the edge of Bournemouth [15 October 1940]. He was leading Blue Flight at the time, and it was 609 Squadron's ninety-ninth accepted claim.

A "practice flight" over Poole Bay turned into an outing to France, with an apparent kill at the end, as he followed a Junkers Ju.88 — which had been over Southampton — to its base on the Cherbourg peninsula, where he left it lurching out of control with flames shooting from the port engine [27 November 1940].

"I've finished an Me.109 — whoopee!" These would be the last words received by radio from John Dundas in Spitfire X4586, over the sea off the Isle of Wight [28 November 1940]. It might have been the Messerschmitt Bf.109E of Major Helmut Wick, leading Jagdeschwader 2, who had 57 white kill-bars painted on his rudder. The Luftwaffe ace and Dundas disappeared on the same day. Neither body was recovered.

Durweston crash — Spitfire R6907 and Pilot Officer John Woodward Allen of 152 Squadron from RAF Warmwell dived into a wood at Field Grove, near Traveller's Rest, Durweston [29 November 1940]. It was thought that he fainted through loss of oxygen. This is one of the few Second World War crash sites to be marked by a plaque, initially on the trunk of a tree killed by the impact, later replaced by a granite memorial [1978].

E

East Holme crash — at Priory Farm, of Messerschmitt Bf.110 (3M+KH) belonging to the 1st Staffel of II Gruppe, Zerstörergeschwader 2, in one of Dorset's busiest days during the Battle of Britain [25 August 1940]. The two crew parachuted into captivity.

Edge — Spitfire pilot **Flying Officer Alexander Rothwell Edge** [1908-85] successfully crash-landed on the Studland beach minefield after a Battle of Britain dog-fight [18 July 1940]. He was rescued from the sea, by the Royal Navy.

Posted to Training Command [2 August 1940] he was promoted to Squadron Leader.

Edward, Prince of Wales, forced down at Swanage — Purbeck's least expected royal visit took place at about 13.15 hours in the afternoon, on 12 July 1933 when the Prince of Wales [1894-1972, briefly King Edward VIII] landed in a cornfield near Godlingston Farm. The Channel coast was being lashed by a gale, and the Prince, after flying over Bournemouth, was heading for Weymouth, to open the harbour and pier reconstruction.

Visibility became poor and the de Havilland Moth was being increasingly bumped by the wind. Prince Edward asked the pilot, Flight-Lieutenant G.H. Fielden, to land in a field. He took his position from the buildings of Swanage Brick and Tile Company, using the chimney stack as a landmark and circling it a couple of times as he descended.

"We thought at first he was going to knock it off," said works director B. P. Codling, referring to the chimney, "but the plane came down nicely in a little wheatfield on the other side of the road from here, on land owned by the Bankes Estate (now National Trust property). The pilot pulled her up by the side of a rick. Afterwards we could find no trace of its descent, the wheat being quite undamaged. Several of our tilers who were near rushed to the assistance of the plane, having seen it in the air, and got the impression it was in difficulties."

The pilot admitted the landing had been far from easy. As for Prince Edward, he was given a lift to Weymouth by Captain F. R. Bacon, from the brickworks. Britain's most fashionable dapper-dresser arrived looking none too spruce, the *Dorset Daily Echo* reported: "His hair was ruffled and his suede shoes were clogged with mud. His trouser ends were bespattered with mud."

Edwards — Hurricane pilot **Flight-Lieutenant Robert Sidney James Edwards** [1916-74], flying P3088 of 56 Squadron from RAF Boscombe Down, was shot down near Weymouth. He was caught by return fire from Dornier Do.17 bombers and Messerschmitt Bf.110s but baled out unhurt [17.00 hours, 30 September 1940].

He would be transferred to Bomber Command, to 9 Squadron at RAF Honington, and would survive the Second World War and long into the Cold War, retiring as Wing Commander in 1963.

8A — squadron code of 298 Squadron, flying Halifax tug-planes from RAF Tarrant Rushton [1943-44].

8Z — squadron code of 295 Squadron, flying Halifax tug-planes for airborne forces, from RAF Hurn [1943-44].

EL — squadron code of 181 Squadron, flying rocket-firing Typhoons on cross-Channel missions from RAF Hurn [1 April-20 June 1944].

Emergency Dispersal Point — of RAF Strike Command, for Valiant and Victor bombers carrying nuclear weapons during times of Cold War tension, was established at Tarrant Rushton [1958]. One of a chain of such airfields, intended to proliferate the number of prime targets and increase the chances of a military survival in the event of a Russian first-strike, this took pressure off the vulnerable front-line East Anglian bases.

The principal users of Tarrant Rushton were Valiants of 148 Squadron from RAF Marham, Norfolk, until their early demise from metal fatigue and the consequent disbandment of the unit [1965].

Empire flying-boats — see entries, for BOAC, *Cabot, Caribou, Clare, Clio, Clyde, Cordelia* and Imperial Airways.

Ensbury Park Aerodrome and Racecourse — in the old Dorset parish of Kinson, now under the houses of Leybourne Avenue and adjoining suburban streets in Northbourne, Bournemouth (Ordnance Survey map reference SZ 080 955). Created by Bournemouth Aviation Company, for the training of Royal Flying Corps pilots in the Great War [1917]. Their activities moved here from Talbot Village Aerodrome. Accidents were inevitable and included that which killed Major John Lockock [22 July 1918].

William Sholto Douglas made the first scheduled commercial peacetime flight from Ensbury Park [6 June 1919], in an ex-military Handley Page 0-400, D8350 of Handley Page Transport Limited, for whom he was the chief pilot. The aircraft was repainted with the civilian identification G-EAAE. Sholto Douglas would become Air Officer Commanding-in-Chief of Fighter Command in the Battle of Britain, and Marshal of the Royal Air Force.

Most post-war flying was for fun, culminating with the Killjoy Stakes which were to bring about their own downfall when Westland Widgeon G-EBPW collided with a Blackburn Bluebird, killing Westland's test pilot, Major Laurence Openshaw [6 June 1927]. A series of accidents prompted official intervention to end the heady days of low-level competitive flights.

It was transferred from the county of Dorset to Hampshire with countryside absorbed into the expanding borough of Bournemouth [1930]. Soon after that it became a housing estate, crossed by Leybourne Avenue and Saxonhurst Road [1932].

INAUGURAL FLIGHT: LIEUTENANT-COLONEL WILLIAM SHOLTO-DOUGLAS TAKING OFF FROM ENSBURY PARK AERODROME, BOURNEMOUTH, IN EX-ROYAL FLYING CORPS HANDLEY PAGE 0-400 D8350 (WHICH BECAME G-EAAE) ON 4 MAY 1919.

MAYORAL RECEPTION: FOR LIEUTENANT-COLONEL WILLIAM SHOLTO-DOUGLAS, THE CHIEF PILOT FOR HANDLEY PAGE TRANSPORT LIMITED, WHO ARRIVED AT ENSBURY PARK ON 6 JUNE 1919 WITH THE FIRST SCHEDULED COMMERCIAL FLIGHT. HE WOULD BE AIR OFFICER COMMANDING-IN-CHIEF OF FIGHTER COMMAND DURING THE BATTLE OF BRITAIN AND RETIRED AS MARSHAL OF THE ROYAL AIR FORCE.

Having thrilled the Bournemouth crowds through 1926, in G-EBOV, his Avro Avian prototype, Squadron Leader H. J. L. "Bert" Hinkler took the world by surprise and flew it from Croydon Aerodrome to Darwin [7 to 22 February 1927]. It was the first solo flight from Great Britain to Australia, with the 11,005-mile route taking in Rome, Malta, Tobruk, Ramleh, Basra, Jask, Karachi, Cawnpore, Calcutta, Rangoon, Victoria Point, Singapore, Bandoeng and Bima. G-EBOV had earned a comfortable retirement and remains on display in the Brisbane Museum. On a lesser level in the scale of human endeavour, Imperial Airways provided "a 14 seater Air Liner" at Ensbury Park and offered Bournemouth residents "Joy Flights" over their homes at 10s-6d each. There were also longer cross-country trips, at noon and 19.30 hours daily, costing £1-1s-0d, which we knew as a guinea.

E7 — squadron code of 570 Squadron, flying Albemarle and Stirling tug-planes for airborne forces from Hurn and Tarrant Rushton [1944].

Euro Direct Airlines — operated from Bournemouth (Hurn) Airport with four flights a day on its service to Amsterdam [winter 1994], which had become Bournemouth's most popular route. A 56-seat, British-built ATP aircraft was introduced for most of the services to Holland and Paris.

An earlier evening flight was also scheduled for the Brussels route [leaving 18.15 hours], which is a half-hour flight time [18.45 arrival].

EASTER MONDAY: THE ENTRANCE TO ENSBURY PARK RACECOURSE AND AERODROME ON A BUSY FLYING DAY IN 1927, WITH BERT HINKLER'S AVRO AVIAN G-EBOV CHASING A DE HAVILLAND MOTH, AND IMPERIAL AIRWAYS ADVERTISING "JOY FLIGHTS" AT 10S-6D EACH.

For the first time, travellers to Paris were offered what was being termed "a genuine day-return in both directions". Flights were leaving Bournemouth at 7.20, 14.35 and 18.40 hours, with return departures from Charles de Gaulle Airport at 06.55, 10.25 and 17.25 hours.

The all-day shuttle between Bournemouth and Exeter, with up to seven flights a day linking the two towns, continued to operate throughout the year. The daily service from Bournemouth to Manchester was increased from once a day to twice a day, giving it day-return status with a morning and evening flight in both directions

Dublin continued to be well covered, with three flights each weekday and one on Sunday, and Aberdeen had a single weekday flight [07.45 departure for 13.10 arrival].

Overseas, Berne received an evening flight [16.05 departure for 20.40 arrival] daily except for Saturday.

CLOSER VIEW: BERT HINKLER'S AVRO AVIAN G-EBOV LIFTING OFF FROM ENSBURY PARK AERODROME ON 6 JUNE 1927, A YEAR BEFORE HE MADE HIS RECORD-BREAKING FLIGHT TO AUSTRALIA, WHERE THE AIRCRAFT IS PRESERVED.

European Helicopter Industries — jointly formed by Westland, of Yeovil and Britain, and the Italian aviation company Augusta, to design and produce the EH-101 [June 1980].

Euroscot Express — daily flight carrier between Bournemouth International Airport and Glasgow, and weekly to and from Edinburgh [1997]. The Edinburgh service then became daily [summer 1998], following which a European daily service was launched to Schiphol Airport, Amsterdam [14 November 1998], with flight numbers MY 141

Fun race: de Havilland Moth G-EBMF awaiting pilot Miss O'Brien, to take part in the Race for the Ladies Purse at Ensbury Park Aerodrome, 5 June 1927.

Taking off: ex-RAF S.E.5t, with Mrs S. C. Elliot-Lynn's G-EBQM (right) momentarily ahead of G-EBPA at the start of the Killjoy Trophy race from Ensbury Park Aerodrome on 18 April 1927.

Fatal finale: Westland Widgeon G-EBPW passing in front of the Racecourse stands at Ensbury Park Aerodrome, moments before test pilot Major L. P. Openshaw collided with a Blackburn Bluebird, on 6 June 1927.

(outgoing), and MY 142 (return), timed from departure to arrival at 2 hours 30 minutes, to allow for loading and unloading, with the actual flying time being 1 hour 30 minutes. Return fares started at £117.50.

Chief Executive Jack Romero announced: "Bournemouth-Amsterdam is a niche market for Euroscot Express and one which is the next logical step in our development. Amsterdam is the destination which is the most demanded by callers to Bournemouth International Airport, and it has featured strongly in all our on-board surveys. It's Europe's fourth most popular destination so we will be opening up a completely new leisure market for people living on the South Coast, and we are already talking to a number of tour operators regarding all-inclusive short breaks to the Netherlands."

Evans — Halifax flyer **Sergeant-Pilot Dennis Evans** [1923-44] was killed when his heavily loaded aircraft stalled shortly after take-off from RAF Hurn, bound for North Africa, and crashed on the Bournemouth suburb of Moordown [22 March 1944]. He was from Middlesex.

Express Air Services — operated from Bournemouth (Hurn) Airport [1970s].

Eyres Field — beside Puddletown Road at Gallows Hill, between Bere Regis and Wool, is the airfield of Dorset Gliding Club (Ordnance Survey map reference SY 845 903).

FREE FRENCH: FLYERS DENYS BOUDARD (LEFT) AND JEAN HEBERT (RIGHT) DEFECTED FROM NAZI-OCCUPIED FRANCE TO CHRISTCHURCH AERODROME BY STEALING A LUFTWAFFE BÜCKER JUNGMANN FROM AN AIRFIELD NEAR CAEN ON 29 APRIL 1941.

F

Falaise — a mansion built in an acre of clifftop at 13 West Overcliff Drive, Bournemouth [1913] was the home of pioneer aviator Sir Alan Cobham [1894-1973]. This red-brick house has a 40 feet lounge with Adam-style fireplaces and a variety of rooms for the purpose of facilitating those home comforts, such as a flower arranging room. The two floors above have eleven bedrooms with the top line of dormer windows looking out across the Purbeck Hills and the English Channel.

Falconet — pilotless Advanced Subsonic Aerial Target developed for the Ministry of Defence by Flight Refuelling Limited of Wimborne [1982]. Propelled by a Microturbo TJA-24 jet engine, at more than 400 miles per hour, and put into service use [1986]. Now well in excess of a thousand launchings [1995].

Farman — pioneer aeroplane builder **Henry Farman** [1874-1958], made the first circuit flight in Europe and thereby won a 50,000-franc prize for flying more than a kilometre [13 January 1908]. Though English-born he was a French resident. By the time of the Reims International Meeting his Farman biplane could achieve ten kilometres in 10 minutes 39 seconds. The 70-horsepower Farman Hydroplane, with Fischer as the pilot, was the best of seven entrants in the world's first seaplane competition, at Monaco [March 1912].

The *Daily Mail* then sponsored Farman to bring this machine to England with crowds on Bournemouth beach being treated to a star performance on its circuit of major holiday resorts.

Fawcett — Spitfire flyer **Sergeant-Pilot Fawcett** of 152 Squadron at RAF Warmwell was killed by the Luftwaffe on the ground, by a machine gun bullet from one of three Heinkel He.111 surprise raiders, as he sat eating lunch [1 April 1941].

Feary — Spitfire flyer **Sergeant-Pilot Alan Norman Feary** [1912-1940] of 609 Squadron from RAF Warmwell was killed in action against the Luftwaffe [7 October 1940]. He was hit by Messerschmitt Bf.109s over Weymouth. Though he baled out from Spitfire N3238, as it crashed at Watercombe Farm, he was too low for his parachute to open. "ONE OF THE FEW", his gravestone reads, in the RAF plot at Warmwell churchyard.

Featherstone — civil servant **Doreen Featherstone** won a flight from Bournemouth International Airport in a charity raffle [September 1996]. She took her ride in a two-seater Cessna and was flown south-east, across Christchurch, towards the Isle of Wight.

"I was nervous of flying, but it seemed too good an opportunity to miss," Ms Featherstone, aged 56, told reporters afterwards. "The pilot was wonderful and put me at my ease. Then I heard him calling 'Mayday, Mayday', and I couldn't believe my ears. We were still over the Solent."

Pilot Peter Heaver attempted to turn inland, towards Sway, to make an emergency landing. He was losing height, however, and clipped electricity cables above Barton-on-Sea golf course.

"There was a terrific flash of light and I thought the plane was on fire, then the window came in," Ms Featherstone said.

Both pilot and passenger escaped unhurt. "I would love to go flying again," the latter remarked.

Fifehead Magdalen crash — Wellington IV bomber Z1312 of 458 (Royal Australian Air Force) Squadron from Holme-on-Spalding Moor, Yorkshire, was hit by flak over Cherbourg and turned for home with its load of twelve 250-lb bombs intact [9 January 1942].

FARMAN WATERPLANE: OTHERWISE KNOWN AS THE HYDROPLANE AND SPONSORED BY THE DAILY MAIL, HENRY FARMAN'S 70-HORSEPOWER MACHINE SEEN BESIDE AND FROM BOURNEMOUTH PIER, WITH THE TOWN'S WEST CLIFF IN THE BACKGROUND.

The crippled aircraft hit power lines when Sergeant Pilot Bert Garland attempted a crash-landing in fields beside Fifehead Wood, Fifehead Magdalen. Four of its bombs detonated with the impact and Sergeants T. L. Brown, A. I. Hewish, P. H. Smith and D. G. Taylor were killed.

The pilot, however, would recover from a coma five days later in Salisbury Hospital. The sixth crewman, Sergeant Ian Highlett, also survived.

Bert Garland [born 1920] returned to Australia and would come back to Dorset to visit the crash site, where he was given souvenir rounds from one of the Wellington's machine-guns, by wartime local boy Peter Custard [September 1996].

The other Australians are buried in Brookwood Military Cemetery, Surrey.

Firsts — see entry for Dorset Firsts, being the listing of the county's aviation achievements.

STUNT FLYER: BUD FISHER, THE FIRST REGULAR USER OF CHRISTCHURCH AERODROME FROM 1931, WITH HIS AVRO 504K BIPLANE.

Fisher — stunt-flyer **Francis Colebourne "Bud" Fisher** was the pioneer aviator at Christchurch [1931-33]. He was flashy and flamboyant, taking passengers up in his Avro 504K biplane, and operated from a field near the town before the creation of Christchurch Aerodrome [1935]. His activities attracted a total of 160 aircraft, including a memorable visit from Sir Alan Cobham's Flying Circus [30 April 1933].

Financially, however, he was less stable, and lived in a tent beside his aeroplane. Despite the hand-to-mouth existence he found the means to organise the short-lived Bournemouth Flying Club. He answered his country's call at the beginning of the Second World War and enlisted in the RAF as a Flying Officer [23 September 1939] and would retire as Squadron Leader. His last known occupation was as a gentleman model, for dinner jackets and lounge suits.

5V — squadron code of 439 (Royal Canadian Air Force) Squadron flying Mark IV Hurricanes from RAF Hurn [18 March-2 April 1944] and returning with rocket-firing Typhoons for cross-Channel missions [19 April-11 May and 20 May-27 June 1944].

FJ — squadron code of 164 (Argentine-British) Squadron, flying rocket-firing Typhoons on cross-Channel missions from RAF Hurn [26 June-17 July 1944].

Fleet crash — of a Dornier Do.17 bomber, at East Fleet Farm, being among the first German aircraft to be brought down in Dorset during the Battle of Britain [25 July 1940]. The pilot, who was the only survivor, handed looted Players cigarettes to his captors, on being taken to John Nobbs's farmhouse. The kill was claimed by Spitfires of 152 Squadron from RAF Warmwell.

Fleet Requirements Unit — provided target-towing and "enemy attacks for the Fleet Air Arm and its aircraft-carriers in the English Channel and South-Western Approaches, operating from Bournemouth (Hurn) Airport [1952]. As well as naval fighters, provided by Airwork Services, the unit progressed from Mosquitoes through a series of ex-RAF jet fighters, such as the Meteor and Hunter, and Canberra bombers painted in distinctive black and yellow stripes. Redeployed to the Royal Naval Air Station at Yeovilton [1972].

Flight Refuelling Limited — the need for a "Petrol Supply Co Ltd" of the skies was predicted in a *Punch* cartoon [1909], first carried out by "Flying Tankerman" Wesley May over Long Beach, California [12 November 1921], and shown to be a practical reality with the supply line from a Vickers Virginia tanker feeding a Westland Wapiti at Hendon Air Pagent [1931]. Turning it into a commercial proposition was jinxed by misfortune. Four died aboard Handley Page W10 tanker G-EBMM as it disintegrated after refuelling Sir Alan Cobham's Courier G-ABXN which was attempting an endurance flight to Karachi [22 September 1934].

Undaunted, he founded his own company, Flight Refuelling Limited, with its name proclaiming that the idea could be made to work [29 October 1934]. The Air Ministry provided two retired Vickers Virginias, J7711 and K2668, which fed each other via a system powered by a primitive windmill, to achieve pumping pressure. This was no more effective than relying on gravity.

Progress was illusory until the Air Ministry loaned an Armstrong Whitworth 23 (K3585) and Handley Page 51 (J9833) and the "Wing Tip" method of hose attachment was used [1937]. Empire flying-boat G-ADUV *Cambria* took off from Short Brothers' factory at Rochester, on the Medway, and was refuelled over Felixstowe by K3585 [1938].

Tandem tankers: Lancastrian G-AHJW of Flight Refuelling Limited (top) feeding Lancastrian G-AHJU, also belonging to Flight Refuelling, having flown over the English Channel from Tarrant Rushton Aerodrome in this photo-call staged for the Daily Graphic.

Berlin Airlift: Lancastrian bulk-fuel tanker of Flight Refuelling Limited from Tarrant Rushton breaking Stalin's blockade, having crossed Soviet-occupied East Germany with petrol for the beleaguered former capital in 1948, which still shows signs of much bombing.

This was repeated numerous times and with other aircraft, such as Harrow tanker G-AFRL fuelling G-AFCU *Cabot* over the ocean terminal at Southampton Docks and above Calshot [1939] in audacious propaganda pictures to show that aviation could provide the liners of the future. Hose nozzles and couplings evolved into integrated fittings.

Then came war which curtailed the peacetime opportunities and initially the situation was too defensive to offer much scope for long-range visionaries. Instead Cobham's company was diverted into producing de-icing systems and Sir Alan was asked by Lord Beaverbrook, the mercurial Minister of Aircraft Production, for help in finding new airfields.

Fears that Malta might fall to the Italians revived thoughts of mid-air refuelling, and the practicalities of towing fighters eastwards across the Mediterranean behind bombers fitted out as tankers. A Wellington was chosen for the towed-fighter tests — leading and feeding a Hurricane — and Cobham's 16-year-old son, Michael, was among the bomber's crew. Group Captain William Proctor Wilson flew the fighter and had several near-death experiences in which the over-stretched tow rope was released with only moments to spare.

Post-war the opportunities mushroomed. War's real gift to Flight Refuelling Limited was six surplus Lancaster bombers that were converted into bulk-fuel tankers. Based in Worcestershire, they came south to rendezvous with the British South American Airways fleet, over the English Channel.

Sir Alan Cobham and BSAA chairman Air Vice Marshal Donald "Pathfinder" Bennett took G-AHJV over the mid-Atlantic and refuelled in mid-ocean, enabling them to make the first non-stop flight from Britain to Bermuda [28 May 1947].

Cobham's fleet now needed its own sizeable aerodrome and this he found between Blandford and Badbury Rings, with a tenancy of redundant RAF Tarrant Rushton [May 1947].

The Russians then blocked land access to the western sectors of Berlin, suddenly causing an international need for airborne bulk-fuel tankers. Flight Refuelling Limited had 12 of them, plus the expertise necessary to break the blockade, and was the petroleum arm of the Berlin Airlift [1948-49].

The United States Air Force was now at the leading edge of aerial fuelling capability, and proved it by sending Boeing B-50A *Lucky Lady II* on a non-stop flight around the world [26 February-2 March 1949]. Flight Refuelling Limited countered by developing more sophisticated probe and drogue technology, which was demonstrated at Tarrant Rushton to a visiting American delegation.

Air Chief Marshal Sir Alec Coryton, who would soon retire to Langton Matravers, took the British cause under his wing and provided Avro Lincoln tanker RA657 and Meteor fighter VZ389 for a series of trials.

It hardly compared with the Americans going once round the globe, but Lancaster G-33-2, flown by Tom Marks, enabled Pat Hornidge's Meteor to stay in the sky, above the English Channel, for an endurance flight of 12 hours 3 minutes [7 August 1949]. The Meteor was refuelled ten times, 3,000 gallons of paraffin were used, and about 3,000 miles, were flown. Hornidge then took the RAF's Lincoln across the Atlantic to show how the Brits were doing it.

USAF B-29 tanker YKB-29T showed that for their part the Americans did things bigger — proving it from Tarrant Rushton with a simultaneous sky-link from wing tips and tail to three British Meteors.

Canberra B2 bomber WH734 was delivered to Tarrant Rushton for conversion to Britain's first jet tanker, its arrival coinciding with the coronation and, appropriately, the climbing of Everest [May 1953].

WH734, intended for trials in refuelling Britain's V-bomber force, remained seconded to Flight Refuelling until after the Falklands War. The first of the new bombers, the Valiant, also converted to tankers, as would the Victors be when onset of metal fatigue caused their premature retirement.

Valiant tankers of 214 Squadron enabled Wing Commander Michael Beetham to take a delta-wing Vulcan bomber of 617 "Dambusters" Squadron non-stop from RAF Scampton to Sydney in 20 hours 3 minutes; an average speed of 573 miles per hour [1961]. Cobham's technology had enabled them to improve upon Sir Alan's pre-war record-breaking flight over the same course, which had taken 36 days.

Flight Refuelling had its main problems on the ground. It was preparing to relinquish its lease on Tarrant Rushton, upon which the control tower would be demolished [1981], and would have to move its aircraft to Hurn. It had already built an extensive factory midway between the two airfields, beside the River Stour east of Wimborne.

The Cold War continued but a lesser dispute would put technology to the test.

In the event we never did bomb Russia, notwithstanding Kenny Everett's exhortation to Young Conservatives, and the great British example of aerial refuelling would occur during the Falklands War [1982]. The Victor tankers of 55 Squadron and 57 Squadron flew more than 3,000 hours, carrying near 5,500 tonnes of fuel, in 600 refuelling link-ups.

Eleven of the Victors were needed for aerial sorties with a Vulcan in operation "Black Buck" which carried out the furthest and longest bombing raid in history — to drop 21 1,000 lb high explosive bombs on or beside Port Stanley airfield [1 May 1982]. Five more refuelling sorties were needed for the bomber, now much lighter, on its way back to Ascension Island. The flight totalled

OVER THE PAGE
GATOW RELIEVED: FOUR LANCASTRIAN TANKERS OF FLIGHT REFUELLING LIMITED ON THE GROUND IN WEST BERLIN IN 1948, IN ONE OF THE CLASSIC PROPAGANDA PHOTOGRAPHS OF THE COLD WAR.

7,860 miles and was the first and only time a V-bomber would be used in anger since Valiants from Malta bombed Egypt during the Suez Crisis of 1956.

Those Victor tankers outlived the Vulcan bombers and would join Chinook fuel-carrying helicopters of 7 Squadron in supplying air and ground needs of allied forces in the Gulf War [1990]. This vindicated the decision of the US Navy to adopt a probe and drogue system. Whatever the nationality, if the aircraft had a probe then the RAF was able to fuel it in the air — and did so, with a fleet that included VC.10 and Lockheed Tristar tankers as well as the faithful Victors.

Target towing became big business, initially with a fleet of Canberra T.22 bombers, and developed into "Threat Simulation" and "Electronic Warfare", these tasks then being carried out by Falcon 20s, bought from Federal Express.

Flight Refuelling as a company and a concept deserves and has received its own book, by Colin Cruddas, which is entitled *In Cobhams'* (sic) *Company* and published by Cobham plc, the new operating name for Flight Refuelling Limited [1994]. My "sic" is for its aberrant apostrophe. Though it passed to son Michael Cobham, this was Sir Alan's company, and writing of "Cobhams" makes for a clumsy plural, in the literary rather than the aviation sense.

Flying-boats — operated from Poole Harbour, which became the main base for Imperial Airways [August 1939] at the time it was being transformed into the British Overseas Airways Corporation [1 January 1940]. The fleet of Short C-class "Empire" flying-boats were evacuated to Poole from Southampton Water.

*MAINTENANCE WORK: ON A CONSOLIDATED CATALINA FLYING-BOAT OF BRITISH AIRWAYS, CIRCA 1946, IN THE SHEDS BESIDE
THE SLIPWAY AND HARD-STANDING AT HAMWORTHY.*

Military flying-boats followed, to RAF Hamworthy, and flew submarine patrols for Coastal Command.

See entries for Airways House; Alcock; *Altair*; *Argentina*; *Bermuda Sky Queen*; *Brazil*; British Airways; British Overseas Airways Corporation; *Cabot*; *Caribou*; *City of Liverpool*; *City of Swanage*; *Clare*; *Clio*; *Clyde*; *Cordelia*; Crashes; GJX; *Golden Hind*; *Guba*; *Hailsham*; *Hamilton*; Hamworthy; *Hythe* class; Imperial Airways; *Inglaterra*; *Maia*; Paraguay; Plymouth class; Poole Harbour crashes; Poole Harbour flying-boats Sandbanks Royal Naval Air Station; Squadrons operating from Dorset; Trots; *Uraguay*; UT; and *Vega*.

FM — squadron code of 257 (Burma) Squadron, flying Mark Ib Typhoons from RAF Warmwell [8 January -12 August 1943; 17 September 1943-20 January 1944] and returning to take their rocket-firing Typhoons on cross-Channel missions from RAF Hurn [2-8 July 1944].

Fontmell Magna crash — Bere Regis pilot David Dawson, flying alone in Cessna Skyhawk G-BMZV, was killed when it stalled and spun into the hilltop pasture above the eastern slope of Longcombe Bottom [21 November 1996]. He had taken off from nearby Compton Abbas Airfield, into a clear blue afternoon sky, after having just landed from Bournemouth International Airport.

Foss — Bridport war author **Sergeant-Pilot Ronald Foss** had gone missing on a Coastal Command flight over the Bay of Biscay [1943]. First to know was his wife who served in the operations room at the same air station. In the event Foss survived and would be picked up from the sea a week later.

He had enough experiences for a book and proceeded to write *In the Drink*, which was followed by *Three of us Live*, and *Famous War Stories*.

Take off: westwards into the wind from the main "Trot" in Poole Harbour, passing the northern side of Brownsea Island in 1945, for a Short "Empire" flying-boat of British Airways.

MILITARY CONVERSION: OF AN EX-BOAC SHORT SUNDERLAND MARK-III FLYING-BOAT, FOR COASTAL COMMAND, WITH GUN TURRET VISIBLE IN THE BOW AND RAF ROUNDEL ON THE FUSELAGE AS SHE SPLASHES DOWN ON SOUTHAMPTON WATER.

EMPIRE BOUND: THE GRACEFUL WAY OF LEAVING ENGLAND AND EUROPE, ABOVE AN ASSEMBLY OF YACHTS, WITH ANOTHER FLYING-BOAT ON HER MOORING (FAR LEFT).

Fox — Hurricane flyer **Sergeant-Pilot Peter Hutton Fox**, in N2434 of 56 Squadron from RAF Boscombe Down, was wounded in the right knee during combat over Portland [16.50 hours, 30 September 1940]. He baled out successfully as the fighter came back to earth on the north side of the lane from Wootton Fitzpane to Monkton Wyld.

Peter Fox also survived a crash in a Magister near Tidworth, Wiltshire [16 November 1940]. His career later saw him based in Dorset, at RAF Warmwell, with 234 Squadron [28 June 1941].

In a cross-Channel operation, flying a Spitfire, he was shot down over France and captured [20 October 1941]. He would be liberated from a prisoner of war camp in Germany [16 April 1945].

Frampton crash — of Blenheim bomber T2439 of 101 Squadron en route back to RAF West Raynham, Norfolk, after a raid on the port of Brest [4 April 1941]. The three crewmen, Sergeants P. T. Burrows, G. B. H. Birdsell and H. R. Perry, were killed instantaneously as the aeroplane exploded on hitting the ground. They had been trying to chart a course to RAF Boscombe Down which is 45 miles to the north-east.

Frisby — Hurricane flyer **Pilot Officer Edward Murray Frisby** [died 1941], in P2987 of 504 Squadron from RAF Filton, found himself damaged in combat and running out of fuel, only four miles from Warmwell Aerodrome, and made a successful forced-landing on rolling chalk downland at Whitcombe [17.00 hours, 30 September 1940].

He would be killed later in the war [5 December 1941] and is buried in St Cuthbert's churchyard, Great Glen, Leicestershire.

VICEREGAL RETURN: OQZG OF BRITISH AIRWAYS STILL IN MILITARY ROUNDELS, TAXIING BETWEEN ARNE AND HAMWORTHY, PREPARING TO TAKE THE VICEROY OF INDIA, FIELD-MARSHAL ARCHIBALD WAVELL, AND HIS PARTY BACK TO THE SUB-CONTINENT IN 1945.

FAMILIAR SIGHT: THROUGHOUT THE 1940S, WHEN POOLE HARBOUR WAS BRITAIN'S MAIN INTERNATIONAL AIRPORT, WITH "EMPIRE" FLYING-BOAT G-AGJJ BEING SEEN BESIDE THE NORTH-WEST CORNER OF BROWNSEA ISLAND.

FR Aviation — Cobham plc's Wimborne-based subsidiary which expanded on the other side of the globe by buying Adelaide-based National Jet Systems for 62 million Australian dollars [2000]. The Australian operation included 13 aircraft flying customs duties for national and state authorities as Surveillance Australia. Civilian flying centred on the provision of twelve British Aerospace BA-146 regional jets, on back-up services for flag-carrier Qantas. Three BA-146 freighters were seconded to Australian Air Express. Services for industry and scientific research included the provision of crews, testing and maintenance facilities for laser airborne depth sounding, through Vision Systems. An Avro RJ70 was being leased to Air Niugini.

ENGINE INSPECTION: WOMEN COXWAINS ON A BRITISH AIRWAYS LAUNCH IN POOLE HARBOUR, ATTACHING IT TO THE MOORING POINT IN THE FORMER FORWARD GUN-TURRET OF A HYTHE-CLASS "SUPERBIRD" FLYING-BOAT IN 1946, WHILE MAINTENANCE MEN CHECK THE SITUATION ON THE WINGS.

Harbour mooring: for BOAC "Speedbird" G-AHYY Portsmouth, off Parkstone.

Hamworthy base: where the flying-boats were grounded, with BOAC "Speedbird" G-AGEW Hanwell on the concrete pad.

'This will give us critical mass in Australia,' said Cobham chief executive Graham Page. He saw the way forward as specialisation in military high-speed training and electronic warfare capabilities. The air forces of Malaysia and Singapore were possible future partners.

F3 — squadron code of 438 (RCAF Wild Cat) Squadron, flying Mark IV Hurricanes from RAF Hurn [18 March-3 April 1944] and returning with rocket-firing Typhoons for cross-Channel missions [19 April-27 June 1944].

FLIGHT REFUELLING: ANGLO-US CO-OPERATION WITH THREE GLOSTER METEORS CLOSING IN FOR FUEL FROM A BOEING B29 SUPERFORTRESS.

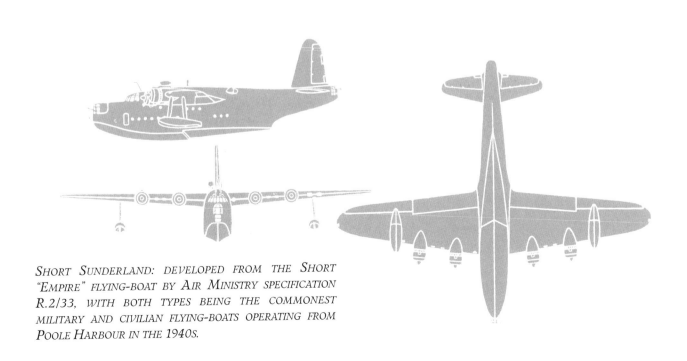

SHORT SUNDERLAND: DEVELOPED FROM THE SHORT "EMPIRE" FLYING-BOAT BY AIR MINISTRY SPECIFICATION R.2/33, WITH BOTH TYPES BEING THE COMMONEST MILITARY AND CIVILIAN FLYING-BOATS OPERATING FROM POOLE HARBOUR IN THE 1940S.

G

Gay — Christchurch Gulf War veteran **Lieutenant Timothy Gay** [1966-95] was killed when his Gazelle helicopter of 705 Naval Air Squadron, from RNAS Culdrose, exploded and crashed into the River Wye at Livox, Gwent [5 October 1995]. It had been flying low along the valley, on a training flight, when it hit power cables.

He once featured in an episode of the BBC television documentary "999" with the rescue of an injured climber which required him to hover within inches of the cliffs at Swanage.

Gee Chain navigation system — ten transmitting stations, nationally, including RAF Worth Matravers in Dorset [1942-70]. Operating in pairs, these provided accurately timed radio pulses for British aircrew, who used the signals to plot their aircraft's position by intersecting hyperbolic lines on a pre-printed lattice chart. The system "revolutionised the effectiveness of the RAF bombing raids" with "targets being found and bombed as never before". The first to use it operationally was a Wellington of 115 Squadron from RAF Watton, Norfolk, captained by Pilot Officer Jack Foster.

The stations continued in operation through the Cold War, but by the late 1960s the Ministry of Defence considered that other ground-based navigation aids and airborne systems had made Gee obsolete, causing the abandonment of the stations and demolition of their tall aerials.

Gerard A. Heineken — see Balloon *Gerard A. Heineken* entry.

Gill — sculptor **Eric Gill** [1882-1940], who created the Briantspuddle war memorial, underwent a notionally aeronautic interlude in Dorset.

In September 1918, Gill was conscripted into the Royal Air Force. Sans beard, he was sent to the Mechanical Transport Camp, at Blandford Camp, to be a driver.

Describing it as "an utterly unfriendly and unChristian place" he found "a terrible lot of waiting around" as the war wound down and its last decimations came from disease rather than conflict. Gill's brother, Kenneth, was "a life just thrown away" in an air crash in France, but at Blandford Eric was more fortunate in being hospitalised with influenza and being able to walk away from the problem. The Royal Air Force Camp was particularly hard hit by the pandemic.

Twenty-nine of the victims died; the majority of them young men from the Recruits Wing. Gill was discharged in November 1918 and never again went beardless. "Nation shall speak peace unto nation," he would engrave in his own typographical lettering on the wall of Broadcasting House. He designed the classic sans-serif typeface that carries his name.

Gillan — Hurricane flyer **Pilot Officer James Gillan** [1914-40], in P3783 of 601 Squadron from RAF Tangmere, was shot down and killed off Portland [10.25 hours, 11 August 1940]. He was a pre-war pilot who had served in Iraq, with the RAF's Persian Gulf Command, in 1936.

Gledhill — Hurricane flyer **Sergeant-Pilot Geoffrey Gledhill** [1921-40] was shot down and killed off the Dorset coast, between White Nothe and Lulworth Cove, in P2978 of 238 Squadron from RAF Middle Wallop [10.45 hours, 11 August 1940]. His body would be washed ashore in France and is buried in the churchyard at Criquebeuf-en-Caux. He had only been with the squadron a week.

GJX — radio pundit code for the Poole Harbour flying-boat base of British Overseas Airways Corporation [1939-48]. The Morse code letters interrupted a continuous tone, at 30 second

Historic aircraft: BOAC "Superbird" G-AFCI Golden Hind, moored off Parkstone, made the last service flight from Poole Harbour in the winter of 1948.

intervals, and were broadcast from a mobile aerial during wartime and then, in peacetime, directly from the Marine Terminal at Salterns Pier.

Glanvilles Wootton crash — Hawker Typhoon R7695 of 266 Squadron, from RAF Warmwell, broke-up in mid air as it flew over the village [24 October 1942].

Golden Hind — named BOAC Superbird G-AFCI would have the distinction of making the last scheduled service flight by a flying-boat from Poole Harbour [winter 1948] when the operational fleet returned to Southampton Water.

Goodman — "One of the Few" **Wing Commander Geoffrey Goodman** [1916-76] is buried in Witchampton churchyard. He was a pre-war pilot who joined the Royal Air Force and was posted to the re-formed 85 Squadron at Debden [1 June 1938]. Flew with them to France, in a Hurricane, on the outbreak of war. Returned injured and later re-joined the squadron at RAF Martlesham Heath [July 1940].

Claimed a Messerschmitt Bf.110 destroyed [30 August 1940] and a Bf.109 fighter [1 September 1940]. Transferred to 29 Squadron at RAF West Malling [November 1942], where his claims were one Dornier Do.217 damaged and a second destroyed. Awarded the Distinguished Flying Cross.

Promoted Flight-Lieutenant and posted to RAF Middle Wallop to command 151 Squadron [October 1943], where in a Mosquito XII night-fighter he accounted for eight enemy aircraft in just two months. Remained with the service after the war, moving to its Engineer Branch, and retiring as a Wing Commander [1969].

Era ends: BOAC named "Superbird" G-AFCI Golden Hind taking off on the last scheduled flight from Poole, seen from the south as she rises from the Main Channel 'Trot' with the tower of St James's parish church, in the Old Town, glimpsed in the background (far left).

Goodwin — pre-war pilot **Flying Officer Henry MacDonald Goodwin** [1915-40], a commissioned Royal Air Force reservist [1935] enlisted for full-time service and came to RAF Warmwell with 609 Squadron [July 1940]. He claimed a Messerschmitt Bf.110 [12 August 1940] and a pair of Junkers Ju.87 "Stukas" over Lyme Bay [13 August 1940] but failed to return from coastal combat in Spitfire N3024 the following day. His body was washed up on the Isle of Wight [24 August 1940] and he is buried at Chaddesley Corbett, Warwickshire.

Gowers — Hurricane pilot **Flying Officer Arthur Vincent Gowers** [1913-43] from Boscombe, Bournemouth, flew with 85 Squadron in France from the beginning of the Second World War until its withdrawal for home defence [22 May 1940].

In the Battle of Britain he accounted for a Messerschmitt Bf.110 one day and a Bf.109 the next [30-31 August 1940]. The following day, however, he was shot down in V7343 over Oxted, Surrey, and baled out with severe burns. Awarded the Distinguished Flying Cross and promoted Flight-Lieutenant, he was later posted to RAF Church Fenton to form the new 183 Squadron [1 November 1942], which he commanded until he was killed [24 October 1943].

Gray — fire hero **Group Captain John Astley Gray DFC** [born 1899] from Maiden Newton was awarded the George Medal [September 1941] for "displaying great bravery in the most appalling circumstances".

Acting Squadron Leader Joseph Aiden MacCarthy, an RAF doctor, received the same award for his part in the incident, when an aeroplane landed at night without its undercarriage and careered into a bomb dump. Gray and MacCarthy ignored the flames and bursting ammunition as they tried to save the crew, until they were overcome by fumes.

Gray had won his Distinguished Flying Cross in the Great War, remained in the RAF as a Flight-Lieutenant in the 1920s, and was promoted Wing Commander in 1938. He would rise to be an Air Vice Marshal [1944] and served with Transport Command after the war.

Guba [G-AGBJ] — the first of the long-range American-built Consolidated Catalina flying-boats to land on the water-runways of Poole Harbour [1 February 1941] for use on the BOAC service to Lisbon in neutral Portugal. The roar of her Pratt and Whitney Twin Wasp engines contrasted with the familiar and somewhat gentler sound of the Bristol Pegasus 9-cylinder radial engines of Short "Empire" flying-boats.

Air Ministry interest in her acquisition dated back to a remarkable pre-war flight. *Guba*, with Captain (later Sir) Patrick Gordon Taylor, Captain R. Rogers, and navigator Captain L. A. Yancey, made the first air crossing of the Indian Ocean [4 June-21 June 1939]. The Australians set off from Sydney to Port Headland (2,600 miles); then attempted to find the Cocos Islands but an obscured sky forced them off course, to Batavia (2,100 miles). From there they island-hopped, via Christmas Island, to Diego Garcia where they met with HMS *Manchester* (1,500 miles). Then they headed for Africa and stepped ashore at Mombassa, Kenya (2,300 miles).

Guest — flyer and politician **Captain the Right Honourable Frederick Edward "Freddie" Guest** [1875-1937] was the third son of the first Baron Wimborne. He was private secretary to cousin Winston Churchill. Guest's first election to Parliament, for East Dorset constituency in 1910, was declared void because his mother, Lady Wimborne, of Canford House, Canford Magna, Poole, had bought votes. Undaunted, she set about his re-election in the third contest that year.

He would become Lloyd George's Chief Whip [1917] and Secretary of State for Air [1921-22]. He established Moortown as his private airfield for the Canford estate and became a Squadron Leader in the Auxiliary Air Force, flying an Avro DH9a bomber with 600 Squadron.

GLIDER TOWING: AN AIRSPEED HORSA OF AIRBORNE FORCES BEHIND A SHORT STIRLING TUG-PLANE OVER CRANBORNE CHASE, IN AN EXERCISE FROM RAF TARRANT RUSHTON.

HAWKER HUNTER: COMING IN TO LAND AT YEOVILTON ROYAL NAVAL AIR STATION.

H

Hamel — pioneer aviator **Gustav Hamel** [1861-1922] visited Meyrick Park, Bournemouth [9-12 April 1914], to give breathtaking displays with his monoplane, taking up passengers ranging from Prince Maurice of Battenburg to the lucky holder of the winning raffle ticket.

As he looped the loop and performed other stunts, including a record 21 loops in a single spiral descent, the world entered the summer that would turn to war, and see the English members of the Battenberg family renouncing their German titles and taking the surname Mountbatten.

Hailsham — BOAC Sunderland flying-boat of the Hythe class [named January 1946] which came to grief in Poole Harbour on returning to England from Singapore [4 March 1946]. The runway "Trots" were shrouded in fog and she lurched off-course into the shallows beside Brownsea Island, becoming a sodden hulk that was later refloated and towed away for scrap.

Hamilton — BOAC flying-boat, outward bound from Hythe on Southampton Water to Poole Harbour to pick up passengers for a flight to Singapore [11 November1947]. Disorientated, in fog, she somehow managed to fly due south, into the 702-feet slope of Brighstone Down, in the centre of the Isle of Wight.

Three of the four crew escaped with their lives, thanks to the cushioning effect of post-war afforestation which had clad the hillside with young pine trees.

Hamworthy — RAF Hamworthy was established for the Sunderland flying-boats of Coastal Command, on anti-submarine duties in the English Channel, South-Western Approaches, and into the Bay of Biscay [August 1942]. Squadron-Leader R.C. Lovelock brought 461 (Royal Australian Air Force) Squadron, with nine Sunderlands, from Mount Batten, Plymouth [31 August 1942].

Squadron headquarters were requisitioned on the north-east shore of Poole Harbour, in the Harbour Yacht Club buildings at Lilliput. This base was initially called RAF Poole but this changed to RAF Hamworthy a week later.

MILITARY BACKGROUND: CIVILIAN BOAC FLYING-BOAT G-AGJN HUDSON MOORED BETWEEN HAMWORTHY AND BROWNSEA ISLAND (LEFT) WITH UT-G FOR GEORGE OF 461 (ROYAL AUSTRALIAN AIR FORCE) SQUADRON FURTHER OFFSHORE.

HAMWORTHY BASE: BOAC "SPEEDBIRD" G-AHER HELMSDALE ON THE HARD-STANDING WITH A SISTER BOAT MOORED IMMEDIATELY OFFSHORE (FAR RIGHT).

ABANDONED BOATS: THE BEGINNING OF THE END WITH SHORT SOLENT MARK-III G-AKNS CITY OF LIVERPOOL AT THE CENTRE OF THIS INACTIVE GROUP AT HAMWORTHY.

BEACHED WHALES: HULKS OF SHORT SOLENT MARK-III G-AKNS CITY OF LIVERPOOL (LANDWARD) AND SOLENT MARK-II G-AHIU SOLWAY, AT HAMWORTHY IN 1959.

SEA HARRIER: CARRYING DROP TANKS, OVER YEOVILTON ROYAL NAVAL AIR STATION, IN 1968.

The Australians operated from Hamworthy during the winter and left in the spring for Pembroke Dock, South Wales [21 April 1943].

They were replaced by 210 Squadron, flying military Catalina flying-boats [May-December 1943]. They were able to fly longer range missions, deep into the Atlantic, with airborne radar causing a decisive kill-rate of German U-boats and turning the tide in the Battle of the Atlantic.

By the end of the year the Catalinas had been withdrawn, to enable the Hamworthy slipway and other facilities to be used for training exercises in Poole Harbour and across the water on the sandy beaches of Shell Bay and Studland in preparation for the invasion of Europe.

Military Sunderland flying-boats returned to RAF Hamworthy for transport duties, rather than attacking U-boats [13 January 1944]. They were operated by 44 Group Transport Command and carried aircrew and other personnel to Karachi, on the route via Gibraltar, Tunis, and Cairo, for the campaign against the Japanese in India and Burma.

The base was hurriedly closed in the hectic run-up to D-Day when its facilities and slipways were needed for the gathering armada of invasion landing craft [March 1944].

Hann — Great War pilot **Cecil Collins Hann** [1895-1916] from Beaminster joined the Royal Flying Corps. He flew over the Western Front and would be killed in the Battle of the Somme [22 October 1916]. The son of Albert and Edith Hann, he is buried at Heily, Mericourt l'Abbé.

Hardacre — Hurricane pilot **Flying Officer John Reginald Hardacre** [1916-40], flying with 504 Squadron from RAF Filton, was shot down and killed in P3414. He was seen falling into the sea off Weymouth [30 September 1940].

His body would be washed ashore near Yarmouth, Isle of Wight [10 October 1940] and buried in All Saints' churchyard at Fawley, Hampshire.

He was born in Birmingham and had joined the RAF in 1938, serving in France [May 1940], and claimed five confirmed victories, there and in the Battle of Britain. His own previous close call had been a day in which he crash-landed in the morning and baled out from a blazing fighter in the afternoon [16 May 1940].

Harriers and the Kestrel — the first vertical landing by a fixed-wing aircraft on an aircraft-carrier took place when a prototype of Hawker Siddeley's project 1127 came down on HMS *Ark Royal* as she steamed at 5-knots east of The Shambles sandbank, off Portland Bill [8 February 1963].

Alfred William "Bill" Bedford [born 1920], Hawker's chief test pilot, was at the controls of the jet that could hover — which led to it being called the Kestrel. The Sea Harrier was developed from the P1127. It was found to take off with increased bomb-loads, at less speed, from ski-ramps rather than traditional flat decks. These appeared on the aircraft-carriers HMS *Invincible* [1978] and HMS *Hermes* [1979], and were incorporated in the next generation of ships, HMS *Illustrious* and the next *Ark Royal*, that were still being built.

The futuristic aircraft made its operational debut with the Fleet Air Arm at Yeovilton [19 September 1979] when 700A Naval Air Squadron was commissioned as the Sea Harrier Intensive Flying Trials Unit. 800, 801 and 899 Naval Air Squadrons were fitted out with Sea Harriers, as were a couple of RAF squadrons with their version of the aircraft, and most would be combat-ready and heading for the South Atlantic within a week of the Argentinian invasion of the Falkland Islands [2 April 1982].

HE — squadron code of 263 Squadron, flying rocket-firing Typhoons on cross-Channel missions from RAF Hurn [10-23 July 1944].

Heathway — the body of bomber crewman **Sergeant R. E. Heathway** of 107 Squadron from Great Massingham, Norfolk, was washed up on Bournemouth beach. He was lost when flak-hit Boston III AL286 crashed into the English Channel during a raid on the docks at Cherbourg [25 April 1942].

Hebert — French flyer **Jean Hebert**, with Denys Boudard, stole a Luftwaffe Bücker Jungmann biplane from an airfield near Caen and flew to Christchurch Aerodrome [29 April 1941]. They joined the Free French Forces. Hebert would be lost over the sea in 1943.

Henstridge Royal Naval Air Station — operated as shore-base HMS Dipper, on the Somerset border at Stalbridge (Ordnance Survey map reference ST 750 205). Effectively a satellite to Yeovilton Royal Naval Air Station.

Built on 355 acres of Blackmore Vale pastures and meadows, north-east of Stalbridge and east of Henstridge Marsh [August 1941] with 18 acres being added at Gibbs Marsh Farm, for an Aircraft Rectification Hangar, as the airfield neared completion.

Commissioned as HMS Dipper and taken over by No.2 Naval Air Fighter School from Yeovilton. Its flying unit, operating Seafire 1Bs, was 761 (Fleet Air Arm) Squadron. Additional accommodation was found in Fifehead Magdalen village.

Deck-landing practising would be its speciality. Indeed it had a dummy deck — the five runways incorporated an area of concrete laid out like the deck of an aircraft-carrier with arrester wires for added realism.

The 42 Spitfires of No.3 Naval Fighter Wing, from Lee on Solent, used Henstridge during the preparations for D-Day [March 1944].

Subsequently, during the hectic training for the Pacific War, Henstridge was the only Naval Fighter School equipped with Seafires [October 1944].

Seafire squadrons were trained there prior to transfer to aircraft-carriers, such as 887 and 894 (Fleet Air Arm) Squadrons which comprised No.24 Royal Navy Fighter Wing which flew from HMS *Indefatigable* in the Pacific theatre [from December 1944].

She became the first British carrier to be hit by a Japanese kamikaze pilot [1 April 1945]. Among the pilots of 887 Squadron was Sub-Lieutenant R. Lygo, who would retire as Admiral Sir Raymond Lygo.

The Naval School of Army Co-operation also used Henstridge until its removal to Northern Ireland [August 1945], and the end of intensive training with the disbanding of 761 Squadron after the war [March 1946].

Henstridge became a satellite airfield for Yeovilton though its aircraft-carrier runway would be brushed off for use in the Korean War period [1949-51], particularly by 767 (Fleet Air Arm) Squadron and the training of deck landing officers. With the departure of 767 Squadron [September 1952] the airfield was effectively inactive.

Cold War tensions revived its fortunes [1954] and much of the deck landing practice now took place at night — to a crescendo of local opposition. This did much to bring about the final military withdrawal [June 1957].

Civilian activities centred on the exploits and ambitions of one man, former Westland's test-pilot Alan Bristow. His Air Whaling Limited, for Antarctic whale spotting [1953-54] was followed by Bristow Helicopters Limited [1954-68]. Four Widgeons were leased to Shell for oil exploration in the Persian Gulf but the enterprise became almost too successful for Henstridge, being moved to Redhill [1958] where it was nearer Bristow's Cranleigh home.

The Admiralty sold-off the land and hangars. For a time it seemed likely that Henstridge would have the aerials for the BBC World Service [1980] but that plan aroused vociferous protests. Instead Aly Aviation returned, for crop-spraying flights, and the central area re-opened to other light aircraft [1986]. The dummy deck survives, being preserved as a unique piece of aviation history, by recent owner Keith R. V. Pierson of Kedgeworth Limited, whose earthmoving machinery was based at Henstridge Airfield in a landscape of wildlife lakes that were of his own creation.

Hewett — Canadian **Flying Officer Duncan Alexander Hewett** [1920-40] flying Hurricane P3084 of 501 Squadron from Middle Wallop, misjudged a dive against low-level reconnaissance Dorniers off Portland and plummetted into the sea [12 July 1940]. The enemy aircraft, which had been searching for a coastal convoy, were driven off by the other five Hurricanes.

HF — squadron code of 183 (Gold Coast) Squadron, flying rocket-firing Typhoons on cross-Channel missions from RAF Hurn [1-14 July 1944].

Hight — New Zealand **Pilot Officer Cecil Henry Hight** [1917-1940] in a Spitfire of 234 Squadron from RAF Middle Wallop, was shot down and killed over Leven Avenue and Walsford Road, Bournemouth, in a Battle of Britain dog-fight [15 August 1940].

He is buried in Boscombe Cemetery, has a memorial plaque in St Peter's Church, and the post-war Pilot Hight Road was named in his honour.

Hinks — Spitfire flyer **Flying Officer C. O. Hinks** of RAF Warmwell was killed during the Battle of Britain [14 September 1940]. He is buried in the RAF plot at Warmwell churchyard.

HH — code letters of 175 Squadron, flying Hurricanes from RAF Warmwell [1942].

Hlavac — Czechoslovakian flyer **Sergeant-Pilot Jaroslav Hlavac** [1914-1940] of 56 Squadron from RAF Boscombe Down was killed when a flight of Messerschmitt Bf.109 fighters shot down his Hurricane at Manor Farm, Worgret, west of Wareham [10 October 1940]. He had only been with the squadron for two days and is buried in the RAF plot at Warmwell churchyard.

Hogg — Spitfire flyer **Pilot Officer Edward Sidney Hogg** [died 1986] of 152 Squadron from Warmwell claimed a half share in the destruction of a Junkers Ju.88 bomber [23 August 1940]. He left the squadron two months later but remained in the Royal Air Force, leaving as Wing Commander at the end of the Second World War.

Hogg — Jersey-born Spitfire flyer **Pilot Officer Richard Malzard Hogg** [1919-40] of 152 Squadron from RAF Warmwell shared in the kills of two Junkers Ju.88 bombers [12 and 21 August 1940].

He was declared "Missing in Action" after being lost over the sea during a day of fierce Battle of Britain dog-fights [25 August 1940]. His body was not recovered.

Holland — Australian orphan and Spitfire flyer **Sergeant-Pilot Kenneth Christopher Holland** [1920-40] from RAF Warmwell claimed a third share of 152 Squadron's kill of a Heinkel He.111 bomber off Portland [15 September 1940]. It probably belonged to Kampfgruppe 55 from Chartres.

He claimed a third share in the kill of a Junkers Ju.88 that was shot down at Ladywell Barn, Imber, Wiltshire, but sustained damage to hydraulic, glycol, and oil pipes [17 September 1940]. He crash-landed on the obstructed concrete runways of a disused aerodrome at Yatesbury.

Two days later he was vectored from Warmwell Aerodrome towards a Junkers Ju.88 bomber [19 September 1940]. Holland was Green One for the afternoon and his partner, Green Two, was left behind and below the cloud. Holland found the target above the cloud at 11,500 feet and fired a total of 2,800 rounds sending it into a vertical dive towards the sea, off the Isle of Wight, with both engines burning.

His next kill would prove doubly fatal. Flying N3173 he brought down one of the Heinkel He.111 bombers (G1+EP) of Kampfgruppe 55 that had devastated the Bristol Aeroplane Company's works at Filton. In doing so he was hit in the head by return fire and both aeroplanes crashed at Church Farm, Woolverton, Somerset [12.00 and 12.02 hours, 25 September 1940]. Born in the Sydney suburb of Manley, Holland also used the surname Ripley and lived with a guardian in Cornwall. His body was cremated at Weymouth Crematorium.

Holmes — Spitfire flyer **Pilot Officer Frederick Henry Holmes** [1919-44] of 152 Squadron from RAF Warmwell claimed the destruction of Junkers Ju.87 [18 August 1940] and a share in the kill of a Junkers Ju.88 [21 August 1940]. Later in the war, as a Flight-Lieutenant with 487 Squadron, he was killed over Germany [4 December 1944] and is buried in the Reichswald War cemetery, near Cleves.

Horner — "Battle of the Beams" **Wing Commander G. K. Horner** of the Special Duties Flight from Christchurch Aerodrome searched out German blind-bombing navigation signals for the Telecommunications Research Establishment at Worth Matravers [1940-42]. He received the hand-over of the new Hurn Aerodrome from the contractors, on behalf of the Air Ministry and the Royal Air Force.

Horsa — troop-carrying glider, made by Airspeed Limited at its factory in Somerford, Christchurch. First used by airborne forces in the invasion of Sicily [9 July 1943], and then in mainland Europe, in Normandy on D-Day, at Arnhem, and landings inside Germany.

Howard — actor and film-maker **Leslie Howard** [1893-1943] stayed at the King's Arms Hotel, Christchurch, whilst working on *The First of the Few*, dramatising the legend of the Spitfire [October 1941]. The film also starred Major David Niven and Rosamund John.

A grass airfield fitted the story of the fighter's creation, with Flight-Lieutenant Joseph "Mutt" Summers making the first flight of Reginald Joseph Mitchell's prototype K5054 from Eastleigh Aerodrome, Southampton [5 March 1936]. RAF Warmwell had been selected for the filming but Howard decided instead to utilise the new concrete runways at RAF Ibsley, near Ringwood, as being not only modern looking for propaganda purposes but technically easier for filming than having to contend with the eight-gun fighters bouncing up and down across the grass.

Howard-Williams — Spitfire flyer in *The First of the Few* **Wing Commander Peter Howard-Williams** [1921-93] retired to Redcotts Lane, Wimborne. During the filming, starring Leslie Howard and David Niven, he was stationed at RAF Ibsley [1941]. Reality was also action-packed at the time, with several kills of enemy aircraft over the New Forest and Dorset coast. He was awarded the Distinguished Flying Cross.

Howell — Spitfire flyer **Flight-Lieutenant Frank Jonathan Howell** [killed 1948] of 609 Squadron from RAF Warmwell parachuted into the sea after a dog-fight off Swanage [8 July 1940]. He would return to the sky for a succession of kills: Junkers Ju.87 [13 August 1940]; Junkers Ju.88 [15 August 1940]; Messerschmitt Bf.110 [7 September 1940]; Junkers Ju.87 [13 September 1940]; Dornier Do.17 [15 September 1940]; Messerschmitt Bf.110 [7 October 1940]; half a share of a Junkers Ju.88 [21 October 1940; 609 Squadron's hundredth victory].

Awarded the Distinguished Flying Cross [25 October 1940]. Posted to RAF Filton to form 118 Squadron [20 February 1941] and later to the Far East where he was captured by the Japanese after the sinking of the battleship HMS Prince of Wales [10 December 1941]/

Post-war, Squadron Leader Howell would be decapitated by the wing of a Vampire as he was filming his jets [9 May 1948].

H2S — airborne "Town Finder" radar for blind bombing of German cities, devised by Group 8 of the Telecommunications Research Establishment, working from a Nissen hut in the grounds of the Establishment's eastern out-station, Leeson House at Langton Matravers [1941-42]. Given its codename for the chemical formula for hydrogen sulphide after Winston Churchill's chief scientific adviser, Professor Frederick Lindemann, snapped "It stinks that we never thought of it before," upon hearing some excuses.

Tested above the Bournemouth conurbation by aircraft of the Telecommunications Flying Unit, initially from a Blenheim bomber flying from Christchurch Aerodrome and then on a specially adapted four-engined Halifax from RAF Hurn [17 April 1942].

Put into production in a top-secret factory beside Northbourne Golf Links at West Howe, Bournemouth. First used operationally, by Pathfinders, to drop flares on Hamburg for a major raid [30-31 January 1943]. Enabled night-bombing of the correct cities — previously Bomber Command had "attacked Hamborn [Duisbury] in mistake for Essen" — for the duration of the Second World War.

Hughes-Rees — Spitfire flyer **Sergeant-Pilot Anthony Hughes-Rees** [1920-43] of 609 Squadron from RAF Warmwell claimed the destruction of a Messerschmitt Bf.110 and then crash-landed his fighter, L1008 after suffering engine failure near Glastonbury [25 September 1940]. He had only been with the squadron a matter of days and would be awarded the Distinguished Flying Medal after increasing his tally to four kills [8 August 1941].

Hughes-Rees was killed in the Middle East, as a Flying Officer with 73 Operational Training Unit [30 April 1943], and is buried in Moascar War Cemetery, Egypt.

Hurn Aerodrome — built on a gravel plain north of the River Stour at Bournemouth, by the Air Ministry on behalf of the Royal Air Force, for 11 Group Fighter Command. Elevation 34 feet above sea level. Three concrete runways were constructed by various engineering firms and attracted their first Luftwaffe bombs at the close of the Battle of Britain [3 December 1940].

Before the war the site had been recommended to Bournemouth Corporation for a municipal aerodrome, by international aviator Sir Alan Cobham.

Three hardened concrete runways, initially 5,200 feet, 4,800 feet and 3,400 feet. Seven large and ten small blister hangars. Pundit Code "KU".

Handed from the contractors to the Air Ministry which passed it to 11 Group Fighter Command. The hand-over ceremony was to Wing Commander G. K. Horner of the Special Duties Flight, from Christchurch Aerodrome [1 August 1941].

Overseas Aircraft Despatch Units and Communications Flights operated from RAF Hurn [1942-44]. The first Liberator landed on 18 January 1942 and many more followed, to be flown onward via Gibraltar and across the Sahara Desert, to operational bases in the Middle East. This aircraft was the RAF version of the bulky high-wing Consolidated B-24 bomber which was powered by four Pratt and Whitney 1,200 horsepower Twin Wasp engines. It became the largest single United States aircraft type of World War Two, 18,482 being delivered, of which the RAF received 1,889.

Hurn became the base — with a large hardened hangar that still survives — for Prime Minister Winston Churchill's personal Liberator and other VIP aircraft [July 1942].

RAF Hurn had then been transferred from Fighter Command to 38 Wing Army Co-Operation Command, with its commanding officer being Group Captain Harold John Granville Ellis Proud [1 June 1942]. The station provided transport support for the 1st Airborne Division.

A flight of six VIP Flying Fortresses, one of which was left behind with failed undercarriage hydraulics, took off from RAF Hurn [3 November 1942] with Lieutenant-General Dwight D.

ROCKET ARMING: TYPHOONS FROM RAF HURN CROSSED THE CHANNEL TO ADVANCED LANDING GROUNDS BEHIND THE D-DAY BEACHES AS THE BATTLE OF NORMANDY UNFOLDED.

Eisenhower and the staff officers of Allied Forces North-West Africa, taking them to the conference in Gibraltar that approved the detailed plans for the invasion of French North Africa.

A total of 180 transport aircraft, including 51 C47 Dakota troop carriers and 61 Boeing B-17 F Flying Fortress bombers, passed through Hurn in Operation Cackle, which was the Hurn-Gibraltar air ferry service that was completed without a single casualty. It provided large elements of the logistical back-up for Operation Torch, in which a combined British and American force involving a total of 107,000 men landed in French North Africa at Casablanca, Oran and Algiers [8 November 1942].

Throughout 1942 work was carried out on the ground, and tested in the air around Hurn, on modifications to bombers such as the Halifax, Whitley, and Stirling, into tow-craft for gliders carrying airborne troops and equipment. In 1943 the Whitleys were replaced by twin-engined

TOWING TROLLEY: WIRES ATTACHED TO THE REAR-WHEEL OF LANCASTRIAN MARK-III G-AGMH OF BRITISH OVERSEAS AIRWAYS, AS IT IS REFUELLED FROM A TANKER, AND THEN TOWED TO DISPERSAL AT HURN AERODROME.

AVRO YORK: BOAC "SUPERBIRD" G-AGSN MARLOW COMING IN TO LAND AT HURN AERODROME.

Albemarles, the first British military aircraft with a tricycle under-carriage. The unit would remain at Hurn until the preparations for D-Day.

The aerodrome's main user, No.38 Wing, Army Co-Operation Command, was reformed as No.38 Group, Airborne Forces [11 October 1943].

Control of Hurn and its 38 Group operators was passed to the Allied Expeditionary Air Force [1 February 1944] in preparation for the invasion of Europe. Massive expansion in capacity was already underway with the two main runways at Hurn being increased in length by half as much again and a square mile of heathland on the north and east sides was churned into a moonscape of yellow sand, crossed by the curves and frying-pan shapes of a complex network of dispersal areas.

Swarms of escort fighters took off or landed back at RAF Hurn throughout the months preceding the invasion of Normandy. This activity was in full swing by the end of the previous year, with 24 Spitfires escorting bombers to Triqueville [22 December 1943] and 37 P-47 bombers taking part in attacks on the Cherbourg peninsula [29 December 1943]. Two flak-damaged B-17 Flying Fortresses also came into Hurn. The station participated in actions that succeeded during the month in destroying eight V1 flying bomb launch sites.

83 Group at Hurn was augmented with an additional three Typhoon squadrons, forming 124 Wing [April 1944].

Crucially, 28 Hurn Typhoons would deliver 96 60-lb rockets and seven tons of bombs on German coastal radar stations; with the deliberate exception of that at Fécamp which was kept intact so that it could report spoof activity aimed at convincing the enemy that the main thrust of the invasion would come further up-Channel, east of the Seine [5 June 1944].

P-61 Black Widow night-fighters of the 9th United States Army Air Force and B-26 Marauders of the American 97th Bombardment Group also operated from Hurn Aerodrome during the D-Day campaign.

OVER THE PAGE

AERIAL AIRPORT: LOOKING SOUTH-WEST, WITH THE ACCESS ROAD AND MERRITOWN (FAR LEFT) AND THE MOORS RIVER ON THE OTHER SIDE (RIGHT) SHOWING HURN AERODROME AND ITS PASSENGER FACILITES (CENTRE FOREGROUND) WITH THE COMMERCIAL AREAS ON THE OTHER SIDE OF THE RUNWAYS.

After the Mosquitoes quit Hurn, to be redeployed at Middle Wallop [1 August 1944], they were replaced by Martin B-26 Marauders of 596, 597 and 598 Squadrons of the 9th Bombardment Group of the United States Army Air Force [23 August 1944]. Their achievements included a spectacular raid on the railway marshalling yards at Corbiel to the south of Paris [14 August 1944]. They were soon to be moved across the Channel to a forward base in Normandy [20 August 1944].

With the transfer of British Overseas Airways Corporation's land-plane operations from Lyneham, Wiltshire, Hurn had the distinction of being Britain's principal civilian airfield.

Civilian operations at what was still RAF Hurn began with the arrival of G-AGJI, a Lancaster transporter of British Overseas Airways Corporation which flew in from Lyneham, Wiltshire [20 January 1944]. More followed, as did the post-war Lancastrians, and Hurn became BOAC's main British base for solid-runways airliners.

BOAC Avro York MW103, given the civilian letters G-AGJA, flew the first wartime service from Hurn to Cairo, via Morocco and across the Sahara Desert [22 April 1944].

The first Lancastrian of BOAC's new fleet, G-AGLF, carried the markings of the RAF's South-East Asia theatre for its 53-hour proving flight from Hurn to Sydney, Australia [23-26 April 1945].

History would be made with the arrival from La Guardia Airport, New York, of a military C-54 Skymaster of Pan American Airways, at the end of a 17-hour flight [18 September 1945]. This was the first time a four-engined land-plane — as distinct from a flying-boat — crossed the Atlantic Ocean on civilian service.

Post-war international flights from Hurn began with BOAC Lancastrian G-AGLV inaugurating the 12,000-miles service to Sydney, Australia [30 May 1945]. Pan American Airways arrived from the opposite direction, with an ex-military C54 Skymaster in a 17 hour flight from New York. British Halifax bombers, converted into Haltons, took over the old flying-boat run, to Nigeria. Then BOAC Lancastrian G-AGMG made its maiden long-haul flight, from Hurn to Buenos Aires [9-18 October 1945]. Avro York G-AGNT took the first 7,000-miles run out of Hurn to Malta and the Middle East and then virtually from Cairo to the Cape, with intermediate stops at Khartoum and Nairobi and destination Johannesburg in South Africa [10 November 1945].

South African Airways shared that route and the Atlantic run was also serviced by American Export Lines and American Overseas Airways. Free Europe entered the running with Koninklijke Luchtvaart Maatschappij, from The Netherlands, and Sabena.

The Americans consolidated their hold of the big airframes of the Atlantic run with the "service of the future" as it was hailed when a Lockheed Constellation made its first ocean crossing and deposited 29 passengers from New York on the tarmac at Hurn after a flight of only 12 hours [1 January 1946]. All that Britain had to offer in competition were the Clipper flying-boats, also American airframe, on the run from Poole Harbour to Baltimore, but these could no longer compete against the landplanes and the service was abandoned [7 March 1946].

Pan American was winning world prizes with the Constellation which was set to achieve the first commercial flight "Round-the-Globe" [29 June 1947]. Its landplanes were also targeting the chunks of European Empire that were not British; such as the Belgian Congo.

All that BOAC and Hurn had to compete with were the N-class Lancastrians, but at least these were coming through in quantity. Some 21 would be delivered [1946-48] and they ousted Dakotas from the mid-range hauls to Africa and India. Fourteen were named, for "N" names from *Nelson* and *Nairn* to *Natal* and *Nepal*.

A further 14 Lancastrians were seconded to British South American Airways, an operating company owned by BOAC, and given their own series of "Star" names. Rather than being celestial names these had the key word first and ranged from *Star Dust* to *Star Watch*. The former would crash in the Andes and the latter was wrecked on a training flight into what was still being called Heath Row. Overall it was a successful subsidiary, with its own charismatic chairman, Air Vice-Marshal Donald "Pathfinder" Bennett who led from the top [1945-48] and flew geographical survey flights across the sub-continent.

Hurn's international role was now threatened as operators were given a new horizon, on the meadows of Heath Row in Middlesex which had been elevated to the status of London Airport [February 1948].

MAINTENANCE SHED: BOAC ENGINEERS PREPARING A LANCASTRIAN AIRLINER AT HURN AERODROME, FOR A FLIGHT ACROSS THE EMPIRE.

Hurn was no longer centre-stage but it remained in the forefront of technology. Flight Refuelling Limited acquired a fleet of Lancastrians as they were withdrawn from passenger flights. The School of Air Traffic Control turned aerial traffic management into an art, teaching radar, blind-landing and queue stacking techniques [from 1949]. The planemakers also arrived, with Vickers Armstrong (Aircraft) Limited flight-testing the first V-bomber, the Vickers Valiant, and setting up a factory to produce their passenger project, which became the Vickers Viscount with work shared between Weybridge and Hurn. Two hundred were built at Hurn.

What was now called Bournemouth (Hurn) Airport also gave a home to Airwork Services who were civilian providers of target-towing flights for the Fleet Air Arm [1952]. Theirs was a general collection of aircraft-carrier machines plus the versatile Mosquito.

Surprise passenger arrivals became increasingly frequent as the notorious smogs closed London Airport and weather conditions often prevented Blackbushe from being used as alternative. Hurn was second in line for diverted flights.

Commonest aircraft at Hurn and over Bournemouth at the end of the 1950s was the Bristol 170 Wayfarer, otherwise known as the Bristol Freighter. This owed its bulbous lines to the Hamilcar gliders that had carried airborne forces from Hurn and Tarrant Rushton during the Second World War. All that seemed different was that it had a pair of engines and the camouflage had given way to the sleek liveries of Silver City Airways and Jersey Airlines; this was the first aerial car-ferry.

Transfers of operations from Eastleigh brought British European Airways and British United Airways, as well as Air Safari and Cambrian Airways to Hurn, with a consequent surge in the number of passengers. High summer in 1961 saw the 50,000 barrier broken for the first time and there was another monthly first for Hurn — that of 1,000 airborne cars [August 1961].

Passenger accommodation was grossly inadequate by modern standards and these expectations were met by the building of a new terminal near the south-east corner of the airfield, at a cost of £250,000 [1963].

Vickers had become a division of the British Aircraft Corporation and their first BAC 1-11, made at Hurn, lifted off to begin a new age of civilian aviation [20 August 1963]. By the time the last of its final version was completed, in the 1-11 475 series, the factory was part of British Aerospace plc [May 1984]. The following month, on news that maintenance work was insufficient to keep it open, the Hurn works was closed.

British European Airways continued to use Hurn until their last scheduled flight in a Vickers Viscount to Jersey [31 March 1966]. The cream of the business was now in package tours and these were seen as the new mass-market opportunity. Channel Airways filled the missing link with Dorset's offshore islands — the Channel

FLY NAVY: SEA VIXEN ABOVE HURN AERODROME WITH A ANOTHER LINKED IN A FLIGHT REFUELLING EXERCISE, WITH A SCIMITAR.

FR FLEET: DASSAULT FALCON JETS ASSEMBLED AT HURN IN 1988 WITH N900FR IN THE FOREGROUND.

Islands — which traditionally regarded Weymouth as their principal mainland port. They also maintained the French connection with a triangle of services that extended to Paris.

Express Air Services and British Island Airways also crossed the Channel and a network of internal flights to British cities was provided by Dan Air, with a fleet of Hawker-Siddely 748s. Hurn also turned out qualified pilots, through the College of Air Training. The Air Traffic Control Evaluation Unit experimented with advanced prototypes of new radars, using the Hurn flights as guinea pigs — though separately from the airfield's actual air traffic system.

The Fleet Requirement Unit moved from Hurn to the Royal Naval Air Station at Yeovilton [1972]. Channel Express became a new name on the Channel Islands run, with Dart Heralds.

Flight Refuelling Limited, having moved its fleet of tankers from Tarrant Rushton to Hurn, expanded into the executive jet business, with a squadron of sleek fighter-like Dassault Falcons, augmented by Cessna Conquests [1988].

That, for now, is the history and the present lies with Bournemouth International Airport as Hurn (Bournemouth) Airport — the 1941-built Hurn Aerodrome — was renamed at the end of the decade [1989].

Hurn crashes — flak-damaged Whirlwind P6983 of 263 Squadron from RAF Filton, Gloucestershire, force-landed at the new RAF Hurn with one engine out of action and the other leaking glycol coolant, after having claimed two Messerschmitt Bf.109s off Cherbourg [6 August 1941].

Spitfire EB687 was written-off on arrival at Hurn, for escort duty, when it collided with a parked Whitley bomber [10 July 1943].

The crew of a Whitley tug-plane were killed when it stalled on take-off and crashed inside the perimeter fence, in what should have been a routine training flight from RAF Hurn [July 1943].

One Sunday afternoon four gliders, of the type used for carrying airborne troops, crashed into the lane leading to East Parley mission church, immediately west of the Hurn Aerodrome [1943].

Hurricane LD972 of 439 (Royal Canadian Air Force) Squadron crashed two miles east of RAF Hurn, into the Avon valley, after colliding with an American P-47 Thunderbolt from USAAF

OVER THE PAGE
POST PLANES: ROYAL MAIL AIR SERVICES, AS OPERATING THROUGH THE NIGHT FROM HURN AERODROME IN 1980, WITH THE ARGOSY'S BOW DOORS OPEN FOR BUSINESS.

CLASS LEADER: BOAC EX-MILITARY "SPEEDBIRD" G-AGJM HYTHE, NAMED FOR THE PREVIOUS FLYING-BOAT BASE IN SOUTHAMPTON WATER, WITH A LAUNCH ALONGSIDE OFF PARKSTONE.

Christchurch that had thrown itself into Canadian practice dog-fights [21 March 1944]. Flight-Lieutenant Norval E. Pollock was killed.

The full details can now be given of the most severely damaged aircraft to return to England from a bombing mission in the Second World War. "Seldom can an aircraft have remained in the sky after having been so badly damaged," the *Daily Telegraph* and the *Sydney Sun* reported around D-Day, but key facts such as the identification of the bomber and its homecoming location were withheld at the time.

LV792, a Halifax Mark III, carried squadron code NP "E" for Easy, with 158 Squadron in No. 4 Group, Bomber Command, from RAF Lissett, near Driffield in Yorkshire. Her crew were:

Pilot — Flying Officer Doug Bancroft of the Royal Australian Air Force.

Navigator — Flying Officer Alwyn Fripp of the Royal Australian Air Force.

Wireless Operator — Sergeant Len Dwan.

Flight Engineer — Sergeant Len Cotterell.

Air Bomber — Flying Officer Eric Tansley.

Mid Gunner — Sergeant Ken Leheup.

Rear Gunner — Sergeant Dave Arundel.

It is Eric Tansley, then of St Albans and now living at Upper Brailes, near Banbury, Oxfordshire, who tells their story.

They took off on the night of 2-3 June 1944, tasked to bomb railway marshalling yards at Trappes, five miles from Versailles, to disrupt German reinforcements bound for Normandy in the aftermath of the impending invasion of Europe. En route home, at Evreux to the north-west of Paris, they were attacked by a German night fighter armed with "Nacht Musik" — an upward firing cannon — which hit the port inner engine of the four-engined bomber which was set on fire and had to be feathered. The port wheel was damaged. The Wireless Operator was wounded as his position was struck and a hole three feet long was blown in the side of the aircraft.

The same shell shattered the radio in the cockpit and holed the perspex over the pilot's head. It also disabled the magnetic compass. A large hole was blown through the starboard wing, inboard of the engine, and through the main petrol tank.

The bomb doors were blown away and the bomb bay set on fire. From the underside of the fuselage both the H2S airborne radar scanner and the DR compass were completely blown away. Eric Tansley surveyed the damage around him: "The fire in the bomb bay was the hydraulic fluid burning, so the flaps fell half down, and later the undercarriage control could only be lowered by the emergency release. All radio and electrics and hydraulics were out of commission."

The Flight Engineer and the Mid Gunner baled out, mistakenly thinking the pilot had given the order to abandon the aircraft. Later the badly injured Wireless Operator baled out and was never heard of again. The Rear Gunner was jammed in his turret and could do nothing until he had hacked his way out with his axe. He then went forward to see the situation: "When he saw us he went back, got his parachute and two fire extinguishers, and tackled the blaze. The flames were leaping high and he soon used up the two extinguishers. Then he beat out the fire with his feet and hands.

The Pilot was unaware that the P4 compass had a piece of shrapnel in it and was stuck on the course being flown at the time of the attack. Air Bomber Tansley resumes his account: "Some time later the Navigator asked the Pilot what course he was flying and Doug replied, 'Oh, about north'. I looked ahead of the cockpit and saw the moon dead ahead. Something registered with me and I said to Doug, an Australian, that we never have moon in the north. His mental view was of the sky in the southern hemisphere. Then he looked around the Pole Star in mid-Channel, by which time we were apprehensive about how far we had flown in a south-westerly direction, and whether we would still reach England on a northerly course."

Though problematic, that new line would prove to be their salvation, as it would keep them clear of the higher cliffs of Dorset to the west and the Isle of Wight to the east. Between these obstacles is a low plateau at the 115-feet contour, rising to 150 feet with rooftops and chimneys, which was enough of a barrier: "The coastal cliffs were only just cleared and landing was made inland, fortunately by chance, on Hurn Aerodrome behind Bournemouth. The bomb bay was still burning. As we came to rest the sight of an RAF ambulance made us realise that we had in fact landed on an aerodrome!"

The combination of low cliffs and an operational base with full-length runways, only four miles inland, occurs in only a handful of locations along the South Coast. The next day the Air Ministry issued its report — leaving out such details — that this was the most severely damaged plane to return to England. The four returnees were rewarded immediately with Distinguished Flying Crosses (for Bancroft, Fripp and Tansley) and a Distinguished Flying Medal (for Arundel). They were debriefed and a plane came to collect them the following day.

Eric Tansley recalls that during the flight, after the cockpit Perspex had shattered, "there was a tremendous draught of air through the plane". He was still wearing his parachute pack on his chest but the wind had ripped it open: "The parachute was all over the place. When we landed at Hurn and went to the be debriefed I gathered my chute in my arms and laid it on the floor outside the office where the debriefing was to take place. When we finally left the debriefing. I looked on the floor and my parachute had disappeared. There was no one about to question and I eventually had to fly back to Lissett without it.

"Later the Equipment Officer came to see me to tell me that I would be charged £70 for not bringing my chute back. I replied that we had not brought the aircraft back either — were we to be charged for that? He said that was a war loss and would be written off. I told him that my chute was also a war loss that could be written off."

LV792 was declared Category B/FB — which was a complete write-off — and then Dave Arundel also went out of commission. He was shot down on returning to operations and taken prisoner of war. Doug Bancroft, however, found the opportunity to return to Hurn and arrange for the instrument panel to be removed from the Halifax as a souvenir.

It went to Australia, to which Bancroft returned a couple of years later, and is now on display in the Royal Australia Air Force Museum at Canberra. Doug Bancroft would have other flying misadventures, including the crash of a Dakota in post-war India, where his heroism earned him the George Medal.

HYTHE CLASS: THIS BEING BOAC "SPEEDBIRD" G-AHEO HALSTEAD, MOORED IN POOLE HARBOUR, IN 1947.

BROWNSEA MOORING: BOAC "SPEEDBIRD" G-AGKW HOTSPUR, SEEN FROM THE NORTH WITH BRANKSEA CASTLE AND BALLARD DOWN GLIMPSED IN THE DISTANCE (RIGHT).

TAXIING WESTWARDS: BOAC FLYING-BOAT G-AGJN HUDSON, BEFORE REPAINTING OF HER REGISTRATION LETTERS AND REMOVAL OF THE GUN TURRET IN THE BOW, OFF BROWNSEA ISLAND (LEFT).

Having baled out of the hole blown in the fuselage where the H2S radar scanner had been, the Engineer met up with French Resistance and went on several operations with them before he reached the invasion forces in Normandy.

The Mid Gunner who jumped with him landed at the opposite end of the same field but found a very different fate. Though given food and civilian clothes by a farmer, and having walked uneventfully for three days, he found himself stumbling on a German arms dump in a wood. He was arrested and the Gestapo threatened to kill him for not revealing the identity of the farmer. Eventually he spent miserable months in a prisoner of war camp in eastern Germany. Despite this, Ken Leheup gradually recovered in peacetime, and enjoyed a long retirement in west Dorset, at Broadwindsor, which ended with his death early in 1999.

News management at the time, as so often happens in war, rather went awry. Envelopes or wires must have been crossed. For it is Pilot Officer Bancroft of Pennant Hills, Sydney, who has the hero's mention in the London *Daily Telegraph*. But it is Flying Officer Tansley from St Albans who appears in the version published in the *Sydney Sun*.

The next notable mishap was when a post-war prototype Airspeed Ambassador, newly made at the firm's Christchurch works, landed at Hurn Aerodrome with the undercarriage retracted, during a practice emergency which became real [January 1950]. One engine had been shut off during take-off to see how she handled. The pilot was George Errington.

Clever aerobatics, a touch too ambitious, caused the spectacular crash of an Argentinian Pampa 1A-63 advanced jet trainer that was practising at Hurn for the Farnborough Air Show [31 August 1992]. Falklands veterans Air Commander Juan Carlos Sapolski and Captain Omar Dario Gelardi were killed instantly as the aircraft "dropped like a stone" from between 500 and 1,000 feet, and hit the ground with "an incredible bang", followed by a fireball.

Witness Gordon Ansty said that something had gone wrong with what was obviously intended as their party piece for the air display: "Their plane kept trying one particularly dangerous trick where it flew up to about 1,000 feet and then dive-bombed vertically, before pulling up at the last minute."

Mrs Lucy Lucas of Merritown Farm said the blue and silver-coloured trainer had been going into spiral dives: "It did two and then it did a third one and the engine seemed to cut out."

A much more recent tragedy occurred when a father and son from Wareham, David and Matthew Samways, were killed when their light aircraft crashed at Bournemouth International Airport [24 December 1999].

Hurricane L1592 — one of three stationed at Christchurch Aerodrome to protect the Special Duty Flight which operated there [1940-42]. This particular machine not only survived an undercarriage failure, collapsing upon touch-down [28 April 1941], but also the remainder of the war and the subsequent peace. It became part of the National Aeronautical Collection that is displayed by the Science Museum in London.

***Hythe* class** — ex-military "Speedbird" flying-boats of British Overseas Airways Corporation, gathered in Poole Harbour and named for the resumption of civilian services to Singapore and Australia [January 1946].

They comprised *Hadfield, Hailsham, Halstead, Hamble, Hamilton, Hanwell, Harlequin, Harwich, Haslemere, Hawkesbury, Henley, Himalaya, Hobart, Honduras, Hotspur, Howard, Hudson, Hungerford, Hunter, Huntingdon,* and *Hythe* (with the latter and the class being named for BOAC's past and future home-base on Southampton Water).

Apart from *Hailsham,* which crashed in Poole Harbour [14 March 1946], and some overseas losses, the survivors returned to Hythe [31 March 1948]. A succession of sales and scrappings led to the total withdrawal of British flying-boat services [30 September 1958].

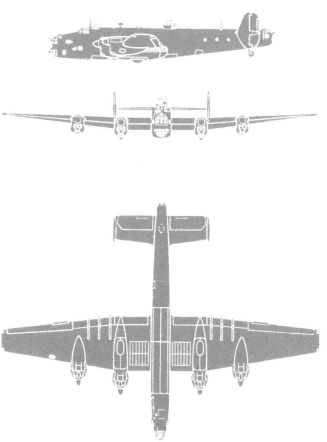

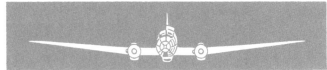

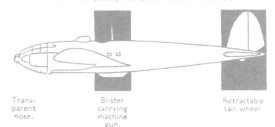

Nose is completely transparent and is "off-centre."

Trans-
parent
nose.

Blister
carrying
machine
gun.

Retractable
tail wheel

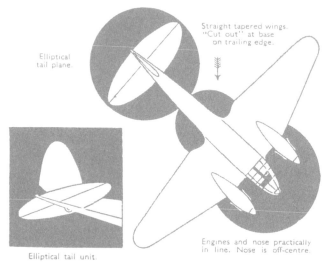

Elliptical
tail plane.

Straight tapered wings.
"Cut out" at base
on trailing edge.

Elliptical tail unit.

Engines and nose practically
in line. Nose is off-centre.

HALIFAX BOMBER: MORE FAMILIAR OVER DORSET IN ITS ROLE AS THE PRINCIPAL TUG-PLANE FOR GLIDERS FROM RAF TARRANT RUSHTON.

HEINKEL HE.III: THE COMMONEST GERMAN BOMBER ATTACKING OR CROSSING DORSET IN THE SECOND WORLD WAR.

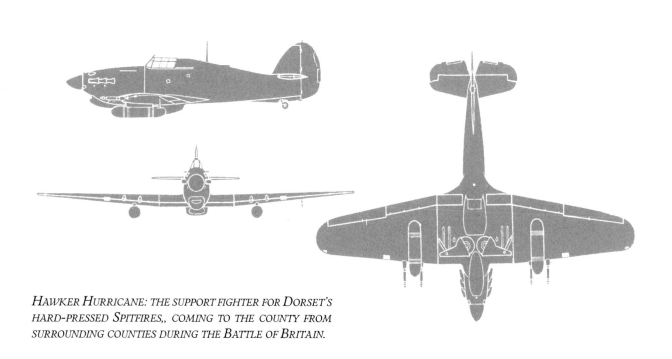

HAWKER HURRICANE: THE SUPPORT FIGHTER FOR DORSET'S HARD-PRESSED SPITFIRES,, COMING TO THE COUNTY FROM SURROUNDING COUNTIES DURING THE BATTLE OF BRITAIN.

I

I8 — squadron code of 440 (RCAF City of Ottawa) Squadron flying Mark IV Hurricanes from RAF Hurn [18 March-3 April 1944] and returning with rocket-firing Typhoons for cross-Channel missions [20 April-28 June 1944].

Imperial Airways — the first British national airline [April 1924] merged with British Airways at the time its flying-boats were transferred from Southampton Water to Poole Harbour [August 1939], and operated as British Overseas Airways Corporation from the new year [1 January 1940]. Its proposed Transatlantic service, if the decade had opened in peace, was headed by Captain Arthur Sidney Wilcockson, who pioneered the proposed route [1937]. He was the manager of the Atlantic Division of Imperial Airways. The future "Pathfinder" Captain Donald Bennett and Captain Jack Kelly-Rogers were his senior pilots.

Pre-war ditchings of Imperial Airways "Empire" flying-boats, prior to the move from Southampton to Poole, started with *Calypso* off the Channel Islands though she would be towed to safety in Cherbourg — and *Cavalier* which broke in two after making an emergency landing in the sea following carburettor icing after taking off from New York for Bermuda [23 January 1939]. The *Capella* was wrecked, but salvageable, at Batavia [12 March 1939]. *Corsair* was stranded in the tropics, having found herself lost in the Belgian Congo and been beached by co-operative natives beside the remote River Dangu. The epic story of her ten-month rescue is pure Biggles.

Meanwhile, *Centurion* up-ended into the Hooghly River, Calcutta, after a misjudged landing [12 June 1939]. Then *Connemara* lit up Southampton water, having caught fire on her mooring at Hythe after flames spread from a fuel barge.

A bargeman was drowned in that accident, and three passengers were lost on the attempted Bermuda run, but otherwise the human casualty list was light. Flying-boats in trouble in the air stood a second chance down on the water; but public confidence in Sir John Reith's Imperial Airways Limited was wobbling as the Air Ministry pushed through legislation to bring about its merger with British Airways.

The war came almost as a relief, bringing an excuse and a respite at a time when increasing weights of mail caused delays and cancellations for passengers as the depleted fleet no longer coped with peacetime expectations.

Transatlantic services started with *Caribou* outbound from Southampton, in formation to Foynes with *Maia* [5 August 1939], and onward alone to Botwood, Newfoundland [6 August 1939]. Captain Jack Kelly-Rogers was in command. As he began the return flight, Captain Donald Bennett took-off in *Cabot*, from Southampton, on the second scheduled service across the Atlantic.

Inglaterra — an ex-BOAC Mark V Sunderland flying-boat from Poole, converted into a Sandringham-3 for carrying 21 passengers and sold to the Argentine airline Dodero [November 1945].

Inness — Spitfire pilot **Flying Officer Richard Frederick Inness** of 152 Squadron from RAF Warmwell, who had left Eton to join the RAF [August 1938], claimed the destruction of a Junkers Ju.88 [26 September 1940], and then a Messerschmitt Bf.109 [27 September 1940].

He became an instructor with 53 Operational Training Unit at RAF Heston [spring 1941] and then commanded 130 Squadron [October 1943], followed by 222 Squadron [February 1944]. Left the RAF as a Squadron Leader [1946].

Isle of Purbeck Light Aeroplane Club — founded by Lieutenant Colonel Louis Strange DSO, MC, DFC and operating from Swanage Aerodrome [1926] which was located in Strange's home parish, between Worth Matravers and St Alban's Head. Flying Officer H.W.R. Banting was the club's chief instructor.

Air Vice-Marshal Sir Sefton Brancker [1877-1930], the Director of Civil Aviation at the Air Ministry, visited the club [23 August 1926]. He was picked up from Hendon in the club's Simmonds Spartan biplane and taken on to Dorchester for the formation meeting of Dorsetshire Aero Club.

Iwerne Minster crash — at The Beeches, beside the main road, of a Messerschmitt Bf.110 (S9+DU) after engine damage in a dog-fight [27 September 1940]. Belonging to Erprobungsgruppe 210, an experimental proving unit from Cherbourg, it had been attempting to take part in an abortive raid on the Parnall Aircraft Company at Yate, near Chipping Sodbury. Pilot Friedrich Ebner made a successful crash-landing but the gunner, Werner Zwick, was taken to Shaftesbury Hospital with major wounds.

LOCKHEED LIGHTNING: THE "FORKED TAILED DEVIL" AS THE LUFTWAFFE DUBBED THE FAST SINGLE-SEAT FIGHTER, OPERATIONAL ACROSS THE CHANNEL WITH THE UNITED STATES ARMY AIR FORCE FROM WARMWELL AERODROME IN 1944.

J

J serial numbers of RAF aircraft:

J7711 Vickers Virginia — see entry for Flight Refuelling Limited.

J9252 Westland Wizard — see entry for Westland Aircraft.

J9565 Westland COW-gun Fighter — see entry for Westland Aircraft.

J9833 Handley Page 51 — see entry for Flight Refuelling Limited.

James — hapless pilot **Lieutenant Vincent R. James** [1920-44] in a P-47 Thunderbolt of 509th Squadron of the 405th Fighter Bomber Group of the United States Army Air Force failed in his take-off from Christchurch Aerodrome and crashed in Foxwood Avenue, Mudford [06.45 hours, 29 June 1944].

Then at 14.00 hours the same day, in another P-47, he again went no further than Foxwood Avenue, this time destroying a bungalow and bringing down another Thunderbolt as his bombs exploded. A total of 16 were killed, including the unlucky pilot, and 18 injured.

Jay — South African **Pilot Officer Dudley Trevor Jay** [1921-40] of 87 Squadron from RAF Exeter claimed two Junkers Ju.87 "Stukas" and a Messerschmitt Bf.109 in combat over Portland [15 August 1940]. In the process he ran out of ammunition as his aircraft was being damaged by return fire. Hurricane R2687 was brought down in a forced-landing at Field Barn Farm beside Chafeys Lake at Radipole, after having narrowly cleared Weymouth's rooftops. The machine was wrecked but Jay was able to walk away.

He was less fortunate when flying over Devon in Hurricane P3404 which was in a mid-air collision with the tail of Flying Officer John Reynolds Cock's machine [24 October 1940]. The latter fighter and its Australian pilot made a successful forced-landing but Jay fell to his death, apparently after hitting the airframe and snagging his parachute, in attempting to bale out.

Remnants of his previous crash, at the rear of what had become No. 3 Chafeys Avenue, would be unearthed by Michael Shepherd when he moved into his new home [1961]. Jay enlisted in 1939 and had gone to France with 87 Squadron. He shot down a Heinkel He.111 on the day that Hitler invaded the Low Countries [10 May 1940]. He is buried at Heavitree in Exeter Higher Cemetery.

Jeff — Hurricane pilot **Flying Officer Robert Voase Jeff** [1913-40] was shot down and killed off Portland, in V7231 of 87 Squadron from RAF Exeter [11.00 hours, 11 August 1940]. Born in Kuala Lumpur, Malaya, of British parents from Tenby, Pembrokeshire, he had joined the RAF in 1936 and was sent to France on the outbreak of war.

He had the distinction of having destroyed the first enemy aircraft to fall on French soil, a Heinkel He.111 bomber [2 November 1939], for which he was awarded the Croix de Guerre and the Distinguished Flying Cross.

Jenkins — early aviator **Lieutenant-Colonel Leslie Jenkins**, from Swanage, served in the Royal Flying Corps and was killed in the Great War, shortly after the RFC was re-titled and became the Royal Air Force [1 April 1918].

Jersey Airlines — operated car-carrying Bristol Freighters, the bulbous Bristol 170 Wayfarer, from Bournemouth (Hurn) Airport [late 1950s]. Carried passengers in two de Havilland Herons, with one on the Jersey service and the other going to Guernsey.

RECORD JUMPER: FREE-FALL PARACHUTIST GWYNNE JOHNS, MAKING ONE OF HIS LESSER JUMPS, FROM A DE HAVILLAND DH 82 TIGER MOTH, OVER CHRISTCHURCH.

Jet Heritage Limited — refurbished historic aircraft, overhauling the avionics and repainting in authentic colours, in workshops at Bournemouth International Airport. Some of their commissions have local associations, such as Christchurch-made de Havilland Vampires T.55 G-BVLM and FB.6 G-BVPO that were given the camouflage of 2 Squadron, Royal Jordan Air Force, before being handed over to the newly formed Royal Jordanian Historic Flight [1955].

The FB.6 was a former target-tug in the Swiss Air Force. Its overhaul was carried out by Eric Hayward and his team. Its place in the workshops was taken by Hawker Hunter F.6A XG160 which had been handed over to the Jordanians at RAF Scampton.

Their classic restoration — Hurn-based and a frequent visitor to air shows — is Gloster Meteor NF.11, G-LOSM / WM167 which was delivered to the RAF [1952], though it never went into squadron service. Its extended nose, being 47 inches longer than the F.8 fighter, housed an Airborne Interception (A1) Mark 10 radar. This was fitted as standard in the NF.11 which became the RAF's first jet-powered night-fighter.

Johns — Bournemouth hardware salesman **Gwynne Johns** became Britain's record-breaking parachutist when he jumped from a plane 22,400 feet above Salisbury Plain and did not pull the ripcord until 90 seconds had elapsed [1937]. He made a post-war comeback by staging his 50th drop at the Southend-on-Sea air pageant [August 1947].

Johnson — aviatrix **Amy Johnson** [1903-1941] landed to a hero's welcome at Talbot Farm, Bournemouth [27 August 1930]. It was four months after she had become the first woman to fly solo from London to Australia, breaking en route the record for a flight between London and India, by touching down in Karachi in six days. Her arrival in Bournemouth, where she transferred to Sir William Morris's best car, was for the purpose of opening a fete in Meyrick Park.

Jones — Spitfire flyer **Pilot Officer John Sinclair Bucknall Jones** [1918-1940] of 152 Squadron from RAF Warmwell was shot down by Messerschmitt Bf.109s, several miles off Lulworth [11 August 1940]. He baled out of R6614 but drowned, being washed ashore in France, and is buried in Sainte Marie Cemetery, Le Havre.

Joubert — controller of the RAF's wartime radar and signals intelligence operations **Air Marshal Sir Philip Joubert** [died 1965] lived at Bucknowle House, Corfe Castle, and then in Canford Cliffs. Nominally the commanding officer of Combined Operations at Poole this was a cover for his main task. In effect he controlled the Telecommunications Research Establishment at Worth Matravers, through the scientific Battle of the Beams. The Luftwaffe unknowingly had its revenge with a bomb that fell on his house, though he was out at the time [March 1941]. He became Air Chief Marshal.

GROUND GESTURE: GWYNNE JOHNS (RIGHT) ABOUT TO GO UP, IN A PRE-WAR DE HAVILLAND GIPSY MOTH, TO JUMP FOR REAL, WITH JOHN POTHECARY (LEFT) BEING HIS PILOT FROM CHRISTCHURCH AERODROME.

PIVOTAL ROLE: AIR CHIEF MARSHAL SIR PHILIP JOUBERT DE LA FERTÉ OF CANFORD CLIFFS AND THE WARTIME TELECOMMUNICATIONS RESEARCH ESTABLISHMENT.

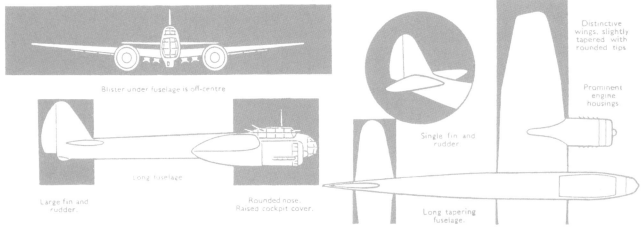

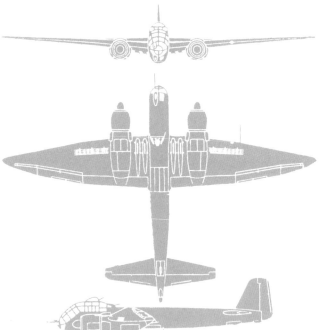

JUNKERS JU.88: FREQUENTLY SEEN OVER DORSET ON BOMBING AND RECONNAISSANCE MISSIONS, CROSSING THE COUNTY BETWEEN BASES ON THE CHERBOURG PENINSULA AND ENGLISH INLAND TARGETS.

STOPPED CLOCKS: ON SAMUELS JEWELLERS IN WINE STREET, BRISTOL (ABOVE) AND ANOTHER JEWELLER'S IN CASTLE STREET (RIGHT), WITH FIRES STILL SMOULDERING ON THE MORNING OF 25 NOVEMBER 1940.

K

K serial numbers of RAF aircraft:

    K2668 Vickers Virginia — see entry for Flight Refuelling Limited.

    K2891 Westland F.7/30 — see entry for Westland Aircraft.

    K3086 Hawker Audax — see entry for Warmwell crashes.

    K3480 Fairey Seal — see entries for Langton Herring and Warmwell crashes.

    K3585 Armstrong Whitworth 23 — see entry for Flight Refuelling Limited.

    K4396 Hawker Audax — see entry for Chesil Beach crashes.

    K5054 Spitfire prototype — see entry for Howard.

    K5544 Hawker Hind — see entry for Warmwell crashes.

    K5985 Swordfish — see entry for Corfe Castle crashes.

    K6057 Westland Wallace — see entry for Owermoigne crashes.

    K6063 Westland Wallace — see entry for Langton Herring crashes.

    K6127 Westland Lysander — see entry for Westland Aircraft.

    K6839 Hawker Hind — see entry for Warmwell crashes.

    K7056 Blenheim — see entry for Warmwell crashes.

    K7594 Fairey Battle — see entry for Chesil Beach crashes.

    K8173 Boulton-Paul Overstrand — see entry for Chesil Beach crashes.

    K8223 Hawker Fury — see entry for Chesil Beach crashes.

    K8271 Hawker Fury — see entry for Chesil Beach crashes.

    K9230 Fairey Battle — see entry for Bournemouth crashes.

    K9880 Spitfire — see entry for Swanage crashes.

    K9882 Spitfire — see entry for Swanage crashes.

    K9901 Spitfire — see entries for Deansly and Portland crashes.

    K9982 Spitfire — see entry for Deansly.

    K9999 Spitfire — see entry for Shepley.

Kadow — German airman **Oberleutnant Gerhard Kadow** became the first pilot to be taken prisoner in the Battle of Britain when he force-landed Messerschmitt Bf.110c (2N+EP) on Povington Heath, Tyneham [12.05 hours, 11 July 1940].

His gunner, Gefreiter Helmut Scholz, was also unhurt. They had flown from Laval to escort Junkers Ju.87 "Stuka" dive-bombers that were attacking Channel shipping off Portland. The Bf.110 belonged to III Gruppe, Zerstörergeschwader 76.

Kay — airborne chaplain **Rev. George Alexander Kay** was killed on D-Day while tending the wounded in Normandy [6 June 1944]. "His father served the church and parish during the war years," a plaque records in Shapwick parish church.

Kearsey — Spitfire flyer **Sergeant Pilot Albert Wallace "Bill" Kearsey** of 152 Squadron from RAF Warmwell claimed a Messerschmitt Bf.110 kill [30 September 1940]. He shared with Pilot Officer Eric "Boy" Marrs the destruction of a Junkers Ju.88 bomber which they found over the Blackmore Vale and put down on a cobbler's shed at Poole [14 November 1940]. Kearsey survived the war.

Kennedy — Australian volunteer **Flight Lieutenant John Connelly Kennedy** [1917-40], flying a Hurricane P2950 of 238 Squadron from Middle Wallop, Hampshire, crashed to his death at South Down, above Chalbury Lodge, Preston, near Weymouth, after a dog-fight [13 July 1940]. He is buried in the RAF plot at RAF Warmwell.

Keymer — Bournemouth car salesman **Sergeant Pilot Michael Keymer** [1916-40], the son of Eastleigh's vicar, joined 65 Squadron at RAF Hornchurch [7 August 1940]. He shared in the destruction of a Messerschmitt Bf.109 a week later but was then shot down, in Spitfire K9909, over the Straits of Dover [22 August 1940]. He is buried on the other side of the Channel, in the churchyard at Bazinghen, France.

KH — squadron code of 403 (RCAF) Squadron, briefly flying Mark LVI Spitfires from RAF Warmwell [4-14 January 1945].

Kimmeridge crashes — Messerschmitt Bf.110 (L1 + FZ) crashed in flames at Swalland Farm, a mile south-east of the village on the Luftwaffe's routed Adlertag (Eagle Day) attack [13 August 1940]. It belonged to Lehrgeschwader 1, a specialist unit formed to test new aircraft of all types, and innovative tactics, under operational conditions.

Another Bf. 110 (3U + DS), belonging to Zerstörergeschwader 26, the Geschwader named Horst Wessel for the Nazi subject of a militant anti-Semitic song which became a national anthem, crash-landed near Gaulter Gap [27 September 1940]. It had three "kill" bars, denoting victories over RAF aircraft. Crewmen Fritz Schupp and Karl Nechwatal were taken prisoner. Their fighter-bomber, which had been taking part in an abortive raid on the Parnall Aircraft Company at Yate, near Chipping Sodbury, was claimed by Spitfires from RAF Warmwell.

Three out of ten North American P-51 Mustang Mark XV fighter-bombers of 2 Squadron Royal Air Force, based at RAF Sawbridge, Hertfordshire, flew into Smedmore Hill when a mission went wrong in poor visibility [26 May 1943]. They had taken off from Thruxton, Hampshire, at 16.50 hours on Ranger Operation Asphalt. This cross-Channel offensive action was to have been against rail movements in the Rennes-Laval area.

They flew south-west in line abreast formation until reaching a wall of fog between Kimmeridge and St Alban's Head. The order to climb was given by Flight-Lieutenant G. Kenning at 17.35 hours.

Seven of the aircraft were able to clear Smedmore Hill but the other three-code letters U, Y and W — crashed into the northern slope. Their three pilots were killed — Flying Officer N.J. Miller, Pilot Officer J. B. McLeod, and Flying Officer D. Hirst.

Kingston Russell crash — into Brickhills Field, near Kingston Russell House, of a Messerschmitt Bf.110C (3U+JP) belonging to the 6th Staffel of Zerstörergeschwader 26 [16.00 hours, 7 October 1940]. It had been defending bombers en route to the Westland Aircraft Company works at Yeovil. Crewmen Obergefreiter Herbert Schilling and Oberfeldwebel Karl Herzog were killed on impact.

Human remains were removed, together with propeller blades, wreckage and identification papers, during an excavation carried out by Andy Saunders [1976]. The flyers' grave is in the German war cemetery at Cannock Chase.

Kirkpatrick — early aviator **Lieutenant Yvone Kirkpatrick** [1899-1975] of Oaklands, Rowlands Hill, Wimborne, joined the Royal Flying Corps [May 1917]. He graduated to a Sopwith Camel on being posted to the Western Front, to join 203 Squadron at Izel le Hameau, near Arras [May 1918]. He had numerous close encounters and at least one crash landing but his worst couple of hours were in the last Allied air offensive [noon, 26 September 1918] when the squadron lost five aircraft on an attack on an aerodrome miles inside German lines. He dropped his bombs, used all his ammunition, and then ran into problems. "Archie", incidentally, means anti-aircraft fire: "I decided to come home. The Archie was awful, along with machine-gun fire on the ground. I was trying to climb up to some of our machines which were going west, when suddenly there was a bang and my engine stopped."

It restarted from his gravity petrol tank, but he was still in trouble. "My engine wasn't going very well and the wind was against me. You should have seen the expression on people's faces. I went over a sunken road and saw two fat old Huns walking calmly along with their hands in their pockets; they simply stared at me with their mouths open. Then I saw two Fokkers up above diving at me. I simply tore round trees and churches with them firing at me."

On landing after the machine gun fire had stopped, among Scottish troops, he found he "had a bullet through my tank, the petrol was pouring out". Things continued to be "rather too exciting now" as the British divisions pushed on through the Hindenburg Line during the following week.

Post-war he took up teaching and spent 33 years at Canford School, between Wimborne and Poole.

Klein — Polish flyer **Sergeant Pilot Zygmunt Klein** [1918-40] of 152 Squadron from RAF Warmwell damaged a Messerschmitt Bf.110 in a dog-fight [7 October 1940]. He ran out of petrol and successfully force-landed on the Devon coast [26 November 1940]. Then he "just disappeared" in Spitfire P9427 over Poole Bay, during a fierce series of engagements with Messerschmitt Bf.109 fighters [28 November 1940]. His body was not recovered.

Knighton Heath Wood — a line of six V-shaped earth-banked dispersal pads for Spitfires survive under the trees at the eastern end of Knighton Heath Wood, on the edge of wartime RAF Warmwell (Ordnance Survey map reference SY 750 887). They merit scheduling as ancient monuments.

The other mound, just south of them and also under trees, is the Bronze Age Huck Barrow. Look out for Battle of Britain period graffiti, such as "152 SQN", on the trunks of beech trees.

Hidden below them are a number of slit-trench air-raid shelters, and more substantial footings and walls of dispersal buildings. The window-less brick-built shelters, above ground on the northern edge of the wood, contain fixtures for bunks and hammocks.

This was very much the nerve centre of the station — on its western side — with the trees being the one element of natural cover and camouflage that nature had provided. Most of the trees were preserved during the course of earthmoving, some of them actually being set in the banks, in order to maximise their contribution to concealment.

During the war this wood extended northwards, with more dispersal pads and air-raid shelters, to the Dorchester-Moreton railway line. This part of the wood has since been lost to an arm of the vast sand and gravel pits.

KS — code letters of the Station Flight at RAF Tarrant Rushton.

KU — pundit code for RAF Hurn, on ten feet high white letters at the airfield and flashed at night in red light Morse code, from a Pundit mobile beacon some miles from the station.

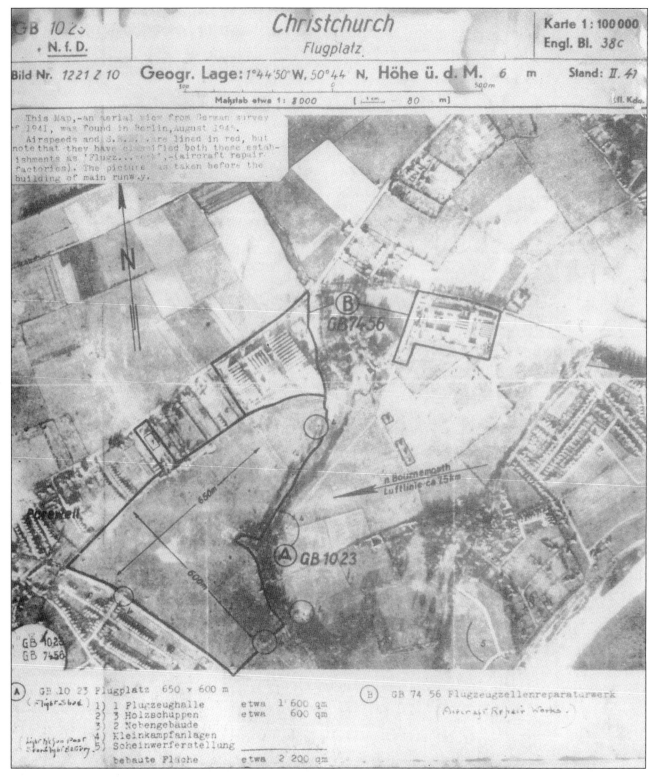

Luftwaffe photograph: air reconnaissance coverage of Dorset in the Second World War was not matched by intelligence on the ground, as this shot from 1941 shows. It is of Christchurch Aerodrome, before the building of the main runway, with the outlined areas to the north being the factories of Airspeed Limited and the Air Defence Research and Development Establishment. Their identification as "Flugzeugzellenreparaturwerk" (Aircraft repair works) underestimates their importance as plane-making and military research establishments. Five "Kleinkampfanlagen" (Light machine-guns posts) are ringed and figure 5 (to the south-east) is a "Scheinwerferstellung" (Searchlight position). The arrowed "Luftlinie" (Flight-line) points towards Bournemouth.

L

L serial numbers of RAF aircraft:

L1008 Spitfire — see entry for Hughes-Rees.

L1069 Spitfire — see entry for Portland crashes.

L1072 Spitfire — see entries for Portland crashes and Reddington.

L1079 Spitfire — see entry for Barran.

L1095 Spitfire — see entry for Portland crashes.

L1552 Hurricane — see entry for Christchurch Aerodrome.

L1562 Hurricane — see entry for Christchurch Aerodrome.

L1592 Hurricane — preserved fighter from the Special Duty Flight at Christchurch; see entries for Christchurch Aerodrome and Hurricane L1592.

L1702 Spitfire — see entry for Shaftesbury crashes.

L1764 Hurricane — see entries for Abbotsbury and Considine.

L2057 Hurricane — see entry for Portland crashes.

L6844 Westland Whirlwind — see entry for Westland Aircraft.

L6870 Westland Lysander — see entry for Stalbridge crash.

L6982 Boulton-Paul Defiant — see entry for Warmwell crashes.

L9405 Blenheim — see entry for Chesil Beach crashes.

Lamb — naval airman **Lieutenant-Commander Peter Melville "Sheepy" Lamb** [1923-2000] had close calls in the sky over Dorset at both ends of his flying career. Initially, as Sub-Lieutenant Lamb,

EXPERIMENTAL AIRCRAFT: THE SAUNDERS-ROE SR-53, WHICH PETER LAMB TOOK TO 56,900 FEET OVER LYME BAY IN 1959, USING ROCKET BOOST.

he crashed into a bungalow, Musoka in Caroline Avenue at Stanpit, while attempting to deliver Seafire NB315 from RNAS Donibristle, on the Firth of Forth, to Christchurch Aerodrome [25 June 1943]. "Not my best landing — engine tired of living," he recorded in his logbook. "Fortunately, I didn't join it."

After recovering from head injuries he was assigned to 800 Royal Naval Air Squadron, flying Seafires in support of assault landings at Salerno and in southern France, followed by service in Burma. After the war, as Chief Test Pilot for Saunders-Roe, he made the 45th, and last, flight with the Saunders-Roe SR-53 mixed power, jet and rocket experimental aircraft [20 October 1959]. The mission was to fly at its maximum height over the sea off Dorset, in the controlled military airspace of Lyme Bay, where he made a near vertical climb. This was powered by the Spectre rocket engine, augmenting the Viper jet engine, with the latter to continue upwards after the rocket propellants had been expended.

MOP HEADED: PETER LAMB IN WARTIME, WITH REGROWN HAIR CONCEALING SCALP WOUNDS FROM HIS CHRISTCHURCH CRASH.

As the speed began to decline, Lamb started to push the nose down for the intended peak of the flight, but then the Viper flamed out and the powerless aircraft peaked at an altitude of 56,900 feet. With plenty of height to spare, Peter Lamb made a 180 degree turn, to head north-eastwards towards land. An unsuccessful attempt was made to light up the Viper at 30,000 feet and another failed attempt took place at 25,000 feet. Lamb at last restarted it at 18,000 feet and crossed Dorset to make a safe landing at Boscombe Down, near Salisbury. It had been a 40 minute flight which established a British record but failed to come anywhere near the existing world height record held by Major V. Ilyushin of the Soviet Union who had reached 94,694 feet [14 July 1959].

Langar — Luftwaffe ace **Hauptmann Langar**, the officer commanding the elite pathfinder Kampfgruppe 100, was killed when his Heinkel He.111 plunged into a hillside near Shaftesbury in low cloud [23 May 1942]. He was trying to evade Squadron Leader John "Cat's Eyes" Cunningham, in a Beaufighter of 604 Squadron from RAF Middle Wallop, in an interception directed by Sopley radar station.

Langton Herring crashes — of Westland Wallace K6063, belonging to 6 Air Training Corps, whilst dropping a drogue over the Chesil Beach Bombing Range [10 March 1939].

A similar drogue-dropping mishap caused the loss of Fairey Seal K3480 from 10 Bombing and Gunnery School at RAF Warmwell [22 April 1940].

Other losses on the range, not identified with a specific parish, are listed under the entry for Chesil Beach crashes.

Langton Matravers crashes — Sptifire R6811 of 152 Squadron from RAF Warmwell successfully crash-landed at Spyway Farm after a Battle of Britain dog-fight [8 August 1940]. It was flown by Pilot Officer Walter Beaumont.

There was drama of a different kind when what should have been an epic endurance flight from Creech Barrow Hill ended with Balloon *Gerard Heineken* bringing down power cables at Coles Farm, Langton Matravers [25 July 1975].

Larichelière — Canadian flyer **Pilot Officer Joseph Emile Paul Larichelière** [1913-40] was shot down and killed off Portland, while in combat with the Hurricanes of 213 Squadron from RAF Exeter [16 August 1940]. He was from Montreal.

le Mesurier — Weymouth College swimmer, runner and rider **Wing Commander Eric Clive le Mesurier** [1915-43], a member of the Alderney family that settled in the town, was one of the pre-war intake into the Royal Air Force. He joined on a short service commission in the Ground Defence Department [1936] and became a Flying Officer [1938].

With the outbreak of war he went to France with the British Expeditionary Force [September 1939]. Mentioned in despatches, he would be awarded the Distinguished Flying Cross and Distinguished Service Order [1941]. He was killed while on active service [23 December 1943].

The family home was The Bungalow in Melcombe Avenue, Weymouth, and he is buried in Radipole churchyard.

Leven — Bryanston old boy **Squadron Leader Richard Leven DFC, DFM** [1921-97] flew and survived a total of 127 bombing missions over enemy territory between the spring of 1941 and early 1945. Fellow Dorset public schoolboy W. H. Auden had a lasting influence on Leven's passion for poetry. Young Leven at that time held Peace Pledge Union sympathies and joined Bryanston's cultural exchange with the school in Salem, Germany, run by Gordonstoun founder Kurt Hahn.

He changed his views about the Nazis in 1939 and joined the Royal Air Force Volunteer Reserve after the outbreak of the war. His father had been an observer in the Royal Flying Corps in the previous war; which left him with lasting injuries from a crash in his Bristol Fighter.

Richard Leven teamed-up with Mike Nolan, from the Irish Republic, who became his navigator for more than a hundred missions. Their targets, generally with a Blenheim, included Boulogne docks, Bremen port, Sylt Island, Sicilian airfields, and Mediterranean shipping.

On returning to Britain, Leven progressed to a Mosquito wing and attacked V1 and V2 rocket sites. London was also within range and his first visit to the Reform Club led to a friendship with spy and defector Guy Burgess and acquaintance with Anthony Blunt.

Post-war he became a film actor, theatre director and circus manager. He lived in a flat at Swiss Cottage.

Lindbergh Road — street close to Castle Lane in the suburb of Moordown, Bournemouth, named for pioneer aviator Colonel Charles Augustus Lindbergh whose *Spirit of St Louis* made the first non-stop crossing of the Atlantic [20-21 May 1927]. Renamed Franklin Road by Bournemouth town coucillors, after Lindbergh expressed pro-Nazi sentiments [January 1943]. Its new name was that of the Anglophile wartime American president, Franklin Delano Roosevelt.

Lindsay Hall — in Lindsay Road, Bournemouth, was the home of the seventh Baron Ventry [1898-1987], Britain's leading post-war expert on airships.

Demolished and rebuilt as quality flats [1992], called Ventry Court.

Littlebredy Relief Landing Ground — established courtesy Lady Williams of Bridehead [1972] on the high chalk plateau south of the village (Ordnance Survey map reference SY 587 871). Receiving up to four Portland helicopters at a time it specialised in handling and hovering.

LODERS CRASH: PILOT JOHN OWNER (LEFT) BESIDE THE GONDOLA OF AN ADMIRALTY AIRSHIP THAT HAD BEEN HEADING FOR POWERSTOCK NAVAL AIR STATION IN THE SUMMER OF 1917.

Loders crash — of a new Zero Airship, on an anti-submarine patrol from Mullion, Cornwall, which was heading inland towards the Admiralty Airship station at Powerstock [summer 1917]. It came too low after passing over Bridport and clipped treetops, coming down on a grassy slope above the branch railway line. Bombs were safely jettisoned and the pilot, John Owner, and his crew suffered only minor bruising.

Lovell-Gregg — heroic New Zealand Hurricane pilot **Squadron Leader Terence Lovell-Gregg** of 87 Squadron, from RAF Exeter, was killed at Abbotsbury during the height of the Battle of Britain [15 August 1940]. Roland Beamont, one of his pilots, returned with the story of how 27-year-old "Shovel" led his men into a mass of German aircraft at 18,000 feet over the sea off Portland. Ignoring adverse odds of fifteen-to-one, he told his men over the radio: "Come on chaps, let's surround them!"

He set about doing the impossible, leading the five of 87 Squadron's Hurricanes which were its only air-worthy machines: "Lovell-Gregg flew straight at the centre of the formation without hesitation or deviation in any way." Shot and burning, he attempted to glide to a crash-landing in The Fleet lagoon, but clipped an oak in the wood beside Abbotsbury Swannery and fell to his death. He is buried in the RAF plot at Warmwell churchyard.

LS — code letters of 297 (Army Co-Operation) Squadron, flying Whitleys from RAF Hurn [1942].

Lulworth crashes — Hurricane P3585 of 213 Squadron from RAF Exeter crash-landed on the "C" Range, Lulworth Camp, after engaging the Luftwaffe [11 August 1940]. Sergeant Pilot Ernest Snowden was unhurt and his fighter repairable.

Jubilant anti-aircraft gunners at Lulworth Camp brought down a Messerschmitt Bf.110 fighter-bomber during a major Battle of Britain attack [27 September 1940]. The stricken aircraft crashed to the ground about a thousand yards from the sea. It had been seen taking part in the abortive raid on the Parnall Aircraft Company at Yate, near Chipping Sodbury.

Another Bf.110, apparently belonging to Zerstörergeschwader 26 and involved in the attack on the Westland Aircraft factory at Yeovil, crashed into the sea 2,000 yards off Arish Mell Gap [7 October

1940]. It was claimed by Spitfires of 609 Squadron from RAF Warmwell.

Spitfire R6639 of 53 Operational Training Unit crashed at West Lulworth whilst attempting a forced-landing [10 September 1941].

There was a huge explosion as a Focke Wulf 190 came in low from over the sea, apparently misjudging its position, and flew straight into the side of Bindon Hill [21 October 1941].

An advanced radar drama ended off the Purbeck coast in May 1969, though what happened is still largely supposition, for papers released in the United States through the Freedom of Information Act are heavily censored. The case concerns a dramatic instance of the occasional tradition throughout the American Forces for suicidal misappropriation of military hardware.

An Assistant Crew Chief, Sergeant Paul Adams Meyer of the 36th Tactical Air Service, United States Air Force, had stolen a 30-ton Lockheed C130E Hercules transporter — one of the last generation of heavy military turbo-props, carrying advanced electronics — from RAF Mildenhall airbase in East Anglia. It belonged to the 513th Tactical Air Wing of the 3rd Air Force, USAFE (United States Air Force, Europe).

Psychologically, Paul Meyer had a problem, it soon emerges from the "USAF Accident/Incident Report." Privacy considerations prevent us knowing the detail, but it seems he married eight weeks earlier in Poquoson, Virgina, before being sent from Langley Air Force Base to Britain. He had been passed over for promotion but there was also a personal difficulty, concerning which he "verbally requested to be returned to Langley AFB to aid his wife in settling the problem".

On Thursday 22 May, Sergeant Meyer "performed his normal duties as assistant crew chief on C-130, SN [Serial Number] 37789, by accompanying the aircraft on a one day flight to Germany. Upon return to RAF Mildenhall he was invited by Sgt. Carpenter to a house party in a nearby town. Sgt. Carpenter loaned Sgt. Meyer a pair of civilian trousers and Sgt. Meyer changed out of his flight clothes at Sgt. Carpenter's barracks. The two sergeants, in company with five other companions proceeded to the party in

HERCULES C-130E: SIMILAR TO THAT OF THE UNITED STATES AIR FORCE WHICH CRASHED OFF LULWORTH IN 1969.

taxicabs at 19.00 CET [Central European Time; following sentence CENSORED]. However, during the later hours he was [word CENSORED] drinking rather heavily, and behaving erratically. He left the house on three or four occasions, going into the yard and generally causing a disturbance." His friends tried to console him but he was last seen "crossing a rooftop and the next they heard he had been arrested by civilian police "and charged with being drunk and disorderly". His mood was changeable: "At times he was co-operative and then would suddenly become sarcastic and belligerent".

The police released him into military custody, during which he attempted to escape through a latrine window, and was eventually returned to his billet after being told he "was restricted to barracks and was grounded".

He "appeared to be preparing for bed" but instead slipped out and stole the vehicle keys of Captain Upton, the 36th Tactical Air Service Materiel Officer. Using the assumed name "Captain Epstein" he requested fuel for Hercules 37789, on hardstand 21: "The POL dispatcher thought it unusual that a captain was requesting fuel, however, it had happened to him before so he hono[u]red the request." Suspicions were not otherwise aroused, despite his physical presence, "as Sgt. Meyer had frequently been on the flight line between 02.00-06.00 using the aircraft high frequency radios to talk to his wife by phone patch through the Tactical Air Command Post at Langley Air Force Base. Also, he had on many occasions shown up two to three hours early on days that his aircraft was scheduled to fly. Since the schedule was not until 10.30 Central European Time. Sgt. Johnson saw no reason to contact Operations, at that early hour, concerning a possible mission change. [Next words CENSORED] missions are frequently changed at the last minute. [Following sentence and the entirety of the next three paragraphs CENSORED.]

"Upon completion of the fuelling operation, aircraft 37789 contained approximately 60,000 pounds of fuel. [Remainder of paragraph CENSORED, as are crucial parts of the preparation for take-off.]

"Staff Sergeant Alexander stopped at Maintenance Control and was informed [by; named CENSORED] that Sgt. Meyer was at his aircraft. SSgt. Alexander decided to check on Sgt. Meyer after delivering the other two crew chiefs to their aircraft. [Sentence CENSORED.]

"As he approached the front of 37789 one of the crew chiefs in the truck noticed that chocks had been removed. Staff Sergeant Alexander stopped his vehicle in front of the aircraft and saw Sgt. Meyer in the pilot's seat. Sgt. Meyer motioned violently for SSgt. Alexander to get out of the way, flashed his taxi lights several times, and moved the throttles into the flight range, near maximum power. Upon observing these actions, considering the safety of the vehicle occupants and not realising the intent for flight, SSgt. Alexander immediately moved his vehicle away from the front of the aircraft. Sgt. Meyer released the brakes and taxied from the hardstand."

He took a minute and a half to proceed "from the beginning of taxi" at 05.06 European Standard Time, through to "beginning to takeoff roll". People were now in panic around the edge of the base, with Staff Sergeant Johnson telling the Law Enforcement Desk Sergeant: "We have a crew chief taxiing an airplane. Stop him."

They almost did, with two patrol vehicles: "The amazingly fast reaction of the Security Police patrols was voided due to the lack of an established and practised procedure on just how to stop an aircraft. Also, confirmation that they had the right aircraft was not received in time nor could the one patrol get permission to use his weapon.

"Sgt. Meyer continued his takeoff roll and made [few words CENSORED] a short field takeoff at 05.08.10 Central European Time. He left the ground in an extreme wing low altitude and began an immediate left turn.

Radar units at both Mildenhall and Lakenheath "tracked the erratic flight path" until the aircraft was about 50 miles south. Meyer flew the plane single-handed into the busiest air lanes in the world, and then vanished, according to contemporary reports. The American investigation found that "contact was not established again until 20 minutes later," by Southern Radar at Sopley.

Defence and ground-control radar systems, at the height of the Cold War, had failed to follow the movements of one of the largest and slowest military aircraft. The *Daily Express* reported that the Hercules "made a hole in Britain's delicate radar system" — for the technically bizarre reason that "the plane was going out, not coming in". Three weeks later there was a statement in Parliament that the plane had been "continuously tracked by British radar".

The fact is that Paul Meyer flew over the River Thames and across Kent on automatic pilot with Mildenhall's control centre only able to register his position when Meyer spoke on his radio. He was using his tried and tested technique to get through to his wife in Virginia. Some claimed that Hercules 37789 was invisible to radar as it carried the latest package of electronics for absorbing radar waves and preventing them from being reflected back to the ground.

By turning right, westwards down the entire length of the English Channel, he minimised the chance of ploughing into a built-up area and also lessened the chances of mid-air collision. As he flew off the Lizard he hooked up to his wife via the radio network, using his tried and tested technique. She, in a desperate early morning call, tried to talk him into flying the plane back to a British airfield. Meyer's conversation "was not monitored or recorded" but he obviously intended flying home across the Atlantic, having requisitioned enough fuel for a full range in excess of 5,000 miles. He seems to have been talked out of it.

Meyer carried out a U-turn over the Scilly Isles and crossed Cornwall and south of Devon to Lyme Bay. An F-100 was scrambled from RAF Lakenheath, and a C-130 from Mildenhall, in an effort to assist Sergeant Meyer by escorting him back to base. Neither established either visual or radio contact. There was anxiety on the ground about the risk of disaster that would inevitably accompany an attempted landing. While an officer who knows the equipment can fly a Hercules without that much difficulty, it is another matter to put the thing back on the ground. The accident investigation does not mention any direct radio contact between Meyer and Mildenhall. Had it been achieved, and smooth-talking developed into a rapport, the runaway Assistant Crew Chief would have been asked to locate various knobs and panels, as a dry-run of landing techniques. One unconfirmed account of such contact having been established claims that in the process he may have touched a red lever for the purpose of which he was unaware. This report claims it was the "destructor"; though his superiors would hardly have called it that over the radio if they had eventually succeeded in making contact. Anyway, the story of the runaway Hercules ended about 40 miles south of Lulworth Cove, at 06.55 Central European Time on Friday 23 May 1969. Paul Meyer and his plane blew up at co-ordinates 50.00 N (latitude), 02.05 W (longitude).

Western security could relax. There was even a convenient explanation for those at Mildenhall — to suggest Meyer had simply tried to ditch in the sea. Said a spokesman: "It takes a highly trained and skilled pilot to land on the sea. There's a strong possibility the plane broke up." Wreckage was found over the next few days: "Sgt. Meyer is still missing and presumed dead of injuries sustained when the aircraft impacted the water."

Lutz — Luftwaffe veteran **Hauptmann Martin Lutz** [1913-40] led the abortive raid on the Parnall Aircraft Company at Yate, near Chipping Sodbury, crashed to his death at Bussey Stool Farm, near Tarrant Gunville [27 September 1940]. The Bf.110 fighter-bomber had been crippled over Bristol. He had served in the Condor Legion in the Spanish Civil War.

Lyme Bay Bombing Range — six miles off Lyme Regis, covering 16 square miles of sea, designated by the Air Ministry for daylight use [August 1939]. An initial limit of 120-lb was imposed on live bombs that could be dropped.

Lyme Bay crashes — numerous Battle of Britain losses from both sides, principally of the Luftwaffe but also defending Hurricanes from RAF Exeter and Spitfires of RAF Warmwell, fell into the sea off the Chesil Beach and Lyme Regis. For the remainder of the war an RAF Air-Sea Rescue launch operated from Lyme Regis. Some days they fell in twos, such as Hurricanes P3766 of 238 Squadron and P3082 of 501 Squadron shot down in the same dog-fight [20 July 1940].

An RAF Canberra bomber crashed into the sea at Lyme Bay during target-towing trials. Two of the crew were killed and one saved [1 May 1970].

Lytchett Matravers crash — Hawker Hind K5382 of the Royal Air Force College crashed near the village, during a low-flying flight that was foiled by pylon cables [26 April 1940].

Lytchett Minster crash — of an American B-17 Flying Fortress, returning from a cross-Channel mission, at Tatchell's Holding on Charity Farm, opposite the Baker's Arms [2 April 1942]. It was a successful emergency landing, followed by the arrival of heavy earth-moving machinery to make a temporary runway, which enabled the bomber to take off, after repairs and refuelling.

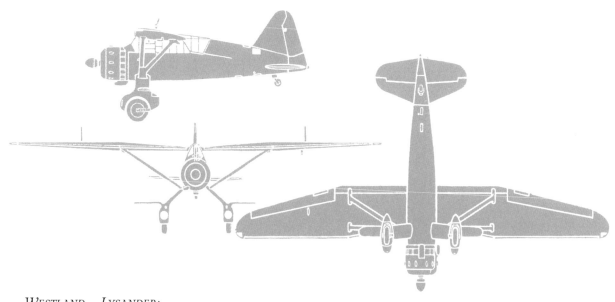

WESTLAND LYSANDER: MADE IN YEOVIL AND OPERATING FROM DORSET ON CLANDESTINE MISSIONS BEHIND ENEMY LINES.

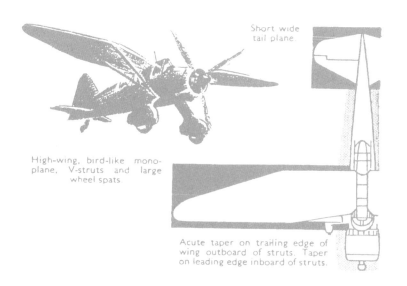

Short wide tail plane

High-wing, bird-like monoplane, V-struts and large wheel spats

Acute taper on trailing edge of wing outboard of struts. Taper on leading edge inboard of struts.

M

Machold — Luftwaffe ace **Oberleutnant Werner Machold**, Staffelkapitan of the 7th Gruppe of Jagdeschwader 2 Richthofen, who had been credited with the fighter wing's hundredth victory over France and was personally congratulated by Field Marshall Hermann Göring, crash-landed at Worth Matravers [6 June 1941]. He was taken prisoner of war.

Maia — British Overseas Airways Corporation Short "Empire" flying-boat (G-ADHK) , converted to a C-class flying-boat [1940] and based at Poole. She had previously been a pioneering composite aircraft as the mother craft, with a cradle above her wings, for the *Mercury* mail-carrying floatplane. *Maia* was destroyed in Poole Harbour by a Heinkel He.111 bomber G1+ES belonging to the 8th Staffel of the 3rd Gruppe, Kampfgeschwader 55, which would be brought down in the attack, off Arne, by anti-aircraft fire [12 May 1941].

Malcolm — air-girl **Miss Betty Malcolm** [1913-36], of Glenmorag, Haig Avenue, Canford Cliffs, Poole, was burnt to death when her aeroplane crashed into a hangar at Alicante, Spain [January 1936]. She was preparing for an attempt on the solo record for the flight between England and Australia.

"I was afraid that Betty would kill herself, but she would not listen," her mother, Edith Malcolm, told the *Daily Mail*. "She pointed to the splendid flights she had made all over Europe since she learned to fly about three years ago, and said she was determined to become famous. Betty would

PIONEERING COMPOSITE: G-ADHK "EMPIRE" FLYING BOAT MAIA *GIVING A PIGGY-BACK RIDE TO THE* MERCURY *MAIL-CARRYING FLOATPLANE — THE FORMER WOULD BE SUNK BY THE LUFTWAFFE IN* POOLE HARBOUR, *IN 1941.*

rush off at a moment's notice without telling anybody where she was going and, with only a few things flung hastily into a suitcase, disappear in her plane across the Channel for weeks on end."

Her father was Brigadier-General Henry Huntly Leith Malcolm [1860-1938].

Manston crash — of Whitley bomber T4299 of 51 Squadron, from RAF Dishforth, Yorkshire, outward bound to attack German battle-cruisers at Brest, brought down at Connegar Farm [3 April 1941]. Sergeant W.N. Brindley was killed but the other four members of the crew baled out successfully. The interception was found to be a case of friendly fire, resulting from misidentification of the twin-engined bomber, and traced to a Hurricane night-fighter, V6960, of 87 Squadron from RAF Exeter.

Mantle — fatally wounded pom-pom gunner **Jack Mantle VC** [1917-40] continued firing as "Stuka" dive-bombers sank anti-aircraft auxiliary HMS *Foylebank* in Portland Harbour. His legs had been shattered as bombs tore the ship apart. Of her 179 crew, 59 were killed, and 60 injured in the attack [4 July 1940]. Leading Seaman Mantle from Southampton had gone to school at Affpuddle. He is buried in Portland Naval Cemetery, on the Verne Common hillside overlooking the dockyard and harbour and would be gazetted for the Victoria Cross — the first of the Battle of Britain and the first to be won for the Royal Navy inside British territorial waters.

Marrs — youthful hero **Pilot Officer Eric Simcox "Boy" Marrs** [1921-41], flying a Spitfire which he named "Old Faithful", with 152 Squadron from RAF Warmwell had his first "kill" disallowed [16 August 1940]. He had his machine covered with oil from it, in a dog-fight over the Isle of Wight, and insisted on claiming the Heinkel He.111: "I don't think it could have got home and I'm pretty sure it didn't. I am counting that as my first."

He put a Junkers Ju.87 "Stuka" of Stukageschwader 77 into the sea off Sussex two days later, in a kill that was confirmed [18 August 1940]. Later that afternoon he went "Tally-ho" again in his second scramble of the day, this time off Portland, and thought he had accounted for a Dornier Do.17, but it managed to limp back to France.

Leading Blue Section, Marrs claimed a third share in the kill of a Junkers Ju.88 that was shot down at Ladywell Barn, Imber, Wiltshire, only three miles from his old school, Dauntsey's [17 September 1940]. Return fire from the stricken bomber smashed his Spitfire's air-cooler and forced him to crash-land at Yatesbury, on the concrete runways of a disused RAF training aerodrome.

Marrs was then parted from "Old Faithful" — in which he had flown 130 hours — though it would also survive to fly again, after restoration and now with a training unit.

Not that this would cramp his style. His next kill was his most flamboyant. Finding a lone Junkers Ju.88 at 23,000 feet above Somerset, he chased it across Exmoor and brought it down to within 50 feet of the hilltops, with ethylene glycol streaming from both engines [27 September 1940]. The stricken bomber reached the Bristol Channel and landed on the beach at Porlock: "I circled round and watched the crew get out. They waved to me and I waved back, and then hordes of civilians came rushing up. I watched the crew taken prisoner, beat up the beach, and then climbed away."

Three days later Marrs had to turn back to Warmwell Aerodrome for his own forced-landing, after German aircraft crippled his Spitfire [30 September 1940]: "I hopped out and went to the MO to get a lot of metal splinters picked out of my leg and wrist. I felt jolly glad to be down on the ground without having caught fire."

He would lead Blue Section at 20,000 feet over the eastern Frome valley on the day that the Luftwaffe did succeed in reaching the Westland Aircraft factory at Yeovil, killing a hundred civilian workers in a direct hit on an air-raid shelter [7 October 1940]. Marrs picked off the last Messerschmitt Bf.110 fighter-bomber of Zerstörergeschwader 26 in an exposed line. It went into the sea and the crew drifted down on to land: "Their parachutes streamed and opened and they began

HUGE CROWD: SURROUNDING WILLIAM McARDLE'S MONOPLANE AFTER HE LANDED IN A FIELD NEAR FORDINGBRIDGE, ON 19 JULY 1910.

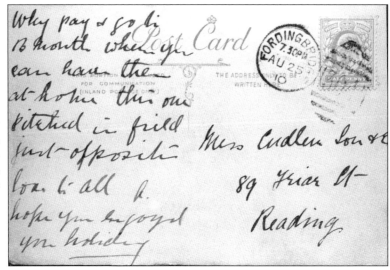

POSTCARD MESSAGE: FROM FORDINGBRIDGE — "WHY PAY TO GO TO BOURNEMOUTH WHEN YOU CAN HAVE THEM AT HOME? THIS ONE PITCHED IN FIELD JUST OPPOSITE."

drifting slowly earthwards. Their aeroplane, left to itself, dived vertically into the sea, making a most wonderful sight and an enormous splash. Everything seemed to have cleared off, so I circled round the two Huns. They took an awful long time to come down on land and I watched the army rush up and capture them."

The rear gunner of a Junkers Ju.88 "landed one plumb in the middle of my windscreen, splintering it in all directions and making it quite opaque" after which he could only be an observer of a combat that continued from the Blackmore Vale to Poole where a colleague, Sergeant Pilot Bill Kearsey, finished it off [14 November 1940].

Marrs avenged the death of a comrade, Pilot Officer A.R. Watson, by creeping up behind the culprit Messerschmitt Bf.109, in its blind spot, to send it flaming into the sea in "the easiest victory I've had" [28 November 1940].

The next was much the same. The target was a single German aircraft that was reportedly entering the Middle Wallop sector [4 January 1941]. Marrs found the Dornier Do.17 above Ringstead Bay and came at it from the sea as it "turned south and dived like stink for the clouds". That was too late as Spitfire R6968 raked it with fire from 400 yards, closing to 250 yards, silencing return fire and setting the engines on fire. It was seen to splash into the sea five miles south-east of Portland Bill. No one survived.

Marrs had an amazingly lucky escape when a bomb crashed through his room at RAF Warmwell [1 April 1941]. He was not there at the time because he was having the Distinguished Flying Cross pinned on his uniform in Buckingham Palace by King George VI.

Celebrated his twentieth birthday [9 July 1941]. Flew to Brest in one of the first long-range offensive missions to be undertaken by the station, which provided fighter escort for 18 Hampden bombers of 44 Squadron and 114 Squadron, in a daylight raid on German capital ships [24 July 1941]. Marrs was killed by German flak, bringing true a Warmwell prophecy that no German fighter pilot was going to take the "Boy".

His body was recovered and is in the military cemetery at Brest.

Marston — Hurricane flyer **Pilot Officer Kenneth John Marston** [1918-40], in P2866 of 56 Squadron from RAF Boscombe Down, force-landed at Longcutts Farm, East Knighton, near Winfrith Newburgh, after combat over Bournemouth [11.30 hours, 30 September 1940].

He stepped clear of the crashed fighter, with shrapnel wounds and minor cuts, but would be killed at the end of the year in a collision beside Middle Wallop Aerodrome [12 December 1940].

McArdle — Bournemouth's first pilot **William McArdle** [born 1875] supplied motor cars to royalty and entrepeneurs from his Motor Mac's garage in Holdenhurst Road. Taught to fly by Louis Bleriot, he became a passionate flying enthusiast, selling the "FINEST GARAGE IN ENGLAND" and moving to France [1909] where he built a shed beside that of aviator Henri Farman at Chalons Camp, near Paris.

MOTOR MAC'S: BOURNEMOUTH'S FIRST RESIDENT AVIATOR, WILLIAM MCARDLE, OWNED 'THE FINEST GARAGE IN ENGLAND' IN HOLDENHURST ROAD.

McArdle then entered into a partnership with rich flyer J. Armstrong Drexel, son of a Philadelphia banker, and returned to England for aviation meetings including the famous Southbourne event. He also ventured into the countryside, as is proved by a postcard showing his monoplane "pitched in a field just opposite" the sender's house near Fordingbridge [19 July 1910].

McArthur — lifelong flyer **Flight-Lieutenant James Henry McArthur** [died 1961] achieved record times on the pre-war service between London and Baghdad and joined the RAF on a short service commission [1936]. He became a test pilot at the Royal Aircraft Establishment, Farnborough [1938], and was posted to 238 Squadron at RAF Middle Wallop in time for the Battle of Britain. During the combat he was transferred from Hurricanes to Spitfires, to command B-Flight of 609 Squadron at RAF Warmwell [1 August 1940] and claimed two Junkers Ju.87 "Stukas" [8 August 1940], a Messerschmitt Bf.110 [11 August 1940], two more [15 August 1940] and a final one [25 August 1940]. Next month he was credited with a Dornier Do.17 [7 September 1940].

Then he had a remarkable escape in combat at 25,000 feet [15 September 1940]. The oxygen supply of his Spitfire failed and he lost consciousness as it plunged towards the ground in a high-speed dive. Somehow he regained awareness and control but pressure changes affected his hearing. He was forced to hand over B-Flight to John Dundas and lost his operational status, being restricted to a 5,000-feet flying ceiling, but his promotion through the RAF continued and he would leave as Wing Commander [1947].

He returned to combat by enlisting with the Royal Canadian Air Force for the Korean War [1951] and resumed his civilian flying career, which ended with his death in a flying accident at Las Vegas [May 1961].

McKeown — veteran navy flyer **Captain David "Paddy" McKeown** [retired 1977] was the commander of HMS Osprey, the Portland shore base. His 35 years flying service for the Royal Navy had taken him up in 52 different types of aircraft, for a total of 4,500 hours airborne, and involved 800 deck landings on sixteen aircraft carriers. He had survived a mid-air collision in a Corsair over southern India in 1945. He was mentioned in despatches when flying a Sea Fury from HMS *Ocean* in the Korean War, and again whilst flying Sea Hawks from HMS *Albion* at Suez [1956].

McNamara — American flyer **Ensign J. F. McNamara**, operating from Portland Royal Naval Air Station, became the first United States aviator to attack a submarine in an "apparently successful" engagement of a German U-boat [1917].

Melbury Abbas crash — in farmland north of Compton Abbas Airfield, being the first fatal accident to an aircraft based there, when a Yak-54 climbed vertically and then went into a spin during an aerobatic sortie [11 August 2001].

The pilot, Chris Philpott [1954-2001], from Swindon, was killed instantly in what should have been a short warm-up before leaving for that afternoon's air show at RAF Kemble, Gloucestershire.

Meyer — for the bizarre story of American ground crewman **Sergeant Paul Adams Meyer** and Lockheed C-130E Hercules 37789, which he stole from RAF Mildenhall [22 May 1969], see the entry for Lulworth crashes [23 May 1969].

Meyrick Park Airfield — used by visiting air display pilots, such as Gustav Hamel, and notable as the only Bournemouth aerodrome that has survived under grass. The early pilots used the cricket pitch that is over-looked by the pavilion (Ordnance Survey map reference SZ 084 922).

Miller — Radipole-born Spitfire flyer **Pilot Officer Rogers Freeman Garland "Mick" Miller** [1920-40] of 609 Squadron at RAF Warmwell claimed half a Dornier kill [13 July 1940]. He would be killed when his fighter collided with a Messerschmitt Bf.110 (3U+FT) at 24,000 feet above Bellamy's Farm, Piddletrenthide [27 September 1940]. Spitfire 4107 crashed on the Cheselbourne side of the parish boundary. Miller is buried in St Nicholas' churchyard, Radford Semele, Warwickshire. His father, Thomas Charles Miller, farmed at Redlands, Radipole, near Weymouth.

Mitchell — Spitfire flyer **Pilot Officer Gordon Thomas Manners Mitchell** [1910-1940] of 609 Squadron from RAF Warmwell was shot down, in L1095, as the Luftwaffe attacked a convoy off Portland [11 July 1940]. His body was later washed up on the Isle of Wight and buried at All Saints' churchyard, Letchworth, Hertfordshire.

MOHD — squadron code of 644 Squadron, flying Halifax tug-planes from RAF Tarrant Rushton [1943-44].

Moortown Aerodrome — private airfield at Canford Magna, near Poole, used by Captain the Right Honourable Freddie Guest of Canford House. He established it when he was appointed Secretary of State for Air [1912] and it continued in use into the 1930s, when he was a Squadron Leader in the Royal Auxiliary Air Force.

Moreton Admiralty Airship Station — established on 355 acres of requisitioned land between the Dorchester to Wareham railway line and the hamlet around Woodsford Castle (Ordnance Survey map reference SY 760 895), in the final year of the Great War [1918].

Buildings were constructed, including airship sheds, gas holders, and repair worksheds. The site was entirely in the parish of Woodsford rather than Moreton but was named for the nearby Moreton Station, to the south-east and opposite the Frampton Arms.

The signing of the Armistice [11 November 1918] caused an immediate halt to the work and no airship ever landed operationally. That said, it has left its mark on the ground, including an access road westwards from Higher Woodsford hamlet and several buildings.

Indeed the site is better preserved than the later Warmwell Aerodrome, on the other side of the railway track, and aviation historians have sometimes confused the two.

Mosquito — parts for wartime de Havilland Mosquitoes, famous for their pathfinding flare-dropping and precision bombing raids, were made by the Airspeed factory at Somerford, Christchurch [1943-44]. Airspeed was owned by de Havilland, though it operated at that time under its own name.

Leslie Dawson, writing in *Wings over Dorset*, states that "over a hundred" Mosquitoes were built at Christchurch — 122 actually — though this fact has not filtered through to the lenghty production placename list displayed at the RAF Museum, in Hendon.

The "Wooden Wonder" continued to be seen in Dorset skies, as Leslie Dawson goes on to record and I can also recall from my childhood. Two night-fighter variants were flown by Flight Refuelling Limited, then at Tarrant Rushton Aerodrome, and their registrations are given as G-ALGU and G-ALGV. Airwork Services operated several.

Three Mark XVIs were overhauled at Hurn, Dawson adds, on being sold to the Israeli Air Force at the time of the Suez crisis [1956]. "Two Christchurch-built Mosquitoes survived into the late 1980s," he concludes.

Others with local associations had by this time ended their days in bonfires, either as acts of deliberate destruction or vandalism — or indeed both — during a series of incidents around Hurn's sprawling perimeter.

Muir — humourist Aircraftsman **Frank Muir** [1920-98] recalled being stationed as a reconnaissance photographic technician under canvas at RAF Warmwell [1941], "with equipment but no aircraft".

MW — code letters of 217 Squadron, flying Avro Ansons on coastal patrols from RAF Warmwell at the beginning of the Second World War.

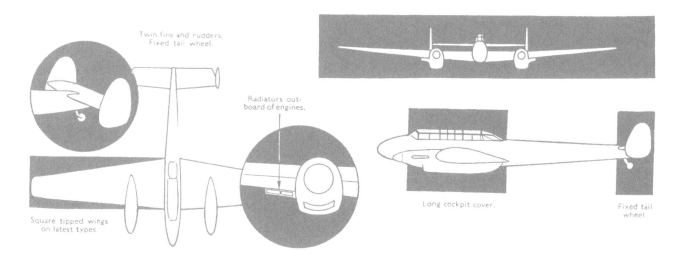

MESSERSCHMITT BF.110: THE LUFTWAFFE'S PRINCIPAL FIGHTER-BOMBER, AS SEEN AND SHOT DOWN ACROSS DORSET.

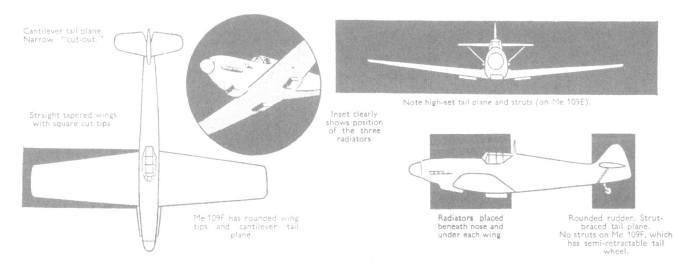

MESSERSCHMITT BF.109E: THE LUFTWAFFE'S ESCORT FIGHTER.

MESSERSCHMITT BF.109: AIRMEN AS ANYWHERE, WAITING FOR THE SIGNAL TO SCRAMBLE ON A CROSS-CHANNEL RAID.

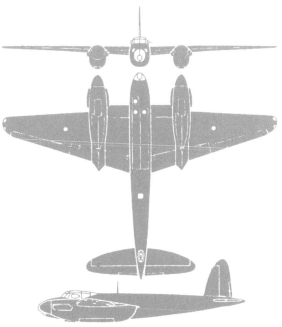

MOSQUITO BOMBER: THE "WOODEN WONDER" ALSO OPERATED AS A NIGHT-FIGHTER FROM RAF HURN, WITH 122 AIRFRAMES BEING MADE AT CHRISTCHURCH.

N

N serial numbers of RAF aircraft:

N255 Parnall Peto — see entry for Peto seaplane.

N2434 Hurricane — see entries for Fox and Wootton Fitzpaine.

N2474 Hurricane — see entry for Shaftesbury crashes.

N2485 Hurricane — see entries for Dixon and Portland crashes.

N2646 Hurricane — see entry for Portland crashes.

N2650 Hurricane — see entry for Portland crashes.

N3024 Spitfire — see entry for Goodwin.

N3039 Spitfire — see entries for Akroyd and Wynford Eagle crash.

N3061 Spitfire — see entry for Weymouth crashes.

N3173 Spitfire — see entry for Holland.

N3223 Spitfire — see entry for Nowierski.

N3231 Spitfire — see entry for Child Okeford crash.

N3282 Spitfire — see entries for Feary and Watercombe crash.

N3980 Miles Magister — see entry for Wareham crashes.

N6648 Tiger Moth — see entry for Thornford crash.

N7551 Miles Master — see entry for Puddletown crash.

National Aviation Displays — Sir Alan Cobham's Flying Circus began its first tour at Hanworth [12 April 1932]. Display days number 122 and 123 reached Bournemouth [12-13 August 1932] with Weymouth chosen for the following day.

Smaller towns did better in the following year's schedules when two tours operated simultaneously. No.2 Tour dropped in on Christchurch [30 April 1933] and Shaftesbury [2 May 1933]. They went deep into the West Country and returned via Sherborne [16 May 1933].

Meanwhile the No.1 Tour were approaching and arrived in Wimborne [20 August 1933]. Petworth, Sussex, was next. Then came Bournemouth, Weymouth and Swanage on successive days [22-24 August 1933].

Flight paths crossed again with the No.2 Tour approaching along the Channel coast and reaching Bridport [28 August 1933] and Lyme Regis [31 August 1933].

The following year Cobham's flyers regrouped as the National Aviation Display. Many of its calls were return visits, such as to Sherborne [15 June 1934], Bournemouth [7 July 1934], and Wimborne [10 July 1934]. Next day, however, it was Blandford's turn, for its first and only air display. There were more return venues the following month, including Lyme Regis [10 August 1934] and Swanage [14 August 1934].

Flying held its grasp on the popular imagination throughout the next spring and summer. Dorset skies saw Cobham's armada again, around Yeovil [1 June 1935], and then the team was split into the Astra Show and the Ferry Show. The former visited Bournemouth [6 July 1935], Christchurch [10 August 1935], Swanage [15 August 1935], Weymouth [16 August 1935], Lyme Regis [19 August 1935] and Wimborne [31 August 1935].

Meantime the Ferry Show also came to Dorset — whilst their comrades were over Swanage — with a visit to Gillingham in Dorset, rather than Kent, as the previous day they had been in Glastonbury and the following day it was Crewkerne's turn.

National Express — the owners of Bournemouth International Airport [from 1994] who then acquired West Midlands Travel and set about extending the main runway at Hurn [1995]. The company's core business is the provision of long distance coach transport. Its diversification into the wider holiday business more than doubled its issued share capital.

Naylor — Canadian flyer **Pilot Officer Naylor** of 418 (City of Edmonton) Squadron was killed when a Mosquito fighter-bomber crashed at Alder Road, Poole [23 July 1944].

Necker Island — 75-acres of the Caribbean, two miles off Virgin Gorda in the British Virgin Islands, owned by Lord Cobham, the founder of Flight Refuelling Limited, who sold it to Richard Branson of Virgin Airways for £300,000 [1979].

Newcombe — naval pilot **Lieutenant Gordon Clifford Newcombe** [1913-39] of West Lulworth was killed flying from the aircraft-carrier HMS *Glorious* [31 January 1939].

Newcombe — RAF flyer **Pilot Officer Jack Stewart Newcombe** [1909-31] of West Lulworth was killed in an accident [26 February 1931].

New Zealand heroes — fighter pilots Squadron Leader Terence Lovell-Gregg and Pilot Officer Cecil Hight were shot down and killed by the Luftwaffe, minutes from each other, in separate Battle of Britain dog-fights over opposite ends of the Dorset coast [18.00 hours, 15 August 1940]. Lovell-Gregg's Hurricane came down at Abbotsbury and Hight's Spitfire fell on Bournemouth.

Lovell-Gregg was from Marlborough, New Zealand, and Hight lived at Stratford, on the other side of the Cook Strait, in North Island.

Nichols — Hurricane flyer **Pilot Officer Dennis Hugh Nichols** [born 1921] of 56 Squadron, from RAF Boscombe Down, was shot down at Alton Pancras whilst on his first combat sortie [7 October 1940]. He parachuted clear of the stricken fighter but had a hard landing and was taken to Dorchester Hospital with a suspected fractured spine.

9U — squadron code of 644 Squadron, flying Halifax tug-planes for airborne forces, from RAF Hurn [1943-44].

NK — squadron code of 118 Squadron, flying Spitfires from RAF Warmwell [9-18 April 1941].

Norman — captain of industry **Sir Arthur Norman** [born 1917], won the Distinguished Flying Cross and bar [1943-44]. He lived at Manston House and retired to Gale Cottage, Hammoon.

Norris — Hurricane flyer **Sergeant Pilot Philip Puchall Norris** [1918-40], in P3348 of 213 Squadron from RAF Exeter, was shot down and killed off Portland [15.42 hours, 13 August 1940]. His body was washed ashore in France and he is buried in Etaples Military Cemetery. He was from Burgess Hill, Sussex.

Nowierski — Polish Spitfire flyer **Pilot Officer Tadeusz Nowierski** [died 1983] of 609 Squadron from RAF Warmwell put a Messerschmitt Bf.109 escort fighter into the sea off Weymouth during the Luftwaffe's Adlertag (Eagle Day) attack [13 August 1940]. He parachuted out of Spitfire N3223, on to Salisbury Plain, when his undercarriage failed [5 October 1940].

Claimed a Messerschmitt Bf.109 destroyed [10 October 1940] and half shares in the kills of a Messerschmitt Bf.110 and a Dornier Do.17 [both 2 December 1940].

Became Polish Liaison Officer to Headquarters, 11 Group Fighter Command [1942] and would be promoted to Group Captain, commanding RAF Dunholme Lodge. Returned to Poland [1947].

NX — squadron code of 131 (County of Kent) Squadron, flying Spitfires on bomber escort duties from RAF Hurn [10-14 July 1943].

NAVAL FIGHTERS: SHOWING THE FOLDING OF THE WINGS IN ORDER TO FIT ON A CARRIER, WITH THE SWORDFISH (ABOVE) AT RNAS YEOVILTON AND THE CHRISTCHURCH CONVERSION OF A SUPERMARINE/AIRSPEED SEAFIRE AT SEA ON A STAMP TO COMMEMORATE THE FIFTIETH ANNIVERSARY OF THE SEAFIRE.

"PEGASUS" AERODROME: NAMED FOR THE EMBLEM OF THE GLIDER PILOT REGIMENT, WITH A HUGE MAINTENANCE HANGAR AT TARRANT RUSHTON, COMMEMORATIVE PLAQUES TO AIRBORNE FORCES AND THE SPECIAL OPERATIONS EXECUTIVE, PLUS A RAINBOW OVER A FLAT SPACIOUSNESS THAT IS RETURNING TO AN AGRICULTURAL LANDSCAPE.

O

O'Brien — Spitfire flyer **Pilot Officer Peter O'Brien** from RAF Warmwell claimed a third share of 152 Squadron's kill of a Heinkel He.111 bomber off Portland [15 September 1940]. It probably belonged to Kampfgruppe 55 from Chartres.

He also scored a third share in the kill of a Junkers Ju.88 that was shot down at Ladywell Barn, Imber, Wiltshire [17 September 1940]. His was the only Spitfire of Blue Section that avoided the bomber's return fire and did not have to crash-land.

Oborne crash — of a German bomber into the hillside below Oborne Wood, east of Sherborne [7 May 1941]. The pilot baled out but the other three members of the crew died in the wreckage. They were buried in Oborne churchyard, until removal of the remains by the Volksbund, to the German war cemetery, Cannock Chase, Staffordshire [1963].

Okeford Fitzpaine crash — apparently of a Hurricane belonging to 56 Squadron from RAF Boscombe Down, on the day the Luftwaffe blitzed Sherborne [30 September 1940]. The pilot parachuted safely.

Olenski — Polish Spitfire pilot **Flying Officer Zbigniew Olenski** [1907-70] flew with 234 Squadron from RAF Warmwell [5 September 1940]. He already had combat experience — having claimed a probable Messerschmitt Bf.109 kill and a definite Bf.110 destruction — which, coupled with a Warsaw aeronautical engineering background, enabled him to suggest modifications to the Mark 1 Spitfire.

This report, which was adopted, led to his move to the Aerodynamics Department of the Royal Aircraft Establishment, Farnborough [28 March 1941]. After the war, on being released from the RAF as a Flight-Lieutenant, he worked for aircraft manufacturers A.V. Roe in Manchester, as an aerodynamicist, and played his part in the creating of the most beautiful aerodynamics of the century — the Avro Vulcan.

1-11 — the "One Eleven" airliner, made by the British Aircraft Corporation, merged into British Aerospace plc, at their works beside Hurn (Bournemouth) Airport [1963-84].

A BAC 1-11 Series 510 airliner, G-AVMO, was flown to Cosford, Shropshire, to join the British Airways collection in the Aerospace Museum [29 December 1992].

Openshaw — test pilot **Major Laurence Openshaw** of Westland Aircraft Limited was killed in an aerial collision at Ensbury Park Aerodrome, Bournemouth [6 June 1927]. His Westland Widgeon was flying at low-level, in a competitive event in full view of the crowded Racecourse stands.

HMS Osprey — Portland Royal Naval Air Station, as it was commissioned for the Air Anti-Submarine Warfare School [24 April 1959].

Ostaszewski-Ostoja — Polish Spitfire pilot **Flying Officer Piotr Ostaszewski-Ostoja** [born 1920], in R6986 of 609 Squadron from RAF Warmwell, was riddled by cannon fire from a Messerschmitt Bf.110 he engaged over Swanage [25 August 1940]. Though his flaps were damaged he succeeded in bringing the fighter and himself back to Warmwell Aerodrome, though the machine was written-off when he overshot the runway and crashed through the perimeter hedge. Damage to the pilot was confined to a minor arm injury. Piotr Ostaszewski-Ostoja would continue to have a reasonably good war, in Mosquito night fighters and then transport duties in South East Asia Command, leaving the RAF in 1946 as Wing Commander. He changed his name to Peter Raymond on deciding to stay in Britain.

Overton — Spitfire flyer **Pilot Officer Charles Nevil Overton** saw his Battle of Britain service with 609 Squadron from RAF Warmwell. Earlier in the war he had been with the squadron over Dunkirk. Along the Dorset coast he claimed a Messerschmitt Bf.109 destroyed [12 August 1940] and two Junkers Ju.87 "Stukas" [13 August 1940].

Posted to the Middle East, with 145 Squadron, he became Flight Commander of the first operational Spitfires in the Western Desert [June 1942] and was released from the RAF as Wing Commander [June 1946].

Owermoigne crashes — Westland Wallace K6057 of 6 Air Training Corps crashed near the hamlet of Holworth, midway between Owermoigne village and the sea [14 January 1938].

A wartime German crash was, apparently, a Messerschmitt Bf.110 fighter-bomber of Zerstörergeschwader 26 which had been involved in the attack on the Westland Aircraft factory at Yeovil [7 October 1940]. It was claimed by Spitfires of 609 Squadron from RAF Warmwell.

Spitfire P8516, a Mark II fighter of 118 Squadron, flew into hills south of the village [4 August 1941].

Oxford — twin-engined advanced trainer produced for the RAF by Airspeed (1934) Limited at its factory in Somerford, Christchurch, and elsewhere. A total of 4,411 were made by the company [1938-45] but taking those from other factories into account the grand total would exceed 8,000.

P

P serial numbers of RAF aircraft:

P1127 Kestrel — see entries for Bedford and Harriers.

P2766 Hurricane — see entry for Portland crashes.

P2866 Hurricane — see entries for Marston and Winfrith Newburgh crashes.

P2872 Hurricane — see entry for Portland crashes.

P2910 Hurricane — see entry for Warmwell crashes.

P2978 Hurricane — see entries for Gledhill and Swanage crashes.

P2987 Hurricane — see entry for Frisby.

P3084 Hurricane — see entries for Hewett and Portland crashes.

P3088 Hurricane — see entries for Edwards and Portland crashes.

P3177 Hurricane — see entry for Portland crashes.

P3200 Hurricane — see entries for Atkinson and Portland crashes.

P3215 Hurricane — see entry for Portland crashes.

P3222 Hurricane — see entry for Cawse.

P3348 Hurricane — see entries for Norris and Portland crashes.

P3404 Hurricane — see entries for Jay and Weymouth crashes.

P3414 Hurricane — see entries for Hardacre and Weymouth crashes.

P3421 Hurricane — see entry for Wareham crashes.

P3585 Hurricane — see entry for Lulworth crashes.

P3598 Hurricane — see entry for Warmwell crashes.

P3599 Hurricane — see entry for Poole Harbour crashes.

P3646 Hurricane — see entry for Don.

P3655 Hurricane — see entries for Portland crashes and Ray.

P3766 Hurricane — see entry for Swanage crashes.

P3774 Hurricane — see entry for Banks.

P3783 Hurricane — see entries for Gillan and Portland crashes.

P3870 Hurricane — see entry for Warmwell crashes.

P3885 Hurricane — see entries for Portland and Smithers.

P3984 Hurricane — see entries for Corfe Castle crashes, Doe, and Poole Harbour crashes.

P4832 Blenheim — see entry for Special Duty Flight.

P6362 Miles Magister — see entry for Worth Matravers crashes.

P6981 Whirlwind — see Warmwell crashes.

P6991 Whirlwind — see Warmwell crashes.

P7014 Whirlwind — see Warmwell crashes.

P7059 Whirlwind — see Warmwell crashes.

P7075 Whirlwind — see Warmwell crashes.

P7096 Whirlwind — see Warmwell crashes.

P7110 Whirlwind — see Warmwell crashes.

P8656 Spitfire — see entry for Winfrith Newburgh crashes.

P9456 Spitfire — see entry for Withall.

Pamphill crash — into Kingston Lacy Park 200 yards north-north-east of Kingston Lacy House, of Halifax bomber DT684 of 58 Squadron from RAF Holmsley South, Hampshire [24 January 1943]. It was on a transit flight to Talbenny, Haverfordwest, and suffered engine failure shortly after its 13.30 hours take-off.

The crew were killed: Flying Officer M. A. Legg of the Royal New Zealand Air Force (aged 32); Flying Officer G. R. Pringle, a Royal Canadian Air Force air observer (29); and Warrant Officers L. E. Gilpin (21) and S. J. Prince (25) also of the RCAF, who were wireless operators and gunners. They are buried in Bransgore churchyard, in the New Forest.

Paraguay — an ex-BOAC Mark V Sunderland flying-boat from Poole, converted into a Sandringham-3 for carrying 21 passengers and sold to the Argentine airline Dodero [November 1945].

Parkinson — Hurricane flyer **Sergeant Pilot Cecil Parkinson** [1915-40] was shot down in flames, 15 miles south of Durlston Head, Swanage [20 July 1940]. Though he baled out of P3766, belonging to 238 Squadron from RAF Middle Wallop, he suffered extensive burns from which he died the following day. He is buried in St Michael's churchyard, Stoke, at Coventry.

Pearson — Christchurch-born **Corporal Daphne Pearson GC** [1911-2000], a vicar's daughter who was serving as a radio operator at RAF Detling, Kent, became the first person to be awarded the George Cross for gallantry in the Second World War. She had received the Empire Gallantry Medal for saving the life of a dazed pilot in a burning bomber, dragging himself clear just before it exploded, after a raid near Dunkirk [31 May 1940]. She flung herself over him as the aircraft exploded and then re-entered the wreckage to try and save another crewman but found he was dead. This award would be replaced by the George Cross by Royal Warrant [31 January 1941].

Pegasus bridge — the Orne canal bridge in Normandy, midway between the D-Day beach-heads and the strategic inland town of Caen, was one of the first objectives in northern France to be captured during the invasion of Europe [01.30 hours, 6 June 1944]. Operation Coup de Main, this surprise attack, was carried out by Major John Howard with "D" company of the 2nd Battalion, Oxford and Buckinghamshire Light Infantry, in one of six gliders of the 6th Airborne Division that had lifted off from RAF Tarrant Rushton [22.56 hours, 5 June 1944], towed by Halifax tug-planes.

The canal bridge would henceforth be known as Pegasus Bridge, from the emblem of the Glider Pilot Regiment, and the nearby swingbridge over the River Orne became Horsa Bridge, from the men's gliders.

Penrose — aviator **Harald Penrose** [born 1904] of Stallen at Nether Compton was the first person to fly higher than the highest point on earth. Repeating the exercise, on the morning of 26 January 1933 as test pilot of the Westland Aircraft Works, he took the Houston-Westland PV-3 aeroplane to a record 35,000 feet over Poole Bay. Air-Commodore P. F. M. Fellowes was in the observer's cockpit. It proved the feasibility of what became, later that year, the first successful flight over Mount Everest, with Commodore and Mrs Fellowes leading the three small aircraft in a Puss Moth. Their exploits enthralled picture house audiences in the film *Wings over Everest*.

As for the first day at 35,000 feet, the flight began at Yeovil at 10.10 am into a 20 mph north-west wind. The aircraft was at its full weight of 4,870 lb and Penrose took her south to south-east to Weymouth bay and the Purbeck coast.

Maximum altitude was reached at 11.24 over Poole Bay, with the temperature at 76 degrees Fahrenheit below zero, the engine's performance (550 horsepower at its normal ceiling of 11,500 feet) reduced to an estimated 150 horsepower, and a speed for a few moments of 140 mph. The wind at that

HIGH FLYER: WESTLAND PV-3 AND THE COMPANY'S TEST PILOT, HARALD PENROSE, WHO TOOK IT UPWARDS OF 30,000 FEET IN A TRIAL FLIGHT OVER POOLE BAY ON 26 JANUARY 1933 AND THEREBY BECAME THE FIRST MAN TO FLY HIGHER THAN THE HIGHEST POINT ON EARTH.

TEST PILOT: HARALD PENROSE, WHO LIVED AT NETHER COMPTON, TOOK UP MORE THAN 400 TYPES AND VARIANTS OF BRITISH AND FOREIGN AIRCRAFT IN HIS PROFESSIONAL CAPACITY DURING THE DECADES BEFORE AND AFTER THE SECOND WORLD WAR.

FAILED EXPERIMENT: PARNALL PETO SEAPLANE N255 BEING LAUNCHED FROM HMS M2, WHICH WAS THE WORLD'S FIRST SUBMARINE AIRCRAFT-CARRIER. BOTH SANK OFF PORTLAND WITH THE LOSS OF 60 LIVES IN JANUARY 1932.

DOOMED FLIGHT: THE PETO FLOAT-PLANE BEING LAUNCHED BY CATAPULT FROM HMS M2 FOR TRIALS WHICH WERE SUCCESSFUL FROM THE AVIATION VIEWPOINT BUT ENDED BY SINKING THE SUBMARINE WHEN ITS HANGAR DOORS FAILED TO CLOSE AFTER THE AIRCRAFT HAD BEEN HOISTED BACK BY CRANE.

height was thought to be about 50 miles an hour.

"My chief concern was whether the controls would operate at such a high altitude," Penrose said after returning to Yeovil at noon, "They worked perfectly, and I was able to demonstrate by working the controls that complete mastery of the machine was maintained. Although I had ice forming over some of my instruments and the control panel and over my face mask and goggle mask, I was perfectly warm owing to my electrically-heated clothing and equipment. As a matter of fact I actually had my goggles more often off than on, because I was so warm."

Earlier in the week, there had been another test, Commodore Fellowes said, and he found that he had to replace his fountain pen with a pencil, because the low pressure at high altitude caused the ink to burst out at the nib.

Penrose told Rodney Legg in 1970 that before taking Fellowes into the upper atmosphere he had tried out the aeroplane himself. That time, when alone, he topped an estimated 30,000 feet and became the first to fly higher than the earth. Then the engine cut out. It had frozen up and he entered into a long glide back to earth, but succeeded in re-starting it as he dropped through the clouds at about 8,000 feet. The cause was a simple icing problem that was cured by adaptations to the fuel pipe and its lagging. He also realised his altimeter was unreliable at great heights (the 35,000 feet of the record being a later ground re-calculation of what the instruments showed at the time as being 38,900 feet).

Over the next two decades, Penrose tested and flew more than 400 types and variations in design of British and foreign aircraft. In the process he returned to his original job as a designer-technician to make major contributions in the development of rotor craft and devising what became the standard system of cabin pressurisation.

On retirement [1968] he embarked on a six-volume history of British aviation from 1903 to the

Second World War.

Pentridge crash — a Robinson R22 two-seater helicopter, flown by 46-year-old instructor Harry Knapp of Bizzi-B Helicopters, crashed while apparently practising manoeuvres beside Bokerley Ditch, in a training flight from Hurn [8 June 1994]. He died in the crash, together with his pupil, 40-year-old Hugh Latham of FR Aviation. Witnesses heard the engine cough and the rotor stop before the helicopter dropped spinning from the sky, scattering wreckage over a kilometer of Martin Down National Nature Reserve, on the south side of the A354.

Peto seaplane — built by George Parnall and Company at Bristol and housed in a hangar built beside the conning tower of big Royal Navy submarine *M2* [launched 1919] which was recommissioned as an aircraft-carrier [1927]. N255 had a 28-feet wing-span that folded to only eight feet. Experimental flights achieved a maximum speed of 113 miles per hour and endurance times of two hours in the air. What seemed like hopeful progress came to an abrupt halt off Dorset, three miles west of Portland Bill, when the submarine dived with its hangar doors open (or faulty), letting in the sea [10.30 hours, 26 January 1932].

She sank to 17 fathoms and the entire crew of 60 submariners — including Peto's pilot and ten men who operated the doors — were drowned. The tiny seaplane was later raised but out of respect it was decided that she should be scrapped, and the project died with her. Salvage attempts to lift the huge submarine were eventually abandoned [8 September 1932] and she was left as a tomb. Divers say the 305-feet hull is still intact, perhaps because it sits on sand, and that the hangar doors remain open.

Phoenix — pilotless rocket-boosted battlefield reconnaissance spy-plane and launcher developed by Flight Refuelling Limited at Wimborne [1980s].

Philippart — first Belgian ace of the Second World War **Pilot Officer Jacques Arthur Laurent Philippart** [1909-40] was shot down and killed over Lyme Bay, west of Portland, by Hauptmann Mayer of I Gruppe, Jagdgeschwader 53 [17.30 hours, 25 August 1940].

Philippart was flying a Hurricane of 213 Squadron from RAF Exeter. He was buried in Exeter Higher Cemetery. In 1949 his remains were exhumed and repatriated, being interred at Evere, Brussels, in the Pelouse d'Honneur Cemetery.

Philpott — stunt pilot **Chris Philpott** [1954-2001] from Swindon was killed in a Yak-54 from Compton Abbas Airfield when it crashed into farmland in the adjoining parish of Melbury Abbas [11 August 2001]. It came down after going into a spin following a vertical climb in what should have been a brief aerobatic rehearsal before departing for an air day at RAF Kemble, Gloucestershire. Philpott, a flight engineer on Boeing 747 airlines, was an experienced display performer at air shows. "He regularly thrilled visitors with his flying sequences," said airfield director Clive Hughes.

Piddlehinton crash — a Spitfire of 609 Squadron from RAF Warmwell crash-landed near the village when its pilot was blinded by glycol fumes after the cooling system of the fighter's Merlin engine had been punctured by gunfire during a Battle of Britain dog-fight [26 July 1940].

Piddletrenthide crashes — of a Messerschmitt Bf.110 (3U+FT) belonging to Zerstörergeschwader 26, the Geschwader named Horst Wessel after the Nazi immortalised in a militant anti-Semitic song which became a national anthem. It was in collision with Pilot Officer Mick Miller's Spitfire of 609 Squadron from RAF Warmwell [27 September 1940].

The German pilot, Georg Jackstedt, parachuted into captivity, but his wireless operator, Emil

Lidtke, was killed. The collision occurred at 24,000 feet above Bellamy's Farm and the aircraft crashed beside its boundary hedge with Dole's Ash Farm. It had been taking part in an abortive raid on the Parnall Aircraft Company at Yate, near Chipping Sodbury.

Miller's Spitfire came down on the Cheselbourne side of the parish boundary.

Pimperne crash — at Nutford Farm, north of Blandford, of a Dornier Do.17 reconnaissance aircraft (5F+OM) the crew of which survived and had their injuries tended in the farmhouse [21 July 1940]. The kill was claimed by Hurricanes of 238 Squadron from RAF Middle Wallop.

Plymouth **class** — Sandringham Mark 5 flying-boats operating from Poole Harbour by British Overseas Airways, on middle-distance routes to the Gulf and India, and onwards to Malaya and Hong Kong [1947-48]. Carrying 22 passengers each, the Poole fleet comprised nine boats: *Pembroke, Penzance, Perth, Pevensey, Poole, Portland, Portmarnock, Portsea* and *Portsmouth*.

PN — squadron code of 41 Squadron, flying Spitfires from RAF Warmwell [7-18 March 1945].

Pollock — Hurricane pilot **Flight Lieutenant Norval E. Pollock** of 439 (Royal Canadian Air Force) Squadron was killed near RAF Hurn when his Hurricane LD972 collided with an American P-47 Thunderbolt from USAAF Christchurch [21 March 1944].

Pooch — bull terrier **Pilot Officer Pooch** was the mascot of 152 Squadron at RAF Warmwell [1940-41].

RAF Poole — as it was known for just one week, being re-named RAF Hamworthy before the arrival of its first military flying-boats [October 1942].

Poole crashes — one of the returning Heinkel He.111 bombers that had devastated the Bristol Aeroplane Company's works at Filton during the Battle of Britain [25 September 1940] was shot down over Poole. Belonging to Kampfgeschwader 55, the bomber (GI +LR) ploughed into Underwood, Westminster Road, Branksome Park. The five crew were killed. This kill was claimed by Hurricanes of 238 Squadron from RAF Middle Wallop.

Sergeant Pilot Bill Kearsey finished off a Junkers Ju.88 bomber which Pilot Officer Eric "Boy" Marrs had engaged over the Blackmore Vale [14 November 1940]. It came down as a fireball, exploding fifty feet from a cobbler's shed, near the corner of Ringwood Road and Herbert Avenue.

A Mosquito of 418 (City of Edmonton) Squadron, from RAF Hurn, crashed 200 yards west of Alder Road Drill Hall, Upper Parkstone [23 July 1944]. It had apparently clipped the roof of a building in Mossley Avenue, during a low-level daylight flight, and exploded shortly after hitting the ground. Pilot Officers Bowhay and Naylor were killed.

Poole Harbour crashes — a Messerschmitt Bf.109 escort fighter was shot down during the Luftwaffe's Adlertag (Eagle Day) attack [13 August 1940]. The pilot, Unteroffizier Wilhelm Hohenseldt, was rescued and made prisoner of war. Pilot Officer Crook, in a Spitfire of 609 Squadron from RAF Warmwell, claimed the kill.

Hurricane P3599 of 238 Squadron was shot down off Poole [1 October 1940]. The squadron then also lost Hurricane P3984 in a Battle of Britain dog-fight over the same spot [10 October 1940]. Though wounded, Pilot Officer Bob Doe, parachuted to a soft landing in "the sewage lagoon" on Brownsea Island, and his fighter sped on into the Isle of Purbeck where it crashed below Corfe Castle.

Sunderland T9111 of 461 (Royal Australian Air Force) Squadron was wrecked off RAF

Hamworthy after it lost power on take-off. Flight-Lieutenant Manger aborted the flight but the flying-boat careered sideways into mud-flats and became a complete write-off [20.55 hours, 21 March 1943]. Though cut and bruised, the twelve crewmen were able to clamber free from the wreckage, and staggered ashore.

An RAF Catalina flying-boat of 210 Squadron, on a training flight, missed the "Trot" off its Hamworthy base and descended in thick fog to disaster beside Round Island, a mile to the south. It fell apart on leaving the water and ripping through cord-grass marshland [04.25 hours, 24 August 1943]. Eight of the twelve crewmen, including Pilot Officer Duff, were killed. The other four were rescued by ratings from the island's naval camp.

In what would be the penultimate chapter of Empire, Field-Marshal Sir Archibald Wavell, Viceroy of India and Supreme Commander Allied Forces in India and Burma, flew out of Poole Harbour aboard a BOAC flying boat bound for Bombay [11 October 1943].

BOAC flying-boat *Hailsham*, returning from Singapore, found the English coast obscured by fog [4 March 1946]. She managed to find the main water-runway "Trot" in Poole Harbour but then veered sideways and damaged her floats in the shallows beside Brownsea Island. No one was hurt but *Hailsham* was inundated by rising tide. She was later pulled clear but only to be towed away for scrap.

Poole Harbour flying-boats — see entries for Airways House; Alcock; *Altair*; *Argentina*; *Bermuda Sky Queen*; *Brazil*; British Overseas Airways Corporation; *Cabot*; *Caribou*; *City of Liverpool*; *City of Swanage*; *Clare*; *Clio*; *Clyde*; *Cordelia*; Crashes; Flying-boats; GJX; *Guba*; *Hailsham*; *Hamilton*; Hamworthy; *Hythe* class; Imperial Airways; *Inglaterra*; *Maia*; *Paraguay*; *Plymouth* class; Poole Harbour crashes; Sandbanks Royal Naval Air Station; Squadrons operating from Dorset; Trots; *Uruguay*; *UT*; and *Vega*.

Portesham crash — a Junkers Ju.87 "Stuka" dive-bomber was shot down between the village and Rodden during the Luftwaffe's routed Adlertag (Eagle Day) attack [13 August 1940]. The kill was claimed by Flight-Lieutenant Derek Boitel-Gill in a Spitfire of 152 Squadron from RAF Warmwell. The dive-bomber was one of those targeted on Middle Wallop Aerodrome, Hampshire.

Portland crashes — a Junkers Ju.88 (B3+DC) was brought down, almost undamaged, in a crash-landing at "The Castles" clifftop beside Blacknor Fort [11 August 1940]. Claimed by a Hurricane of 213 Squadron from RAF Exeter, its "B3" markings indicated it belonged to Kampfgeschwader 54, a bomber wing whose death's head emblem — Totenkopf — appeared on the fuselage just aft of the transparent nose.

The sea off Portland saw numerous casualties through the Battle of Britain and for almost the duration of the Second World War. Most of the aircraft belonged to the Luftwaffe but they were joined by many defending Spitfires and Hurricanes.

The following losses were inflicted on the Royal Air Force over the sea off Portland in Battle of Britain dog-fights:

Spitfire of 609 Squadron [9 July 1940].

Spitfires L1069 and L1095 of 609 Squadron and Hurricane N2485 of 501 Squadron [11 July 1940].

Hurricane P3084 of 501 Squadron [12 July 1940].

Spitfire K9901 of 152 Squadron [25 July 1940].

Hurricanes L2057, P3783, P3885 and R4092 of 601 Squadron [11 August 1940].

Hurricane N2650 of 213 Squadron [11 August 1940].

Hurricanes P3348 of 213 Squadron and P3177 of 238 Squadron [13 August 1940].

Hurricanes P2872 and P3215 of 87 Squadron [15 August 1940].

Hurricanes N2646, P2766 and P3200 of 213 Squadron, and Spitfire R6810 of 152 Squadron

BOUND STONE: ROYAL NAVY WESSEX HELICOPTER XS868 FROM PORTLAND LOWERING THE REPLACEMENT BOUNDARY STONE FOR THE ISLAND, ON TO THE PEBBLES OF THE CHESIL BEACH OFF THE FLEET AT CHICKERELL.

[25 August 1940].

Spitfire R6831 of 152 Squadron [27 August 1940].

Hurricanes P3655 and P3088 of 56 Squadron, and Spitfire L1072 of 152 Squadron [30 September 1940].

Hurricane P3421 of 56 Squadron [10 October 1940].

The following fighters were also shot down off the Dorset coast after interceptions that began over Portland:

Spitfire R6614 of 152 Squadron and Hurricane R4097 of 238 Squadron [11 August 1940].

Spitfire R6985 of 234 Squadron [15 August 1940].

German losses into the English Channel are recorded with less accuracy but the following, at least, were seen from Portland:

Junkers Ju.87 [9 July 1940].

Heinkel He.111 [15 September 1940].

Dornier Do.17 [4 January 1941].

A Royal Navy Whirlwind helicopter crashed at Portland [9 October 1968].

Another ditched in the sea at Portland Harbour [20 June 1969].

Three were killed and four saved when a Royal Navy Wessex helicopter crashed in the sea off Portland during a photographic reconnaissance exercise [20 May 1971].

The next helicopter to ditch in the sea was a Royal Navy Sea King [13 January 1972], followed a month later by a Navy Wessex, also off Portland [16 February 1972].

One of the most embarrassing air crashes of all time occurred off Portland as a Sea Harrier FRS.1 of 801 Naval Air Squadron from RNAS Yeovilton was being put through its paces by Lieutenant Paul Simmonds-Short. He made a high speed low-level approach towards the aircraft carrier HMS *Ark Royal*, on which senior officers of the Royal Navy and visiting members of the international

PORTLAND BASE: END OF AN EARLIER ERA, WITH A SEA HAWK AND CAPTAIN DAVID "PADDY" MCKEOWN BEING TOWED INTO RETIREMENT ON 5 MAY 1977.

NATO Council watched the flight demonstration unfold [4 October 1989].

The Harrier then clipped the warship's radar antenna — damaging its wing-tip, reaction jet, and outrigger undercarriage. It survived the collision and returned to Yeovilton but low-speed handling checks resulted in it being refused clearance for a safe landing.

The pilot was told to take the fighter back to Lyme Bay and eject over open sea, ten nautical miles west of Portland, where he was picked up uninjured by a naval helicopter. No one aboard the carrier had been hurt. Only their pride.

Portland Royal Naval Air Station — established on The Mere Marshes in the corner of Portland Harbour between the Chesil Beach and Portland Castle, for float-planes during the Great War [26 September 1916]. Initially designated HMS Sereptia. Expansion followed, including a seaplane shed, and the lagoon beside the oil tanks became the home-base for the 12 Short and Wright float-planes of No. 416 and 417 Flights, comprising 241 Squadron [1918].

Extension of this into the vast acreage of modern concrete and tarmac (Ordnance Survey map reference SY 682 743) is much more recent. Quarry waste was not dumped across the entirety of The Mere until the middle of the Cold War [1959].

Renamed HMS Osprey [24 April 1959].

Posener — South African volunteer **Pilot Officer Frederick Hyam Posener** [1917-40], flying Spitfire K9880 of 152 Squadron from RAF Warmwell, was shot down off Swanage in a Battle of Britain dog-fight [20 July 1940]. It was his second operational sortie. He was one of only 21 South African pilots who took part in the battle.

Powell — Malmesbury's Member of Parliament **Walter Powell** was whisked away into the sky, never to be seen again, from Cliff Close, Eype, Symondsbury [10 December 1881]. The War Office hot-air balloon *Saladin*, on secondment to the Meteorological Society, was the cause of the misadventure. Its remains, though without those of the MP, were discovered on the slopes of the Sierra del Piedroza in the mountains of Spain [20 January 1882].

Powerstock Admiralty Airship Station — as it was sometimes called, being above Gray's Farm in this parish, is listed here under its official designation as Toller Admiralty Airship Station.

Powerstock crash — of Wellington X9785 belonging to 218 Squadron from RAF Marham, Norfolk, which had been on a mission to bomb German capital ships in the French Atlantic port of Brest [16 December 1941]. Five of the crew baled out over Chilfrome and the pilot, Sergeant Vezina, successfully brought his crippled aircraft to a crash-landing at Holm Farm, above West Milton. The starboard engine had failed.

PR — code letters of 609 (West Riding) Squadron flying Spitfires from RAF Warmwell [1940-41].

Proud — pre-war **Group Captain Harold John Granville Ellis Proud** [born 1906] joined the RAF in 1924. He became station commander of RAF Hurn for 38 Wing Army Co-operation Command, providing transport for the 1st Airborne Division [1942-43]. Reached the rank of Air Commodore and commanded the Far East Base, Singapore [1949-51].

Puddletown crash — Miles Master N7551 of the Central Gunnery School, flying from RAF Warmwell, was abandoned out of control over Puddletown Heath [22 April 1940].

Pulham crash — Beaufighter R2438 of 307 (Lwowski [Polish]) Squadron from RAF Exeter force-landed in a field 200 yards south-east of Pulham parish church (15.15 hours, 29 December 1941). The port engine had cut out and the night-fighter, a Mark IIf airframe carrying Air Interception radar, landed wheels-up.

Though the machine was extensively damaged it would be categorised as repairable at contractors. Sergeant Pilot R. Sniezkowski and Sergeant Observer Z. Domanski walked apparently unharmed from the wreckage, though the pilot had sustained serious internal injuries which later came to light. Information from Richard Danilo of Preston, Lancashire.

Pytlak — Hurricane flyer **Pilot Officer T. W. Pytlak** of 302 (Poznanski) Squadron at RAF Warmwell was killed in a flying accident [9 September 1941]. The Polish Squadron had arrived at the station four days earlier. He was aged 22 and is buried in the RAF plot at Warmwell churchyard.

POOLE DEPARTURE: OF MAJOR BROOKS, THE WHITE RAJ OF SARAWAK, RETURNING HOME ON BOAC FLYING-BOAT HARWICH IN 1945, FOLLOWING THE OUSTING OF JAPANESE INVADERS FROM BRITISH BORNEO.

POOLE SUPPLIES: BRITISH AIRWAYS STEWARDESSES (RIGHT) WITH A SEAWOMAN (LEFT) GREETING THEM FROM A LAUNCH BESIDE SHAMBLES STEPS, POOLE QUAY, AS THEY EMBARK ON THE FIRST STAGE OF AN OUTWARD-BOUND FLIGHT FROM POOLE HARBOUR.

PORTLAND RECORD: TEST PILOT BILL BEDFORD BRINGS THE HAWKER P.1127 — FORERUNNER OF THE HARRIER — DOWN ON HMS ARK ROYAL OFF DORSET'S SHAMBLES SANDBANK ON 8 FEBRUARY 1963, IN THE FIRST VERTICAL LANDING OF A JET ON TO A SHIP.

Q

Qantas Empire Airways — the Australian airline, took delivery of *Coogee*, *Coorong*, and *Corio* from the Imperial Airways C-class fleet of Empire flying-boats that were being dispersed from Southampton Water to Poole Harbour [1939]. *Coorong* and *Corio* would later be exchanged for ex-Poole flying-boat *Calypso* and *Centaurus*.

Back in Europe, *Coorong* joined sister flying-boat *Cambria*, from the Poole fleet in evacuating 469 of the 30,000 British, Australian and New Zealand troops garrisoning the island of Crete, in the teeth of German airborne invasion [May 1941]. Thirteen flights were made across the Mediterranean, from Suda Bay to Alexandria.

Qantas, the acronym of the Queensland and Northern Territory Aerial Service, is the airline of the Australian Commonwealth. Its links with Hurn and BOAC led to a joint service between Britain and Australia, which resumed when the war in Europe ended.

Lancastrian G-AGLV of British Overseas Airways Corporation lifted off from Hurn in the inaugural flight, via Lydda in British Palestine (now Lod, Israel) and Karachi in British India (now in Pakistan), for Sydney, Australia. Of eleven seats, only six were occupied for the 12,000 mile flight which became the world's longest post-war scheduled service [30 May 1945].

QV — squadron code of 19 Squadron, flying Spitfires from RAF Warmwell [1-14 June 1942].

BOMB ARMING: OF A 250-POUND WEAPON IN 1943, UNDER THE WING OF A WESTLAND WHIRLWIND AT A SANDBAGGED DISPERSAL BAY BESIDE KINIGHTON HEATH WOOD ON THE EDGE OF RAF WARMWELL.

RADAR RESEARCH: SITE B OF THE TOP-SECRET TELECOMMUNICATIONS RESEARCH ESTABLISHMENT AT WORTH MATRAVERS IN A VIEW FROM THE EAST LATE IN 1940, SHOWING EXPANSION CONTINUING AND BLAST-WALLS AROUND THE HUTS.

AVRO FOUNDER: HUMPHREY VERDON ROE, SEEN WITH ONE OF HIS BIPLANES, LIVED ON PORTLAND WITH DR MARIE STOPES — WHO HAD HER FAME IN THE PIONEERING OF CONTRACEPTION.

R

R serial numbers of RAF aircraft:

R2438 Beaufighter — see entry for Pulham crash.

R2687 Hurricane — see entry for Jay.

R4092 Hurricane — see entries for Demetriadi and Portland crashes.

R4097 Hurricane — see entry for Portland crashes and Walch.

R4099 Hurricane — see entry for Atkinson.

R6607 Spitfire — see entries for Chaldon Herring and Shepperd.

R6614 Spitfire — see entry for Portland crashes.

R6634 Spitfire — see entry for Swanage crashes.

R6831 Spitfire — see entries for Beaumont and Portland crashes.

R6907 Spitfire — see entry for Durweston crash.

R6910 Spitfire — see entry for Akroyd.

R6985 Spitfire — see entry for Portland crashes.

R6986 Spitfire — see entry for Ostaszewski-Ostoja.

R6915 Spitfire — preserved fighter from RAF Warmwell; see entries for Agazarian, Dundas, and Spitfire R6915.

R7016 Spitfire — see entry for Beaumont.

R7142 Spitfire — see entry for Corfe Castle crashes.

R7695 Typhoon — see entry for Glanvilles Wootton crash.

R8663 Typhoon — see entry for Chilfrome crash.

R9306 Stirling — see entry for Church Knowle crashes.

RAK — squadron code of 604 (County of Middlesex) Squadron, flying Mosquito night-fighters from RAF Hurn [3 May-13 July 1944].

Ray — Hurricane flyer **Sergeant Pilot Ronald Wilfred Ray** [died 1985], of 56 Squadron from RAF Boscombe Down, sustained damage to himself and P3655 in a dog-fight over Bournemouth. He succeeded, however, in making a forced-landing at Longcutts Farm, East Knighton, near Winfrith Newburgh [11.35 hours, 30 September 1940].

Though taken out of combat with a broken arm and other wounds he would return to action over the Humber, with 604 Squadron in 1943, and would claim two German bombers.

Rayment — Blenheim pilot **Flight-Lieutenant Douglas Rayment** of the Special Duty Flight from RAF Christchurch was lost at sea, 33 miles south of St Alban's Head [17 July 1941]. He had told his gunner, Sergeant R. Sadler, to fire at a mystery object, thought to be a weather balloon, floating in the water: "There you are, have a go. You can't miss!" Two bursts of machine-gun fire followed and the aircraft's wireless then went dead. No one ever knew what happened.

Raymond — for Polish pilot **Wing Commander Peter Raymond** see entry for Piotr Ostaszewski-Ostoja, his birth-name.

RB — squadron code of 66 Squadron, flying Spitfires on bomber escort duties from RAF Hurn [10-14 July 1943].

Rebbeck — Bournemouth-born **Rear-Admiral Sir Edward Rebbeck** [born 1901] served in the Great War in HMS *Erin*, and in the Second World War in HMS *Birmingham*, before making his mark on naval aviation. He was Commanding Officer to Anthorn Royal Naval Air Station [1946], ADC to the Queen [1952], and Rear-Admiral Reserve Aircraft, up to retirement [1952-55]. Then he spent a decade working for the Vickers Group.

Reddington — Spitfire flyer **Sergeant-Pilot Leslie Arthur Edwin Reddington** [1919-40] of 152 Squadron from RAF Warmwell was shot down into the sea on the day that the Luftwaffe blitzed Sherborne [30 September 1940]. His fighter, L1072, crashed into the sea. Reddington's body was not recovered but his widow was pregnant in Coventry with their second daughter; Lesley Reddington was born in February 1941.

Rees — navigator **Flight-Sergeant F. W. Rees** of Bomber Command was killed at the age of 33 [29 March 1945]. He is buried in Radipole churchyard, Weymouth.

Rhodes-Moorhouse — first flyer to win the Victoria Cross **Lieutenant William Barnard Rhodes-Moorhouse VC, RFC**, [1887-1915], "DIED APRIL 27th 1915 AT MERVILLE, FRANCE, FROM WOUNDS RECEIVED IN BOMBING COURTRAI, AGED 27 YEARS. IN SACRED LOVING MEMORY. PER ARDUA AD ASTRA." The inscriptions in a railed plot overlooking Parnham House and Beaminster gloss over the superlative. He had provided the Royal Flying Corps with its first Victoria Cross.

He had taken off at 15.00 hours on 26 April 1915 in a BE 2b biplane, from Merville, to drop a hundred pound bomb on a railway bridge over the River Lys at Courtrai in German-occupied Belgium. To do so he flew at three hundred feet through a hail of bullets, mainly unleashed from the church belfry, and the bomb hit its target — temporarily tearing up the track. Rhodes-Moorhouse and the BE 2b were equally shot-up but limped back together to Merville. There the flyer was resigned to his fate, with massive gunshot wounds to his thigh and abdomen.

"I am not a brave man," he told the chaplain, "but I have tried to do my duty." He survived only 24 hours.

Such was the admiration of his commanding officer that he implemented William's request that his body should be shipped home to Dorset — itself a rare honour as it was a wish denied to almost all the other dead heroes.

HEROIC FIRST: THE VERY FIRST VICTORIA CROSS FOR THE ROYAL AIR FORCE — THEN THE ROYAL FLYING CORPS — WAS WON IN APRIL 1915 BY LIEUTENANT WILLIAM BARNARD RHODES-MOORHOUSE FROM PARNHAM HOUSE, BEAMINSTER.

William has another claim to fame — in the carefree days of pre-war aviation he had been the first to fly through the Golden Gate at San Francisco.

Parnham House had been bought by his Maori mother in 1913. There he left a widow, Linda, and a baby son, William Henry Rhodes-Moorhouse [1914-40] who would follow his father's example in the next war and win a Distinguished Flying Cross for 601 (County of London) Squadron in the Battle of Britain. At its close, on 6 September 1940, his Hurricane was shot down near Tonbridge, Kent. His ashes were returned to the Parnham plot. Linda had now lost both her husband and her son — at the same ages and from the same cause.

The aside to his father's story is that William Barnard Rhodes-Moorhouse made the first crossing of the English Channel to carry passengers. They were two in number, being his wife and a friend, whom he flew from Douai, via Boulogne, to Dungness and Bethersden, in Kent [4 August 1912]. There the Breguet tractor-biplane had to make a crash-landing, in poor visibility, though the pilot and passengers were unhurt.

Ridgeway crash — precise south Dorset parish not know, of a belly-landed Heinkel He.111 H-8 bomber [5 April 1941]. The crew were unhurt and taken prisoner. They had been attacking Channel shipping and ended up in Dorset through a navigational error.

Ringstead Radio Station — two huge elevated rectangular steel structures, comprising a latticework of girders and cables, dominating the low cliffs beside the site of mediaeval Ringstead village on the west side of Ringstead Bay in the parish of Osmington (Ordnance Survey map reference SY 745 814). Operational through the height of the Cold War [1957-75] until removal after being rendered obsolete by satellite technology.

They comprised an ultra-shortwave tropospheric scatter station of the United States Air Force, receiving signals from the command bunker at High Wycombe, via a series of "beacons" within visual range. The last ones, on the Dorset Downs, were the masts at Bulbarrow, which relayed incoming transmissions from the penultimate station, at Wincombe Hill, Shaftesbury.

From the coast at Ringstead the communications system beamed its messages via the troposphere to the Spanish border.

Robinson — Spitfire flyer **Sergeant-Pilot Denis Norman Robinson** of 152 Squadron from RAF Warmwell crashed at Bestwall, Wareham, after a Battle of Britain dog-fight over Swanage [8 August 1940]. He had a remarkable escape — the fuselage of K9894 ended up standing vertically, with the propeller embedded in the meadow, and he was able to jump down on to the grass.

He had claimed a Messerschmitt Bf.109 in the first week of that busy month [5 August 1940], and returned to the sky to account for another [15 August 1940]. He then had a Junkers Ju.87 [17 August 1940] and finally a Junkers Ju.88 [4 September 1940] before being posted to RAF Upavon, Wiltshire [26 September 1940].

Robinson survived the war and became a civilian pilot [1946-78].

Robinson — former Hurricane pilot **Squadron Leader Michael Lister Robinson** [1917-42] left 238 Squadron at RAF Chilbolton, from which he had been defending the Dorset coast, to take charge of Spitfires of 609 Squadron at RAF Warmwell [4 October 1940]. He came with several Messerschmitt claims and would share in two more Bf.110s within days during the attack on the Westland Aircraft Company at Yeovil [7 October 1940].

Eight more Messerschmitts, Bf.109s, were claimed in a rapid tally of kills, plus one probable destruction [8 May-24 July 1941]. Robinson was then gazetted with the Distinguished Service Order [5 August 1941] and posted to Biggin Hill.

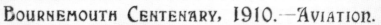

Last Flight of the Hon C.S. Rolls, Killed at Bournemouth July 12

Daily News. July 13. 1910

IN FLIGHT AT BOURNEMOUTH.

CRASH SCENE: THE CHIEF OF POLICE AT SOUTHBOURNE, BOURNEMOUTH, WARNS OFF PHOTOGRAPHERS AS A CROWD GATHERS AROUND THE WRECKAGE OF THE WRIGHT FLYER FLOWN BY CHARLES STEWART ROLLS.

MONMOUTH MEMORIAL: IN THE HOME TOWN OF CHARLES STEWART ROLLS, WHO ALSO LIVES ON BY HAVING CONTRIBUTED THE FIRST ELEMENT OF THE NAME OF THE FAMOUS CAR AND ENGINE MAKERS, ROLLS-ROYCE.

It was as leader to Tangmere Wing, heading 340 Squadron, that he failed to return from a sweep along the English Channel [10 April 1942]. Michael Robinson was the son of Sir Roy Robinson [1883-1952], chairman of the Forestry Commission, who was created first Baron Robinson of Kielder Forest [1947].

Roe — pioneer aviator **Humphrey Verdon Roe** [1878-1949], second husband of contraception advocate Dr Marie Stopes, lived at the Higher Lighthouse, Portland.

His *Who's Who* entry explains how he came to make flying machines: "From 1909 onwards, when flying seemed to be a dream, his foresight and faith in its future led him to devote the whole of his capital and talents to helping his brother Sir Alliott Verdon-Roe, to establish the Avro bi-plane."

They founded plane-makers A.V. Roe and Company Limited. Humphrey left in 1917 to join the Royal Flying Corps, in France, and was wounded on active service [1918].

Rolls — pioneer automobile manufacturer and aviator, the **Honourable Charles Stewart Rolls** [1877-1910] was the first Briton to be killed in an aeroplane crash. His biplane, a Wright Flyer carrying number "18" on the tail, stalled in an air-display at Southbourne, Bournemouth [12 July 1910]. The accident is commemorated by a plaque in the grounds of St Peter's School, in St Catherine's Road.

Apart from the manner of his death, Rolls had already accumulated a list of aeronautic records. He was one of the first four resident Englishmen to fly, as passengers, courtesy Wilbur Wright [8 October 1908]. More notably, Rolls would be the first person to fly from England to France [18.30 to 19.13 hours, 2 June 1910]. He had taken off and returned to Broadlees, Dover, and thus accomplished the additional feats of being the first to make a non-stop two-way crossing, and the first to land at a pre-arranged spot without damaging his aeroplane.

Rowley — Bournemouth-born **Squadron Leader Clive Rowley** [born 1951], a veteran of the Falklands and the Gulf War, where he flew Tornadoes, joined the RAF Memorial Flight at Coningsby, Lincolnshire [1995]. He flew into Hurn in the Flight's Spitfire [August 1997] to see his parents, Southbourne hairdressers Cliff and Phyllis Rowley, who retired to Mudeford. The Flight was en route to an air show in Devon.

Royal Naval Air Landing Ship 50 — the vessel in Portland Harbour with more helicopter landings to her credit than any other vessel in the Royal Navy or, perhaps anywhere in the world. Recorded upwards of 100,000 drops before the Navy quit Portland.

Royal Navy Seaplane School — moved from Calshot on Southampton Water to Sandbanks, beside Poole Harbour [15 May 1940].

RINGSTEAD RADIO: DURING THE COLD WAR THIS TWIN SET OF APPARATUS, FACING WEYMOUTH BAY AND PORTLAND (TOP RIGHT), BEAMED AND RECEIVED ULTRA-SHORTWAVE COMMAND AND CONTROL SIGNALS BOUNCED OFF THE STRATOSPHERE, LINKING THE UNITED STATES AIR FORCE COMMAND BUNKER AT HIGH WYCOMBE WITH ITS COUNTERPART IN SPAIN.

WORLD FIRST: LIEUTENANT CHARLES RUMNEY SAMSON TAKING OFF FROM A MOVING SHIP OFF PORTLAND IN MAY 1912.

S

Saladin — War Office gas-filled balloon 60 feet high and 30 feet across, made at the Royal Gun Factory, Woolwich Arsenal [1878], last seen on the Dorset coast, above Symondsbury and then disappearing across Lyme Bay [16.15 hours, 10 December 1881].

The ill-fated flight began from Bath [14.00 hours] and was carrying out cloud measurements of temperature and water-vapour for the Meteorological Society. The occupants underestimated the northerly wind and the perilous implications of their seaward flight-path.

The balloon clipped a clifftop pasture at Cliff Close, Eype's Mouth, throwing two of the occupants clear as well as much-needed ballast. Captain James Templer was left on the ground, crewman Agg Gardner was pulled 80 feet by a line and broke his leg, and their Parliamentary guest — Malmesbury MP Walter Powell — rose alone into the dusk and was never seen again.

Wreckage of what was presumed to be the balloon, though sans Member of Parliament, would be discovered on the slopes of Sierra del Piedroza in the mountains of Spain [20 January 1882].

Salmet — French aviator **Henri Salmet** was sponsored by the Daily Mail to give air displays around Britain and became the principal pilot at the Louis Bleriot Flying School in Hendon. His popular flight demonstrations included an example of how not to do it when on landing he was blinded by the sun and ran into a tree at Tuckton, between Bournemouth and Christchurch [1913]. The Bleriot monoplane was mangled but Salmet stepped from the wreckage with only a cut to show for it, and his passenger Hatton Turner was unhurt.

One of Salmet's return visits was to Meyrick Park where he delivered Father Christmas, whose time in town just happened to coincide with the absence from his office of department store owner Cyril Beale.

Salter — the world's first female Tornado pilot **Flight-Lieutenant Jo Salter** [born 1968] from Bournemouth qualified as a combat pilot and joined 617 "Dambusters" Squadron at RAF Lossiemouth, Scotland [1995]. "I never feel fear," she was quoted as saying at the press briefing that made her front-page national news. "The Air Force is an armed force and you have to expect to go into combat."

Unmarried, she said she was "just one of the boys", but left future options open: "I would like to have children one day and in the Air Force you can have maternity leave. But I would hate to give up my career."

Her training had cost the RAF £3 million, the same as her male counterparts, and she received a permanent commission which will last until 2007.

Jo Salter would be taken to task for her "never feel fear" remark, and find an able defender in sometime Lieutenant-Commander John Kilbracken RNVR, writing as Lord Kilbracken: "It was far from being my experience, during five wartime years, flying mostly Swordfish biplanes, that all pilots have 'a healthy fear for their aircraft'.

"Fear may come when the flak starts flying or the elastic breaks (our euphemism for the engine failing), but no one should be flying who ever feels afraid when at the controls of a magnificent, well-maintained flying machine in peacetime, except in a dire emergency."

Samson — Manchester-born naval **Lieutenant Charles Rumney Samson** [1883-1931] took a certificate as an air pilot [1911] and carried out the first sea-plane experiments, the first cross-country night flights, and the first flight from a moving ship [3 May 1912]. That, together with two more flights later in the day, took place in a Short S.38 float-plane from the battleship HMS *Hibernia*

Sinking feeling: Commander Basil Hobbs's G-EALP, a Supermarine Sea Lion, went down here, off Bournemouth Pier, when one of his floats filled with water in September 1919.

Controversial victory: Guido Jannello on Bournemouth beach, having won the Schneider Trophy race in September 1919, despite missing much of the course by going the wrong side of a buoy in Studland Bay.

HAMMERSLEY'S SEAPLANE: G-EALG, AN AVRO 589, FLOWN BY CAPTAIN H. A. HAMMERSLEY IN THE 1919 SCHNEIDER TROPHY RACE, SEEN OFF BOURNEMOUTH'S EAST CLIFF IN 1919.

LATER CONTENDER: AN ITALIAN MACCHI M.67 ON THE SLIPWAY AT CALSHOT IN 1929.

as she sailed across Weymouth Bay at 10.5 knots in the Portland Naval Review. The S.38 had pusher propellers. King George V was duly impressed and commanded him to dine aboard the royal yacht *Victoria and Albert*.

Lieutenant Samson went on to have a remarkable war, from the siege of Antwerp and the first Battle of Ypres to the Dardanelles and the coast of Syria, where he commanded HMS *Ben-My-Chree*. He was promoted Wing Commander in the Royal Naval Air Service [January 1918] and Lieutenant-Colonel in the Royal Air Force. By the end of the Great War he had accumulated the Chevalier Legion of Honour, Croix de Guerre, five mentions in despatches, and the Distinguished Service Order and bar. He went on to be a Group Captain in the RAF [1919], Air Commodore [1922], and retired to write his autobiographical account of *Flight and Flights* [1930].

Samways — father and son **David Samways** [1949-99] and **Matthew Samways** [1975-99], from Wareham, were killed in a light aircraft at Hurn [24 December 1999]. The accident took place at Bournemouth International Airport.

Sandbanks Royal Naval Air Station — known to Poole people as HMS Tadpole, because it functioned as the Royal Naval Seaplane School and handled beginners with float-planes that were dwarfed by the flying-boats of British Overseas Airways Corporation and Coastal Command that were the regular users of Poole Harbour. Established for training Fleet Air Arm pilots as a satellite station to HMS Daedalus shore-base at Lee-on-Solent [15 May 1940]. Situated on the north-west side of the peninsula where it requisitioned the Royal Motor Yatch Club (Ordnance Survey map reference SZ 044 877).

Withdrew to Lee-on-Solent as the offensive war became busier, with Poole Harbour filling with flying-boats and invasion craft [15 October 1943].

Sandes — Spitfire flyer **Pilot Officer L. D. Sandes** of RAF Warmwell was awarded the Distinguished Flying Cross. He would be killed, aged twenty-eight [26 March 1941], and is buried in the RAF plot at Warmwell cemetery.

Saville — "Missing in Action" **Flight-Lieutenant John Saville** of 439 (Royal Canadian Air Force) Squadron, flying a rocket-firing Typhoon from RAF Hurn [5 June 1944], epitomised the skill, courage and sacrifice of the aerial contribution that caused the D-Day landings to be relatively unopposed. A Guernsey diver, Mick Peters, would find the remains of lost Typhoon MN210 [1982]. It lies near Moulinet Reef in Havelet Bay, where it had been downed by German flak as the Typhoons destroyed German radar apparatus at Fort George, in the vital "blinding" of the enemy's early-warning system before the invasion armada embarked.

It had been his third attack on Fort George. Not only had he taken part in a raid carried out by 439 Squadron and 440 Squadron two days earlier [3 June 1944], but Johnny Saville had also made a sortie to the same target earlier on D-Day minus 1. In the 1980s, divers were authorized to remove all small surface items that might attract looters — such as a silk parachute which was in mint condition — but the Ministry of Defence discouraged further investigation of the site because of the likelihood that human remains were present.

Schneider International Seaplane Race — known as the Schneider Trophy, donated by French munitions heir Jacques Schneider, resumed off Dorset after the Great War with its third race being held in Poole Bay [10 September 1919]. The contest was between seaplanes, which at this time were biplanes with floats, and it started from Bournemouth Pier with an anti-clockwise circuit of 20 nautical miles via turning points off Durlston Head and Hengistbury Head.

FINAL VICTORY: THAT OF FLAG OFFICER H. R. D. WAGHORN IN 1931, IN A SUPERMARINE S.6, ENABLED BRITAIN TO RETAIN THE SCHNEIDER TROPHY IN PERPETUITY.

The Royal Navy battleships HMS *Barham* and HMS *Malaya*, both of 31,100-tons and mounting eight 15-inch guns, anchored inside the triangle.

Elite flyers arrived from all over Britain and much of war-torn Europe. What followed was a fiasco.

Lunch and what went with it, aboard the yatch *Ombra*, clouded the judgment of the organising officials from the Royal Aero Club. They overlooked the restricted and deteriorating visibility and proceeded to start the race in a thick "sea-fret" as one of the Bournemouth residents called it. Fog caused chaos and the race was called off, a new time set, and then brought forward by an hour. This effectively disqualified the French team who were using the extra time to repair their floats.

The revised time still had the flyers going off into both fog and dusk. As the light failed the leading aeroplane, a Savoia flying-boat flown by Guido Jannello, made its turns at a reserve buoy moored in Studland Bay, instead of continuing down to the south-eastern corner of the Purbeck coast. This gave the Italian team an astonishing lead, though as it was virtually dark no one had a clear idea of where anyone had flown.

The Royal Aero Club compounded the problem by first declaring the race void, then accepting an Italian appeal and awarding Jannello the £1,000 prize, and having this decision revoked by the Federation Aeronautique Internationale.

An incidental hiccup was the sinking of Supermarine Sea Lion G-EALP, which had been flown by Commander Basil Hobbs, off Bournemouth Pier. It was later lifted, taken to pieces on the beach, and sent to London where it was reassembled and put on display in the Science Museum.

Scholz — German airman **Gefreiter Helmut Scholz**, the gunner of Messerschmitt Bf.110c (2N+EP), together with the pilot, was the first crewman to be taken prisoner in the Battle of Britain, when they crash-landed on Povington Heath, Tyneham [12.05 hours, 11 July 1940]. Oberleutnant Gerhard Kadow was also unhurt and the fighter-bomber suffered little more than twisted propellers and a dented fuselage.

School of Air Traffic Control — established at Hurn Aerodrome to teach the new art of air traffic management [1949-62]. Radar, blind-landing, and queue stacking techniques revolutionised the possibilities for the mass movement of people and planes, with operations around the clock. Britain's first generation of experts learnt their trade in Bournemouth.

Scoble — parascending enthusiast **Chris Scoble** [born 1950] of Rushall Lane, Lytchett Matravers, designed and put into production the Sunrider para-motor. It fits on the user's back and enables take-off from level ground. "It is just about the perfect flying machine," he says. "You can put it on the back seat of the car, assemble it in three or four minutes, and then be airborne from just about anywhere."

SD — Squadron code on the Mark IIa Spitfires of 501 (City of Bristol) Squadron, flying from RAF Ibsley, between Ringwood and Fordingbridge, and regular visitors to the Dorset sky [1941-42]. They provided evocative wartime footage for the film 'The First of the Few', which was filmed at Ibsley and over the Isle of Wight.

Sea crashes — virtually countless off the Dorset coast during World War Two; in my book on the conflict I have detailed well over a hundred losses and the total must be at least double. Upwards of three-quarters belonged to the Luftwaffe.

SEAFIRE CONVERSION: THE MARITIME VARIANT OF THE FAMOUS SPITFIRE, ADAPTED FOR USE ON ROYAL NAVY CARRIERS, AT THE AIRSPEED WORKS IN SOMERFORD, CHRISTCHURCH.

In this present book the "Crashes" entry lists a representative quantity from both sides. Post-war losses have been in the testing and training of military aircraft.

An RAF Hunter ditched in the sea off Dorset [15 July 1968]. The pilot was rescued.

An RAF Phantom was lost off the Dorset coast with its two crew killed [13 May 1970].

Sea Venom — jet fighter, produced for the Fleet Air Arm by the de Havilland factory at Somerford, Christchurch [1950s]. See entry for de Havilland Aircraft Company Limited.

Sea Vixen — jet fighter, produced for the Royal Navy and its aircraft-carriers by the de Havilland factory at Somerford, through the late 1950s and up to the plant's closure and removal to Chester [1962]. See entry for de Havilland Aircraft Company Limited.

Sea Vixen XJ580 — the last to fly for the Royal Navy [1982], going to Flight Refuelling Limited at Hurn, and then purchased by the Sea Vixen Society [1984] for return to Somerford as a "tribute to the aviation history of Christchurch, 1932-62". It now guards a Queensway megastore on the site of the former factory.

7C — squadron code of 296 Squadron, flying Albemarle troop-carriers from RAF Hurn [1943].

Shaftesbury crashes — rising to fly over Dorset's hilltop town, during the Battle of Britain, Spitfire L1702 of 238 Squadron collided with Hurricane N2474 [30 September 1940].

The Heinkel He.111 flown by Hauptmann Langar, officer commanding the elite Kampfgruppe 100, flew into a hillside near Shaftesbury whilst trying to escape from an interception directed by Sopley radar station [23 May 1942]. The attacking Beaufighter of 604 Squadron was flown by Squadron Leader John "Cat's Eyes" Cunningham from RAF Middle Wallop. Langar had lost his bearings in dense cloud and rain. No shot had been fired.

Shapwick crash — at Crab Farm, between the village and Badbury Rings, of Hurricane V6792 belonging to 238 Squadron from RAF Chilbolton, Hampshire [5 November 1940]. It had been shot down by Messerschmitt Bf.109s over Bournemouth. Pilot Officer Brian Considine had baled out above Sturminster Marshall.

Shepley — Spitfire flyer **Pilot Officer Douglas Clayton Shepley** [1918-40], in K9999 of 152 Squadron from RAF Warmwell, was shot down and killed by gunners of Junkers Ju.88 bombers, within sight of the Isle of Wight [12 August 1940].

His death would be avenged by his mother, who raised £5,700 in south Yorkshire to buy Mark Vb Spitfire W3649, for 609 Squadron in 1941. Famously, it was the machine flown by Wing Commander Victor Beamish when he spotted the German warships Scharnhorst and Gneisenau, as they made their Channel Dash [12 February 1942].

The memorial to both aircraft is the Shepley Spitfire public house at Totley, Yorkshire.

Shepperd — Spitfire flyer **Sergeant Pilot Edmund Eric Shepperd** [1917-40] of 152 Squadron from RAF Warmwell claimed four kills during the Battle of Britain: a Messerschmitt Bf.109 [25 July 1940]; a Junkers Ju.88 [12 August 1940]; a Junkers Ju.87 [18 August 1940]; and a second Ju.88 [7 October 1940]. He was killed when Spitfire R6607 unaccountably plunged into the ground at Tadnoll Mill, north of Chaldon Herring [18 October 1940].

He is buried at Binstead, where he was born, in the Isle of Wight.

Sherborne Conservative Fete — provided some of the first public flights over the Dorset countryside when pioneer aviator Herbert Spencer took up passengers in his biplane [5 August 1912].

Sherborne crashes — at Burdon's Nurseries, Oborne Road, of a Hurricane belonging to 87 Squadron from RAF Exeter, which was one of the defending aircraft on the afternoon when the town was devastated by Luftwaffe bombs [16.40 hours, 30 September 1940]. Sergeant Pilot Herbert Walton baled out and was taken to the Yeatman Hospital, Sherborne, with minor injuries.

A Hurricane of 238 Squadron from RAF Chilbolton is said to have crashed near Sherborne after a dog-fight with Messerschmitt Bf.110s. Pilot Officer Aubrey Richard Covington baled out unhurt and claimed he had accounted for two Bf.110s earlier in the day [1 October 1940].

Shillingstone crash — at "Nutmead" [7 October 1940], but this has been found to be an error for Netmead, Child Okeford, and is described under the entry for that parish.

Short — Spitfire flyer **Sergeant Pilot Jimmy Short** of 152 Squadron from RAF Warmwell parachuted into captivity when his fighter was shot down by Messerschmitt Bf.109s as he escorted Hampden bombers that were attacking the French port of Brest [24 July 1941].

Silver City Airways — transferred their fleet of Bristol 170 Wayfarers, better known as the Bristol Freighter, from Southampton to Bournemouth (Hurn) Airport [1959]. Ran a constant summertime car-ferry shuttle service from Hurn to the Channel Islands.

622 Gliding School — based at Christchurch Aerodrome until its move to Old Sarum, Wiltshire [1963], and from there to Upavon.

Smith — novelist **Frederick Escreet Smith**, author of *633 Squadron* and thirty other successful novels, lives in Hathaway Road, Southbourne, Bournemouth.

Smith — Typhoon flyer **Pilot Officer Graham Smith** of 263 Squadron was killed when he failed to pull out of a low roll whist taking part in the official welcome for the 474th Fighter Group of the United States Army Air Force on their arrival at RAF Warmwell [12 March 1944].

Smithers — Hurricane flyer and stockbroker **Pilot Officer Julian Langley Smithers** [1916-40], in P3885 of 601 Squadron from RAF Tangmere, was shot down off Portland [10.23 hours, 11 August 1940]. His body was later washed up on the French coast and he is buried in Sainte Marie Cemetery at Le Havre. He was from Knockholt, Kent.

MR. HERBERT SPENCER
WINNER OF NUMEROUS COMPETITIONS AT BROOKLANDS

FLIGHTS AT SHERBORNE CONSERVATIVE FETE
ON MONDAY, AUGUST 5TH, 1912

PASSENGER FLIGHTS: HERBERT SPENCER PROVIDED THE HIGH POINT FOR THE CONSERVATIVE FETE, OVER SHERBORNE PARK IN AUGUST 1912.

Solway — one of the two Sunderland flying-boat hulks abandoned in Poole Harbour when British Overseas Airways Corporation departed for Southampton Water [1948]. *City of Liverpool* was the other.

Solway was the outer of the two fuselages stranded at Lower Hamworthy, where they were finally beached like stranded whales [1958-59].

She had been built as Short's S.1307 and converted to a Mark 2 Solent, call-sign G-AHIU.

Sopley — **RAF Sopley** radar station [1940-74] began operations with the deployment of a mobile Type 15 ground-to-air antenna, in a field four miles north of Christchurch, on the estate of Lord Manners between the River Avon and the New Forest [25 December 1940]. The radar unit had been developed by the Telecommunications Research Establishment at Worth Matravers and built at Somerford, Christchurch, by the Air Defence Experimental Establishment.

Experiments began with aerial interceptions, through combat guidance to 604 Squadron at RAF Middle Wallop, and the two stations celebrated their first radar-controlled kill three months later [4 March 1941].

What became Southern Radar continued to operate from its underground bunker through the height of the Cold War. "Through freedom to the stars" and "Guard the Flight" declared its mottos. Above-ground buildings at the station became a camp for refugees from the Vietnam war [1978].

Southbourne Aerodrome — laid out as a 3,140-yard racecourse between Belle Vue Road and Church Road in Bournemouth's eastern suburb, created for a major pioneering aviation meeting [1910], and now remembered on a plaque [1978] in the grounds of St Peter's School in St Catherine's Road (Ordnance Survey map reference SZ 147 915): "This stone commemorates the Hon. CHARLES STEWART ROLLS who was killed in a flying accident near this spot on the 12th July 1910, the first Briton to die in powered flight."

MOBILE RADAR: TYPE 15 ANTENNA IN ONE OF LORD MANNERS' FIELDS AT SOPLEY, NEAR CHRISTCHURCH, WHERE AIRBORNE INTERCEPTION EQUIPMENT WAS INSTALLED ON CHRISTMAS DAY IN 1940.

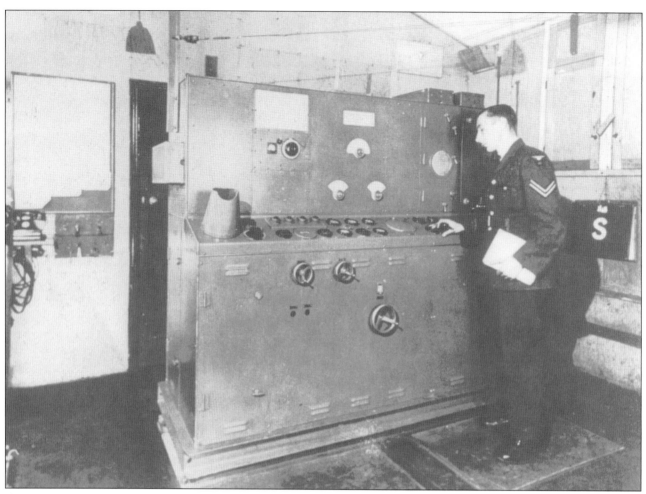

SOPLEY UNDERGROUND: "THE WELL" AS IT WAS CALLED, WITH A TYPE 7 TRANSMITTER RECEIVER IN ITS BUNKER AT THE END OF THE SECOND WORLD WAR, HAVING SCORED A NOTABLE TALLY OF NIGHT-FIGHTER INTERCEPTIONS.

SOUTHERN RADAR: RAF SOPLEY CONTINUED TO BE THE EYES OF THE HOME DEFENCE THROUGH THE COLD WAR.

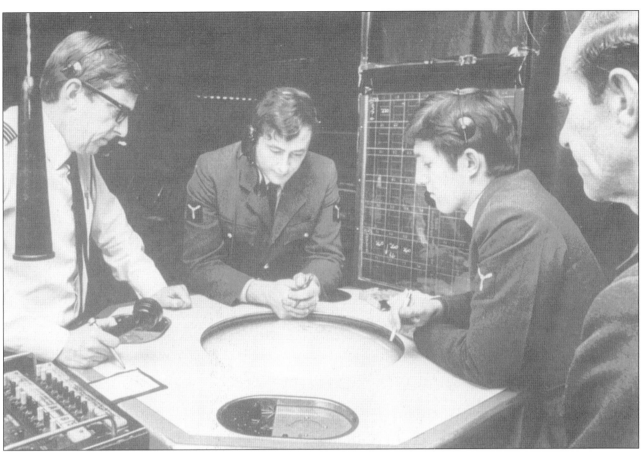

OPERATIONS ROOM: COURSE PLOTTING AT "THE FONT", 100 FEET BENEATH RAF SOPLEY IN 1972, WITH TWO MILITARY AIR TRAFFIC CONTROLLERS BEING WATCHED BY SUPERVISOR FLIGHT-LIEUTENANT BRIAN JONES (LEFT) AND THE COMMANDING OFFICER, WING COMMANDER PETER WOOD.

FINAL INSPECTION: AIR COMMODORE WILLIAM POPE, AIR OFFICER COMMANDING OF MILITARY AIR TRAFFIC OPERATIONS, TALKING TO A WRAF ASSISTANT AT THE RADAR CONSOLE IN THE UNDERGROUND OPERATIONS ROOM AT RAF SOPLEY IN MAY 1974. BEHIND AIR COMMODORE POPE STANDS FLIGHT-LIEUTENANT JIM KYLE (FAR RIGHT) WHO FLEW TYPHOONS FROM NEEDS OAR POINT AND HURN IN 1944.

CLOSING CEREMONY: AIR COMMODORE WILLIAM POPE RETURNING THE SALUTE OF PARADE COMMANDER FLIGHT-LIEUTENANT BRIAN JONES IN "THE WELL" DEEP BELOW RAF SOPLEY, ON 11 SEPTEMBER 1974. ITS ABOVE-GROUND BUILDINGS AND BILLETS WOULD BECOME A TEMPORARY HOME FOR VIETNAMESE REFUGEES IN 1978.

Other early aviators who attended the meeting, and survived a number of lesser mishaps, included Edmond Audemars, in *Demoiselle* (crashed) and *Infuriated Grasshopper*; George A. Barnes in *Humber*; Louis Bleriot, as guest visitor; "Colonel" Samuel Franklin Cody in *Cody's Cathedral*; Claude Grahame-White, taking up passengers in his *Autobus*; Captain Bertram Dickson in a Farman biplane; and Leon Morane, winning the sea-flight race; plus a Wright Brothers' Flyer from the new production line at Short's Shellbeach factory in the Isle of Sheppy, Kent.

Speare — wartime **Wing Commander Richard Douglas Speare DSO, DFC** [killed 1945] was the son of Major and Mrs Fraser William Speare of Annandale, Barrie Road, Moordown, Bournemouth.

Special Duty Flight — under the control of the Air Ministry and put at the disposal of the Christchurch-based Air Defence and Research Development Establishment at Worth Matravers. Arrived at Christchurch Aerodrome, from St Athan, Glamorgan [8 May 1940]. It then comprised six Ansons, four Blenheims, two Harrows, two Fairey Battles, and three "Special Aircraft". These were adapted versions of the Hurricane and Anson and a High Altitude Machine.

Among their first tasks, using three Ansons, was to attempt to track the course of a German "beam", a radio directional signal for the navigation of bombers [21 June 1940].

Blenheim P4832, flown by Flight-Lieutenant Douglas L. Rayment, would be lost over the English Channel, 33 miles south of St Alban's Head, when he told his gunner, Sergeant R. Sadler, to engage a mystery object which they spotted floating on the sea: "There you are, have a go. You can't miss!" Two bursts of machine-gun fire were followed by the aircraft's radio going dead [17 July 1941].

The flight moved from Christchurch to take control of the brand new RAF Hurn [1 August 1941]. After having completed the move it was renamed, as the Research Section of recently formed Telecommunications Flying Unit [10 November 1941].

Spencer — pioneer flyer **Herbert Spencer**, the "winner of numerous competitions at Brooklands" provided passenger flights at Sherborne Conservative Fete [5 August 1912].

Spitfire — the legendary fighter of the Battle of Britain, flying from RAF Warmwell in the Frome valley east of Dorchester, which was the only front-line base between Exeter and Eastleigh during the hot and hectic summer of 1940.

Spitfire R6915 — the surviving airframe from the Dorset skies during the Battle of Britain, when it was flown by Pilot Officer Noel le Chavalier Agazarian and also by Flight-Lieutenant John Dundas, of 609 Squadron from RAF Warmwell. It is suspended along with one of its adverseries, a Messerschmitt Bf.109, over the main hall in the Imperial War Museum, Lambeth Road, London SE1.

Squadrons operating from Dorset in World War Two:

19 Squadron — briefly flew Mark Vb Spitfires from RAF Warmwell [1-14 June 1942]. Motto:"Possunt quia posse videntur" — "They can because they think they can". Squadron code: "QV".

41 Squadron — briefly flew Mark XIV Spitfires from RAF Warmwell [7-18 March 1945]. Motto: "Seek and destroy". Squadron code: "PN".

66 Squadron — flew Spitfires brom RAF Hurn on escort duties, to protect American Flying Fortress bombers as they crossed the English Channel on daylight raids [10-14 July 1943]. Motto: "Cavete praemonui" — "Beware, I have given warning". Squadron code "RB".

118 Squadron — briefly flew Mark I and IIa Spitfires from RAF Warmwell [9-18 April 1941]. Motto: "Occido redeoque" — "I kill and return". Squadron code: "NK".

125 (Newfoundland) Squadron — flew Mark XVII Mosquito night-fighters from RAF Hurn [25 March-31 July 1944]. They were controlled by Starlight, as Sopley radar was codenamed, and carried out defensive interceptions over central southern England during the D-Day period. Motto: "Nunquam domandi" — "Never to be tamed". Squadron code: "VA".

130 Squadron — briefly flew Spitfires from RAF Warmwell, with a mix of Mark IIa, Va and Vb machines [30 November-5 December 1941]. Motto: "Strong to serve". Squadron code: "AP".

131 (County of Kent) Squadron — flew Spitfires from RAF Hurn on escort duties, to protect American Flying Fortresses as they crossed the English Channel on daylight raids [10-14 July 1943]. Motto: "Invicta" — "Unconquered". Squadron code: "NX".

152 (Hyderabad) Squadron — posted from RAF Acklington, Northumberland, flying into RAF Warmwell with Mark I Spitfires as the Battle of Britain gained momentum [12 July 1940]. Later equipped with Mark II Spitfires [14 March 1941] as losses were replaced. They were transferred to the newly opened RAF Portreath, Cornwall [9 April 1941]. Motto: "Faithful Ally". Squadron Code: "UM".

164 (Argentine-British) Squadron — flew Mark IV Hurricanes from RAF Warmwell [20 June-6 August 1943]. Returned with Mark Ib Typhoons to RAF Hurn, shortly after D-Day [20 June-17 July 1944]. Motto: "Firmes Volamos" — "Firmly we fly". Squadron code: "FJ".

170 (Army Co-Operational) Squadron — flew Mustangs from RAF Hurn, in forward reconnaissance and army-support roles [1942]. Squadron code: "BN".

174 (Mauritius) Squadron — flew Mark IIb Hurricanes from RAF Warmwell [1-21 September 1942]. Motto: "Attack". Squadron code: "XP".

175 Squadron — formed at RAF Warmwell and equipped with Mark IIb Hurricanes [3 March 1942]. They departed in the autumn to RAF Harrowbeer, Devon [10 October 1942], and returned briefly with Mark Ib Typhoons [21 November-4 December 1944]. Motto: "Stop at nothing". Squadron code: "HH".

181 Squadron — flew rocket-firing Mark Ib Typhoons from RAF Hurn through the D-Day period [1 April-20 June 1944]. Came back to Dorset in the winter, to RAF Warmwell [12 January-3 February 1945]. Motto: "Irriumus vastatum" — "We rush in and destroy". Squadron code: "EL".

182 Squadron — flew rocket-firing Mark Ib Typhoons from RAF Hurn through the D-Day period [1 April-20 June 1944]. Came back to Dorset in the winter to RAF Warmwell [3-21 February 1945]. Motto: "Fearless I direct my flight". Squadron code: "XM".

183 (Gold Coast) Squadron — flew rocket-firing Mark Ib Typhoons from RAF Hurn during the Battle of Normandy [1-14 July 1944]. Motto: "Versatility". Squadron code: "HF".

WARMWELL SPITFIRE: MARK I SURVIVOR R6915 OF 609 SQUADRON, DOMINATING THE BATTLE OF BRITAIN DISPLAY IN THE IMPERIAL WAR MUSEUM, SOUTH LAMBETH.

184 Squadron — flew Mark Ib Typhoons from RAF Warmwell [4-18 December 1944] and returned at the end of the war [7-28 May 1945].

193 (Fellowship of Bellows) Squadron — flew rocket-firing Mark Ib Typhoons from RAF Hurn during the Battle of Normandy [3-14 July 1944]. Motto: "Aeram et terram imperare" — "To govern the air and the earth". Squadron code: "DP".

197 Squadron — flew Mark Ib Typhoons from RAF Hurn during the Battle of Normandy [3-20 July 1944]. Motto: "Findimus caelum" — "We cleave the sky". Squadron code: "OV".

198 Squadron — flew rocket-firing Mark Ib Typhoons from RAF Hurn shortly after D-Day [22 June-1 July 1944]. Motto: "Igni renatus" — "Born again in fire". Squadron code: "TP".

210 Squadron — flew Catalina flying-boats of Coastal Command on long-range anti-submarine patrols over the Atlantic, from RAF Hamworthy [May-December 1943]. Motto: "Yn y nwyfre yn hedfan" — "Hovering in the heavens". Squadron code: "DA".

217 Squadron — flew Avro Ansons on coastal patrols, from RAF Warmwell [1939-40]. Motto: "Woe to the unwary". Squadron code: "MW".

234 (Madras Presidency) Squadron — flew into RAF Warmwell with Mark I Spitfires [24 February 1941]. Changed to Mark II Spitfires, improvised with an unjettisonable fuel drop-tank added to the centre of the port wing, to extend their flying range for escort duties on offensive operations against the Brest peninsula [2 July 1941]. These dismayed the pilots who were appalled at the compromising of the fighter's legendary manoeuvrability. Towards the end of the year they were transferred to RAF Ibsley, Hampshire [5 November 1941], where they would be re-equipped with Mark Vb Spitfires. From this aerodrome, between Ringwood and Fordingbridge, they continued to be regular visitors to Dorset skies.

They returned to RAF Warmwell [23 March 1942], but only for a fortnight, before moving on to Cornwall.

Motto: "Ignem mortemque despuimus" — "We spit fire and death". Squadron code: "AZ".

241 Squadron — flew Short and Wright float-planes from Portland Royal Naval Air Station and operated DH6 patrol aircraft from Chickerell Aerodrome, on being formed at the close of the Great War [August-December 1918]. Motto: "Find and forewarn".

245 (Northern Rhodesia) Squadron — briefly flew Mark Ib Typhoons from RAF Warmwell [19 December 1944-6 January 1945]. Squadron code not known.

247 (China-British) Squadron — briefly flew rocket-firing Mark Ib Typhoons from RAF Hurn through the D-Day period [24 April-20 June 1944]. Came back to Dorset in the winter, to RAF Warmwell [21 February-7 March 1945]. Motto: "Rise from the east". Squadron code: "ZY".

253 (Hyderabad State) Squadron — operated DH6 patrol aircraft on coastal anti-submarine flights from Chickerell Aerodrome, at its formation towards the close of the Great War [June-August 1918]. Motto: "Come one, come all".

257 (Burma) Squadron — flew Mark Ib Typhoons from RAF Warmwell [8 January-12 August 1943] and then returned a month later [17 September 1943-20 January 1944]. They were briefly posted to RAF Hurn during the Battle of Normandy [2-8 July 1944]. Motto: "Thay myay gyee shin shwe hti" — "Death or glory". Squadron code: "FM".

263 Squadron — flew Whirlwinds from RAF Warmwell [19-23 December 1941] and returned the following autumn [13 September 1942-20 February 1943]. After a short break they were back again [15 March-19 June 1943] and then re-equipped with Mark Ib Typhoons [12 July-5 December 1943]. They came back to Warmwell in the spring [6-19 March 1944]. During the Battle of Normandy they were briefly stationed at RAF Hurn [10-23 July 1944]. Motto: "Ex ungue Ieonis" — "From his claws one knows the lion". Squadron code: "HE".

266 (Rhodesia) Squadron — flew Mark Ib Typhoons from RAF Warmwell [21 September 1942-8 January 1943]. Briefly stationed at RAF Hurn during the Battle of Normandy [13-20 July 1944]. Motto: "Hlabezezulu" — "The stabber of the sky". Squadron code: "ZH".

277 Squadron — operated three Walrus amphibians and six Air-Sea Rescue Spitfires from RAF Warmwell [1943-44] and RAF Hurn [18-29 August 1944]. They then returned to Warmwell Aerodrome. Motto: "Quaerendo servamus" — "We save by seeking". Squadron code: "BA".

295 Squadron — flew Halifax tug-planes towing Horsa gliders, from RAF Hurn [1943-44], temporarily departing to take part in airborne landing during the invasion of Sicily [9 July 1943]. Left for RAF Harwell [14 March 1944]. Motto: "In caelo auxilium" — "Aid from the skies". Squadron code: "8Z".

296 (Army Co-Operational) Squadron — flew Whitleys from RAF Hurn, making paratroop drops for the 1st Airborne Division [1942]. Re-equipped with Albemarle troop-carriers and left to take part in the invasion of Sicily [9 July 1943]. Left for RAF Brize Norton [14 March 1944]. Motto: "Prepared for all things". Squadron code: "7C".

297 (Army Co-Operation) Squadron — flew Whitleys from RAF Hurn [1942] on Special Duties across the Channel, dropping agents for the Special Operations Executive and supplies for resistance groups. They left for RAF Stoney Cross [spring 1944] and from there to Brize Norton. Squadron code: "LS".

298 Squadron — flew Halifax tug-planes, towing gliders, from RAF Tarrant Rushton [1943-44]. Motto: "Silent we strike". Squadron code: "8A".

302 (Poznanski) Squadron — flew Hurricane IIb fighters from RAF Warmwell [5 September-11 October 1941] and returned briefly, re-equipped with the Mark Vb Spitfire [27 April-1 May 1942]. They were a Polish squadron. Squadron code: "WX".

312 Squadron — a Czech unit, briefly flew Mark Vb and Vc Spitfires from RAF Warmwell [20-24 April 1942; 19-31 May 1942] and then made a longer return visit [20 February-14 March 1943]. Motto: "Non multi sed multa" — "Not many men but many deeds". Squadron code: "DU".

401 (Royal Canadian Air Force / Ram) Squadron — briefly flew Mark IXb Spitfires from RAF Warmell [24 October-4 November 1944]. Motto: "Mors cellerima hostibus" — "Very swift death to the enemy". Squadron code: "YO".

402 (Royal Canadian Air Force / Winnipeg Bear) Squadron — flew Mark IIb Hurricanes from RAF Warmwell, on ground-attack offensive sweeps over Normandy and Brittany [6 November 1941-4 March 1942]. These were the "Hurri-bomber" variant of the Hawker Hurricane.

The squadron returned to Warmwell with Mark XIVe Spitfires [14 January-2 February 1945]. Squadron code: "AE".

403 (Royal Canadian Air Force) Squadron — briefly flew Mark XVI Spitfires from RAF Warmwell [4-14 January 1945]. Motto: "Stalk and strike". Squadron code: "KH".

411 (Royal Canadian Air Force) Squadron — briefly flew Mark IXe Spitfires from RAF Warmwell [15-23 October 1944]. Motto: "Inimicus inimico" — "Hostile to an enemy". Squadron code: "DB".

412 (Royal Canadian Air Force) Squadron — briefly flew Mark Vb Spitfires from RAF Hurn [1-6 March 1943]. Motto: "Promptus advindictum" — "Swift to avenge". Squadron code: "VZ".

418 (City of Edmonton) Squadron — briefly flew Mark II Mosquito night-fighters from RAF Hurn, during the Battle of Normandy [14-29 July 1944]. Motto: "Piyautailili" — "Defend even unto death". Squadron code: "TH".

438 (Royal Canadian Air Force) Squadron — flew Mark IV Hurricanes from RAF Hurn [18 March-3 April 1944] and returned re-equipped with rocket-firing Mark Ib Typhoons for the D-Day period [19 April-27 June 1944]. Came back to Dorset the following spring, to RAF Warmwell [19 March-3 April 1945]. Motto: "Going down". Squadron code: "F3".

439 (Royal Canadian Air Force) Squadron — flew Mark IV Hurricanes from RAF Hurn [18 March-2 April 1944] and returned for another short period [19 April-11 May 1944]. They were then re-equipped with rocket-firing Mark Ib Typhoons and were stationed at Hurn through the D-Day period [20 May-27 June 1944]. Came back to Dorset, to RAF Warmwell, towards the end of the war [3-22 April 1945]. Motto: "Fangs of death". Squadron code: "5V".

440 (Royal Canadian Air Force) Squadron — flew Mark IV Hurricanes from RAF Hurn [18 March-3 April 1944] and returned re-equipped with Mark Ib Typhoons for the D-Day period [20 April-28 June 1944]. Came back to Dorset to RAF Warmwell, for the final fortnight of the war [23 April-8 May 1945]. Motto: "Ka Ganawaitah Saguenay" — "He who guards the Saguenay". Squadron code: "I8".

433 (Royal Canadian Air Force / Hornet) Squadron — briefly flew Mark IXb Spitfires from RAF Warmwell [18 December 1944-3 January 1945]. Motto: "Our sting is death". Squadron code: "21".

461 (Royal Australian Air Force) Squadron — flew Sunderland flying-boats from RAF Hamworthy [31 August 1942-21 April 1943]. Carried out anti-submarine duties for Coastal Command in the English Channel and South-Western Approaches. Motto: "They shall not pass unseen". Squadron code: "UT".

504 (County of Nottingham) Squadron — flew Spitfires from RAF Hurn on escort duties, to protect American Flying Fortress bombers as they crossed the English Channel on daylight raids [10-14 July 1943]. Motto: "Vindicat in ventis" — "It avenges in the wind". Squadron code: "TM".

570 Squadron — flew Albemarle troop and glider transports from RAF Hurn. Left for Harwell [14 March 1944]. Motto: "Impetum deducimus" — "We launch the spearhead". Squadron code: "E7".

601 (County of London) Squadron — its Hurricanes were visitors to RAF Warmwell, to escort war Premier Winston Churchill to Paris, for secret talks on the collapse of France after the German invasion [31 May 1940]. Squadron code: "UF".

604 (County of Middlesex) Squadron — flew Mark XIII Mosquitoes from RAF Hurn, through the D-Day period [3 May-13 July 1944]. Motto: "Si vis pacem, para bellum" — "If you want peace, prepare for war". Squadron code: "RAK".

609 (West Riding) Squadron — flew Mark I Spitfires from RAF Warmwell, throughout the Battle of Britain. Initially they were day visitors to the station, from Middle Wallop, Hampshire, to which they returned each night [16 July-2 October 1940]. They then were based full-time at Warmwell [until 24 February 1941]. Motto: "Tally Ho!". Squadron code: "PR".

633 Squadron — fictional Royal Air Force unit created by Bournemouth author Frederick Escreet Smith, based around the real-life precision bombing raids carried out by Mosquitoes during the final year of the war in Europe.

644 Squadron — flew Halifax tug-planes, towing gliders, from RAF Tarrant Rushton [1943-44]. Motto: "Dentes draconis serimus" — "We saw the dragon's teeth". Squadron code: "9U".

737 Royal Naval Air Squadron — reformed with Westland Whirlwind helicopters for airborne anti-submarine training at Portland Royal Naval Air Station [24 April 1959].

765 Fleet Air Arm Squadron — operated Walrus amphibians and Seafox float-planes, later Vought Kingfisher float-planes, from Royal Naval Air Station Sandbanks [June 1941-15 October 1943].

772 Fleet Air Arm Squadron — flew Swordfish biplanes as a Fleet Requirements Unit in Portland Harbour [September 1939], attached to the Anti-Submarine School, until removal to Dunoon and Campbelltown following the Luftwaffe's occupation of airfields on the Cherbourg peninsula [July 1940].

793 Fleet Air Arm Squadron — trained at Chickerell Aerodrome [1939-40].

815 Royal Naval Air Squadron — flew Lynx helicopters from Portland Royal Naval Air Station in anti-submarine training flights [1975-88].

829 Royal Naval Air Squadron — flew Lynx helicopters from Portland Royal Naval Air Station in anti-submarine training flights [1975-90].

Stainforth — Weymouth College old boy **Wing Commander George Stainforth** [killed October 1942] rose to fame in 1931 when he took the world airspeed record in Schneider trophy flights. He pushed his Supermarine S-6B round the Spithead course at an average speed of 340 miles per hour and raised the world's absolute speed record to 379.05 mph. Other records included flying upside down for a duration of eleven minutes seven seconds and the title of RAF revolver champion.

Finally, as Wing Commander in the Middle East, he was the oldest fighter pilot serving in that theatre. He was shot down in night fighting, his particular forte.

Stalbridge crash — of Lysander L6860 belonging to 41 Operational Training Unit of the Royal Air Force [7 October 1941].

Staples — Spitfire flyer **Pilot Officer Michael Staples** of 609 Squadron from RAF Warmwell was shot down in one of the dog-fights over the Blackmore Vale following the bombing of the Westland Aircraft factory at Yeovil [7 October 1940]. He was seriously injured in the leg and baled out at 21,000 feet, as the fighter began its plunge into riverside meadows at Child Okeford. Staples recovered in Blandford Cottage Hospital, but never rejoined his squadron.

Starfish — codename of the Major Strategic Night Decoy at the west end of Brownsea Island in Poole Harbour. It successfully drew bombs intended for RAF Hamworthy [25 May 1942] and saved Poole and Bournemouth from a total of 1,000 tons of high explosive.

Starlight — codename for RAF Sopley, north of Christchurch, for its direction of night-fighters to intercept German aircraft [1942-44].

Station 416 — Advance Landing Group Christchurch, converted into a base for P-47 Thunderbolt fighter-bombers [7 March-11 July 1944] of the 9th United States Army Air Force by laying temporary wire-mesh runways across the grass at Christchurch Aerodrome, Somerford.

Station 454 — RAF Warmwell during its secondment to the 474th Fighter Group of the United States Army Air Force [12 March-15 August 1944], flying Lockheed P-38 Lightnings.

Steborowski — Polish Hurricane pilot **Flying Officer Michal Jan Steborowski** [1909-40] was shot down and killed off the Dorset coast, between White Nothe and Lulworth Cove in P3819 of 238 Squadron from RAF Middle Wallop [10.45 hours, 11 August 1940].

Steeple crashes — in the south-east corner of the parish, on the northern side of Smedmore Hill, of three North American P-51 Mustang Mark XV fighter-bombers belonging to 2 Squadron Royal Air Force, based at RAF Sawbridgeworth, Hertfordshire, but flying from Thruxton in Hampshire [26 May 1943]. They had taken off at 16.50 hours on Ranger Operation Asphalt. This cross-Channel offensive action was to have been against rail movements in the Rennes-Laval area.

They flew south-west in line abrest formation of ten aircraft, until reaching a wall of fog between Kimmeridge and St Alban's Head, where the order to climb was given by Flight-Lieutenant G. Kenning at 17.35 hours.

Seven of the aircraft were able to clear Smedmore Hill but the other three-code letters U, Y and W — crashed into the north-facing slope. Their three pilots were killed — Flying Officer W. J. Miller, Pilot Officer J. B. McLeod, and Flying Officer D. Hirst.

The remaining Mustangs returned to Thruxton after having failed to locate the missing aircraft. Flying Officer M.F. Dunkerley returned late with hydraulic failure but was able to effect a safe landing. The operation was then cancelled.

VETERAN FLYER: NO OTHER MATCHED THE RECORD OF SQUADRON LEADER LOUIS ARBON STRANGE OF WORTH MATRAVERS, WHO WAS IN AERIAL COMBAT THROUGHOUT THE GREAT WAR AND RETURNED TO ACTIVE SERVICE IN FRANCE IN 1940, BRINGING A HURRICANE HOME AND GOING ON TO TRAIN PARATROOPS.

Strange — pioneer aviator **Lieutenant-Colonel / Wing Commander Louis Arbon Strange** [1891-1966] was born at Keynston Mill, Tarrant Keynston; moved to East Almer, Sturminster Marshall; farmed at Worth Matravers; had a caravan at Warmwell; left for a derelict cottage near Wincanton; retired to Winterborne Kingston; and is buried in Worth Matravers churchyard.

Visited the Bournemouth Aviation Meeting and mounted guard with the Dorsetshire Yeomanry on the body of crashed avaitor Honourable Charles Rolls [July 1910]. Went up for his first flight with Lewis Turner of Sturminster Newton, from Race Down, Blandford [1911], and learned to fly at Hendon [1913]. Predicted the use of aeroplanes for military reconnaissance and became one of the first Britons to copy Frenchman Adolphe Pegoud's "upside-down-loop". Specialised in unconventional "ragtime flying" and won the first leg of the London-Manchester-London Air Race, 35 minutes ahead of the next of the seven flyers, but was then immobilised at Trafford Park as the heavyweight Lord Mayor, leading 100,000 spectators, clambered aboard and snapped a bracing wire that then smashed the propeller [20 June 1914]. He also won dummy bombing contests, dropping bags of flour to within 25 feet of the target, from 300 feet. By now Lieutenant Strange was seconded by the Dorsetshire Yeomanry to the Royal Flying Corps [May 1914], training at Upavon on Salisbury Plain. Landed on his Yeomanry chums in Crichel Park, terrifying their horses, to collect bets. Ordered to report to 5 Squadron, at Gosport, on the declaration of war [4 August 1914].

He was the last of 37 RFC pilots to fly four squadrons from rendezvous at Dover to the war in France, and the only one to do so with a Lewis machine-gun, in Henry Farman F-20 No.341 [06.00 hours, 14 August 1914]. Only seven of these first flyers would survive the Great War; Strange doing so still in squadron service, decorated with the Distinguished Service Order, Distinguished Flying Cross, and Military Cross.

A "very good recce" proved the value of aerial reconnaissance, showing the German First Army was no longer heading for Paris, and Strange became the first flyer to fire a machine-gun at the enemy, and among the first to attack ground troops, with petrol bombs. Likewise he was one of the first to shoot down a German aircraft, a two-seater Aviatik, with the Lewis gun from his new Avro-504, above Armentieres [22 November 1914]. The war was not over by Christmas, but it was supposed to be a day off from hostilities. Strange broke off from the hampers and chocolates, courtesy Queen Mary, and flew alone across the silent lines to deliver a present to the Germans at Fives Aerodrome, Lille — they ran for cover as a football bounced across the grass [25 December 1914].

Promoted Captain Strange and transferred to a BE-2c of 6 Squadron, he bombed two trains at Coutrai station, from 50 feet, in the first tactical bombing in history. Witnessed the first poison gas attack of the war, in the Ypres salient [22 April 1915].

He was provided with a single-seater Martinsyde Scout, armed with a Lewis gun, but this was hit by a German Albatross on its first flight, rupturing the oil tank. Strange reverted to Hendon-style aerobatics and flew upside-down in a roll to land on a track in hop-fields.

Later, at 8,000 feet above Menin, his gun jammed as he attacked an Aviatik. Wedging the stick between his knees and trying to change the drum, he found the Martinsyde going into a spin and hurling him from the cockpit. He literally hung on for his life from the inverted machine, clinging to the troublesome drum of the gun he had been trying to free, and kicked his way back into the cockpit, where he "jammed on full aileron and elevator" and fell "into my seat with a bump". Despite jammed controls he managed to pull out of the dive at the last possible moment and return to his aerodrome.

Acted as a decoy for Major Lanoe Hawker, luring two German aircraft to their doom under the gunfire from Hawker's new Bristol Scout [15 July 1915]. Two kills in one day was just about unprecedented and Hawker was awarded the first Victoria Cross for aerial combat. Captain Strange was by now the longest serving pilot on the Western Front; he was ordered to depart for Dorset on home leave [2 August 1915]. From here he progressed to the new 12 Squadron, forming at Netheravon, as Flight Commander, and took it from Hawkinge to France. His presence at St-Omer was unauthorised, however, and Major-General H.M. Trenchard caught him attaching a Lewis gun to a BE-2c. "Go home at once, Strange," Trenchard boomed, "in that machine, now". He pointed to a dilapidated Maurice Farman [September 1915].

His next task, at Gosport, was to form and command 23 Squadron, in Avro No.4741 [21 September 1915] with orders to have it trained and operational by 1 January 1916. In fact they did not receive their full quota of FE-2b fighters for another couple of weeks [18 January 1916] and illness prevented him taking them to the Western Front. Acute appendicitis led to emergency surgery at Cosham Military Hospital during which he was sewn-up with a swab mislaid in his stomach. It would keep him in the Home Establishment for two years, convincing the RFC that gunnery training was an imperative, and that flying at low level also had to be practised. He commanded the Machine Gun School at Hythe and turned it into No.1 School of Air Gunnery, increasing its output from 20 trainees a month to 120. In the process he rebelled against tented accommodation and requisitioned the Imperial Hotel, part of the Town Hall, Tilling and Stevens Omnibus Company, Lympne Aerodrome, and the Golf Links ("for a rifle range"). It also gave him the excuse to slip across to France, visiting the French School of Aerial Gunnery at Cazeaux and his best friend Lanoe Hawker with his aggressive 24 Squadron; whose DH-2s had the reputation amongst Germans and Allies alike as being the only flyers who were a fair match for the feared Fokker Eindekker and its cowling-mounted Parabellum machine-gun. It would be the last time Major Hawker would meet his old friend; Manfred von Richthofen in his personalised Albatross D-2 prevented Hawker's escape at treetop height and shot him through the back of the head with a fatal burst from twin Spandau guns firing through the arc of his propeller.

Back in Britain, promoted Lieutenant-Colonel, Louis Strange was appointed Assistant Commander of the Central Flying School at Upavon, Wiltshire [April 1917]. He not only unbanned aerobatics but taught them, and returned yet again to France to see the rapidly developing tactics in front-line fighting and fly combat patrols with 60 Squadron, in a Nieuport Scout [June 1917]. Home again, he then appointed himself as the test pilot at Upavon of new and adapted machines.

Younger brother Ben Strange joined him as an instructor at Upavon, from where they both flew back to Dorset, before leaving for France and an SE-5 of 40 Squadron. On the integration of the Royal Flying Corps and the Royal Naval Air Service, henceforth the Royal Air Force [1 April 1918], Louis Strange was given command of No.23 (Training Wing) and conducted King George V and Queen Mary around his Cranwell base, having flown from Waddington and failed to find the aerodrome in mist. He landed in a field three miles away and walked from there to his royal rendezvous.

His wish to return to combat in France was eventually granted, to command 80 Wing, newly formed under General Ludlow Hewitt.

He found the reconnaissance function had extended into offensive ground support for the Army and attacks on bases behind enemy lines. For this purpose he had 2 and 4 Squadrons of the Australian Flying Corps (with the SE-5); 46 Squadron of the RAF (with the Camel); 88 Squadron of the RAF (with the Bristol Fighter); and 103 Squadron of the RAF (with the DH-9). Additionally, 54 Squadron and 92 Squadron of the RAF were promised later, when they became operational.

Strange concentrated his efforts on attacking German airfields to destroy aeroplanes on the ground — arguing that tactical strikes would be far more effective than trying to shoot them down in the air. He flew to his squadrons almost every day and joined them on patrols and bombing raids. In one engagement he was "thoroughly sat upon by four Fokkers" and destroyed one and damaged another, but then had his Camel almost ripped apart by friendly fire when he made the basic mistake of making a victory swoop across Allied lines and was mistaken for the enemy. Some things had not changed. If in doubt, open fire; that was the rule of survival on the ground.

His greatest "show" came with organising and leading, with Australian ace Captain Harry Cobby, the entire 65 aircraft of 80 Wing in a devastating ground attack that delivered 150 bombs and 20,000 rounds of gunfire into Bruno von Leutzer's aerodrome at Haubourdin [15 August 1918]. All 65 returned safely.

The following day he repeated the performance, with no one aware of the target until Louis Strange appeared on the airfield with a reconnaissance photograph of the German aerodrome at Lomme. "All yours," he told Cobby, and again followed his left wing-tip. It was a ditto situation of complete destruction with "all the six hangars enveloped in black smoke clouds, edged with reddish-yellow flames". The Germans had moved in anti-aircraft guns but it was still a ditto situation, of the previous day's result, with both Haubourdin and Lomme being abandoned for the duration of the war. Cobby wrote of Strange: "He was one of those persons with more than the average issue of guts. All he wanted was to be let loose in any old sort of trouble ... I used to devote a lot of time to studying where one met with most 'hate' so that Strange would get a bellyful next time he wanted to get out!"

He also had reunions with Ben Strange by flying a couple of times into Bryas where his brother was an over-enthusiastic newly promoted Flight Commander for hard-pressed 40 Squadron. As he sensed, Ben would be lost on a dawn patrol, shot down after destroying a Hun in a dogfight over Cambrai [24 September 1918]: "Ben had gone to join all those other good friends of his and mine."

The citation for Louis Strange's DFC credits him with organising the low-flying raids by 80 Wing and examples an occasion [30 October 1918] when "he accompanied one of these raids against an aerodrome; watching the work of his machines, he waited until they had finished then dropped his bombs from 100 feet altitude on hangars that were undamaged, then attacked troops and transport in the vicinity of the aerodrome. Whilst thus engaged he saw eight Fokkers flying above him; at once he climbed and attacked them single-handed; having driven one down out of control he was fiercely engaged by the other seven, but he maintained the combat until rescued by a patrol of our Scouts."

The last days of the war saw a German rout and as well as airfields the Wing attacked retreating columns, with "many lorries burnt and destroyed by direct hits, many casualties caused amongst massed troops on the roads".

An orderly woke Strange with an "Urgent" message [02.00 hours, 11 November 1918]: "HOSTILITIES will cease at 11.00 today and no operations should be undertaken which cannot be completed by that hour" ... "Then I turned over and went to sleep again, dimly wondering what on earth we were going to do with ourselves in the morning without a war." The following day he flew his battered Camel to a reunion with wife Marjorie at Sutton Scotney on the Hampshire Downs and introduced himself to his son Brian, aged two months. His final endurance in the backlash of war, after 1,000 hours of wartime flying, was the influenza pandemic that carried off so many of the young and the fit who had considered themselves survivors.

In peacetime he took command of the Flying Wing of the Royal Air Force Cadet College, Cranwell, under Air Marshal Charles Longcroft, retiring as Lieutenant-Colonel Strange of the Dorsetshire Regiment [1922] to the family farm, now 1,300 acres at Worth Matravers. Inevitably, selling milk through drought and depression was pedestrian compared with the life that was still in his blood. The age of long-distance flight was all over the newspapers and newsreels. He was determined to play his part and became a director of Spartan Aircraft until, as Spartan Airlines Limited, it merged with Hillman's Airways and United Airways [1935].

Establishing the Swanage and Isle of Purbeck Light Aeroplane Club [1926] was followed by London-Berlin non-stop flights in his Simmonds Spartan with two up [24 October 1928]. The return flight was also non-stop and two up [27 October 1928]. These exploits are documented in his memoirs, *Recollections of an Airman* [1933], and expanded in *Flying Rebel: The story of Louis Strange*, by parachutist and novelist Group Captain Peter Hearn [1994].

That gives both halves in what soon becomes an amazing biography. Louis Strange returned to the sky for the Second World War, as Acting Pilot Officer Strange with 24 Squadron at Hendon [April 1940], flew to France and repaired abandoned Hurricanes at Merville, one of which he took back to Manston, chased by Messerschmitt Me.109s, on being ordered to return to England "as best he could". That added a bar to his Great War DFC. He then flew back to Paris and brought the last of 24 Squadron's Rapides out of France. Air Minister Harold Balfour took his hat off to him, with congratulations for showing "that the old men when put to it can do as well as the youngsters".

Sir Peter Masefield, a fellow pilot of the 1930s, wrote: "Strange revelled in action, flew with gusto, cheerfully rebelled against the rigid order of things, and endeared himself to a host of friends and colleagues, though not always to higher authorities." Richard Townshend bickers: "Louis Strange was one of the most electrifying personalities I ever met."

His next posting was to the new Parachute Training School at RAF Ringway, Manchester [24 June 1940]. He found himself Squadron Leader Strange, en route to the Parachute Development Unit at RAF Henlow. Pioneer aviator Lord Egerton loaned him Tatton Park, Cheshire, as the drop-zone, and Louis Strange at age 49 made the first jump of his life, from one of his four Whitleys [13 July 1940]. Others followed, in the call of wartime duty rather than for the thrill of the thing, from the removed rear gun-turret of the bomber. They soon decided it made more sense to jump through the bombing hole in the fuselage.

Troop-carrying gliders followed, delivered by road from the Airspeed factory at Christchurch. Strange flew operations for the secret war, over occupied Europe, and dropped a Dutch naval operative near Leiden [August 1940]. A "large-scale" parachute exercise was provided for General Bernard Montgomery at Shrewton on Salisbury Plain [3 December 1940]. Winston Churchill visited the airborne forces at Ringway [26 April 1941] and was told by Strange that "we could have trained ten times the number". He went on to an indiscretion, criticising delays and indecision between the Air Ministry and War Office, in the fall-out from which he was relieved of his post.

His next job, at RAF Speke, Liverpool, was training pilots for Hurricats — seaborne catapult-launched Hurricanes — in the new Merchant Ships Fighter Unit [12 May 1941]. Characteristically, Strange would be the first to fly rocket-launched Sea Hurricane 7253 from a ramped platform at Speke, demolishing "all top secrecy ... also the protecting screen, which the blast of the rockets blew almost out of the aerodrome". He calculated 0 to 75 mph in 80 feet "with G-force distorting one's face, flash, and 200 feet over the Mersey". Rockets were much more fun than the other end of the procedure, which was preparing for "ditching and dinghy". They trained pilots for 804 Royal Naval Air Squadron of the Fleet Air Arm, at RNAS Sydenham, Belfast, for the Battle of the Atlantic.

Strange's next command was RAF Valley, Anglesey, and he then joined No.11 Group Fighter Command Headquarters at RAF Uxbridge. Wing Commander Strange's following station command was RAF Hawkinge [18 December 1942] and from there to No.12 Group Fighter Command Headquarters at RAF Watnall, Nottingham. Next it was the new No.46 Group Transport Command Headquarters, a London-based offshoot of No.38 Group at Netheravon, Wiltshire, and the return to Airborne Training [27 December 1943]. That gave him a Dakota and a 150-aircraft mass drop of paras, once more at Shrewton [14 April 1943].

He appointed himself Group observer for D-Day, aboard the first Dakota of the leading squadron of the 6th Airborne Division, with Squadron Leader "Dusty" Miller [6 June 1944]. They crossed the Channel between Arundel Castle and Littlehampton and on the other side saw 100 Lancasters bombing the German coastal defences at Merville, with the drop-zone 15 minutes away, where the red warning light came on "for the longest four seconds in a man's life". The hand goes down on Number One's shoulder as it turns to green, with all 16 dropping in eight seconds, as two more sticks of 16 descended from Dakotas two and three: "For a moment the great aircraft felt very lonely and empty. The urge to follow those splendid troops was almost irresistible."

So he did, landing with 20 Dakotas on a hastily bulldozed strip, in sight of the enemy, henceforth No.46 Group Advanced Headquarters [15 June 1944]. Inward came personnel and supplies; outwards in the next three months went 50,000 wounded from the Battle of Normandy. He based himself in a rectory at Magny, near Bayeux, and established six airstrips. From there they made the leaps to Evreux, Bernay, and Orly, in Paris. They were told it had been allocated to the Americans and were given Le Bourget instead, still technically in German hands, but in fact abandoned and mined. "The RAF Ensign was run up over the control tower" [10.00 hours, 30 August 1944], and opened for flights thanks to the efforts of German prisoners and the French, a week before the promised arrival of an Airfield Construction Company.

A grass strip was next, at Amiens, where they became 111 Wing and the priority for the Dakotas was fuel, in jerrycans, for tanks of 30th Armoured Corps and the fighters of the 2nd Tactical Air Force. From here he landed in arable stubble beside Nivelles Airfield, Belgium, and found himself in the care of the Belgian Resistance who took him into Brussels for one of the greatest parties in history, "like the densest football crowd ever seen, swaying, singing and cheering continuously . . . hugging and kissing the troops". He hung the sign "111 Wing RAF" on the door of the Astoria Hotel and then took over the Chateau Lillois, to the popping of more champagne corks.

His early criticism of what became the Arnhem debacle led this time to a part in planning the final airborne operations of the war — across the Rhine and to protect prisoner of war camps — as Assistant Deputy Chief of Staff at the Headquarters 1st Allied Airborne Army, linking the four American and two British Airborne Divisions (now effectively reduced to one). He was the only officer from the Royal Flying Corps at the start of the Great War who also ended the Second World War with combat responsibilities. Demobilisation was followed by what could have been a lifetime of squadron reunions. When he could, he attended by air, such as at the age of 68 when he flew himself from Thruxton to RAF Coltishall [1960]. He had flown 115 different aircraft types, from a Caudron and the Claude Grahame-White Box Kite [1913] to an Auster Taylorcraft [1949] and the Venom jet fighter [1955].

Amid all this he suffered a clinical depression verging on hypomania and was certified insane at his wife's instigation, on which he discharged himself, and left Marjorie for dilapidated Campson Cottage near Wincanton.

The place at Worth where he used to land became known as Aerodrome Field — indeed he called it "Swanage Aerodrome" — and was subsequently the village football pitch.

Stratton crash — what appears to have been a Junkers Ju.87 "Stuka" or a Messerschmitt Bf.110 fighter-bomber crashed behind Grimstone viaduct, in Stratton parish, as the RAF ripped through the Luftwaffe's Adlertag (Eagle Day) attack [13 August 1940].

Strickland — Hurricane pilot **Flying Officer James Murray Strickland** [1919-41] had an eventful Battle of Britain in combat across Dorset. Serving with 213 Squadron from RAF Exeter he put down a Junkers Ju.88 bomber (B3+DC) in style beside Blacknor Fort, Portland [11 August 1940]. He also survived his own crash-landings, after being shot down near Redhill [27 September 1940] and then over Swanage [15 October 1940].

He was awarded the Distinguished Flying Cross [22 October 1940] but his luck would run out when flying a Spitfire from Portreath, in an accident the following year [14 August 1941]. Born in Iloilo, Phillipines, of British parents, he is buried at Ivybridge Cemetery, Devon.

Stringfellow — aviation pioneer **John Stringfellow** [1799-1883], working in Chard, devised a series of steam-powered models that he believed to be capable of flight. The first was designed in collaboration with William Samuel Henson [1812-88] who would emigrate to America. Their monoplane, the Aerial Steam Carriage, had a 20-feet wing-span and was driven by twin pusher propellers [1847]. It was launched from an inclined ramp. Henson's model of the Aerial Steam Carriage is now in the London Science Museum. Claims for sustained flight of this and others of Stringfellow's design are regarded, at best, as unproven. Imaginary prints of such machines flying over the Pyramids and the Taj Mahal were greeted with ridicule.

Studland crashes — on the beach, then a minefield, by Flying Officer Alexander Rothwell Edge's Spitfire, of 609 Squadron from RAF Warmwell [18 July 1940]. Though covered by sea it would be salvaged and fly again. Edge, who was unhurt, was picked up by the Royal Navy.

Later in the Battle of Britain, a returning Heinkel He.111 bomber that had taken part in devastating the Bristol Aeroplane Company's works at Filton [25 September 1940], crash-landed at Westfield Farm, Studland. Wine waiter Theo Janku took the crew prisoner with an unloaded Home Guard rifle; villagers treated them kindly when it was realised there were casualties. Flight mechanic Josef Attrichter died a few minutes later.

Their bomber (G1+BH) belonged to Kampfgeschwader 55 and the kill was claimed by Hurricanes of 238 Squadron from RAF Middle Wallop.

The Heinkel was relatively undamaged and would be salvaged and reassembled for Cardiff war weapons week.

Sturminster Marshall crashes — Heinkel He.111 (1G+AC), returning to France after bombing Bristol docks, crashed in flames at Sturminster Marshall [12 August 1940]. It belonged to Kampfgeschwader 27 and was being flown by a Gruppenkommander.

During the Cold War an F-111 swing-wing fighter-bomber of the 20th Tactical Wing of the United States Air Force plunged into a hill half a mile from Mapperton, west of Sturminster Marshall [29 April 1980]. The crewmen were Jack Hines of Pennsylvania and Richard Franks of New York. Both were killed, and the impact left a 15-feet crater with wreckage strewn over 500 yards. Cattle panicked in the fields.

It was the second F-111 that had come low over Winterborne Zelston, Bere Regis, and then the hamlet of Almer. The first plane was not involved in the crash and returned safely to its base, Upper Heyford in Oxfordshire. They had been on a routine training flight and were unarmed.

Royal Navy helicopters later landed to help collect wreckage. Because of its sophisticated and secret electronics, Dorset police declared the area a restricted zone.

Mapperton — the farm's placename — caused some confusion for the recovery teams. One helicopter landed at Maperton village near Wincanton (22 miles to the north-west). It dropped into a paddock close to the country mansion of singer Georgie Fame, before realising the mistake.

A kit-built Montgomery-Bensen B&M Autogyro — similar to that apparently flown by Sean Connery as James Bond in the film You Only Live Twice — crashed on the north side of the A31 near the Stag Gate entrance to Charborough Park [11 December 1993]. Professional pilot Paul Crook [1936-93], who flew Falcon jets for FR Aviation from Hurn (Bournemouth) Airport, was killed instantly as the "flying motorbike" dropped like a stone. He was on a test flight to decide whether to buy one — there were said to be only fifteen such machines in the country.

Both machine and pilot had been in working order. Crook probably caused the crash, investigators concluded, by his own instinctive fixed-wing reactions. On encountering turbulence, as he climbed to 200-feet, he had moved the control column forward. This would increase the speed of a normal aircraft and therefore create lift. An autogyro handles differently, with its top rotor reducing speed, so the machine stalled and nose-dived.

Sunrider — para-motor for mobile parachuting, enabling take-off from level ground instead of a hilltop or aircraft, designed and built by Chris Scoble at his home in Rushall Lane, Lytchett Matravers. The motor is attached to the enthusiast's back.

Sutcliffe — RAF chaplain **Rev John Farrar Sutcliffe**, from Shillingstone, was killed in an air crash in North Africa [18 September 1942].

Sutton — electronics engineer **Robert Sutton** [1905-98] developed the "Sutton Tube", a practical and tunable low-noise oscillator, in the wartime Telecommunications Research Establishment, at Worth Matravers and Langton Matravers [September 1940]. A modification, containing a low pressure gas, was nicknamed the "Soft Sutton" and came into use as a switching device. His team included Frank Skinner who developed a silicon-crystal mixer [early 1941].

Sutton continued to make electronic gadgets, at the post-war Services Electronics Research Laboratory, Baldock, and maintained a lifelong interest in aviation, which culminated in learning to fly a helicopter, at the age of 90.

Sutton Waldron crash — at Vale Farm, of Spitfire X4472 of 609 Squadron from RAF Warmwell, during the dog-fights following the bombing of the Westland Aircraft Company works at Yeovil [16.00 hours, 7 October 1940]. Flight-Lieutenant Frank Howell stayed with his aircraft and made a successful forced-landing. The fighter was repairable.

Swanage Aerodrome — opened with a flying display [16 August 1928] and was located in the parish of Worth Matravers, on The Plain between the village and St Alban's Head. Operated by the Isle of Purbeck Light Aeroplane Club and organised by veteran local flyer Lieutenant-Colonel Louis Strange.

Swanage crashes — of a Messerschmitt Bf.110 in the Battle of Britain, claimed by Flying Officer John Dundas flying a Spitfire of 609 Squadron from RAF Warmwell [11 August 1940].

Brian Sharpe of Tunbridge Wells has informed me of another wartime crash, this time one of ours: "On a Saturday afternoon I recall a Spitfire came low over the bay and town with engine spluttering and crashed through a hedge at Ulwell, close to Godlingston brickworks. I believe the pilot was killed."

There were many more crashes, from both sides, into the sea. Swanage had an RAF Air-Sea Rescue launch that operated in this particularly busy central sector of the English Channel, from Portland Bill in Dorset to St Catherine's Point in the Isle of Wight.

Battle of Britain losses inflicted on the RAF off Swanage included:

Spitfire of 609 Squadron from RAF Warmwell [8 July 1940].

Spitfire R6634 of 609 Squadron shot down by the gunner of a Junkers Ju.88 bomber [18 July 1940].

Hurricane P3766 of 238 Squadron [20 July 1940].

Hurricane of 501 Squadron [20 July 1940].

Spitfire K9880 of 152 Squadron [20 July 1940].

Hurricane P2978 of 238 Squadron [11 August 1940].

Spitfire K9882 of 152 Squadron [26 September 1940].

Swanage, City of — see entry for *City of Swanage*.

Swanage RAF Hospital — established towards the end of the Great War for convalescent cases. Captain Clement Perronet Sells of the Royal Army Medical Corps "died on July 4th 1919 at RAF Hospital Swanage, of illness contracted on Active Service, Aged 29 years".

He is buried in Northbrook Road Cemetery. A nearby stone is to Flight-Lieutenant P. L. T. Lewin of the RAF who died on 9 September 1919.

Sydling St Nicholas crashes — of a Messerschmitt Bf.109 shot down at Hundred Acres Field, Spriggs Farm [16.40 hours, 30 September 1940]. It belonged to the 5th Staffel of fighter wing Jagdgeschwader 2 Richthofen. It came from the south and the pilot, Unteroffizier Alois Dollinger, had baled out over Grimstone, near Stratton. The parachute failed to open and he fell to his death. The Black-2 had flown from Octeville, Le Havre, and was escorting the Luftwaffe attack that ended with bombs being jettisoned on Sherborne. This was the longest range of all the Bf.109 crashes of 1940.

A Junkers Ju.88 bomber (9K+SN), heading for the Westland Aircraft factory at Yeovil, was brought down on Tappers Hill, above the hamlet of Up Sydling [16.20 hours, 7 October 1940]. The kill was claimed jointly by Sergeant Pilot Edmund Shepperd of 152 Squadron from RAF Warmwell and Flying Officer Bob Doe in a Hurricane of 238 Squadron from RAF Chilbolton.

All four members of the German crew baled out successfully and were taken prisoner of war, after being rounded up by shotgun, following which the farm labourers were said to have performed a victory dance around the wreckage. The crewmen were Oberleutnant Sigurd Dey, Leutnant Friedrick Bein, Oberfeldwebel Christian Koenig, and Oberfeldwebel Josef Troll.

The bomber belonged to the 5th Staffel of II Gruppe Kampfgruppe 51.

Sylvester — Hurricane flyer **Pilot Officer Edmund John Hilary Sylvester** [1914-40] of 501 Squadron, which had recently returned from France, was shot down over the sea between the Isle of Purbeck and Cherbourg peninsula [20 July 1940]. Born at Trowbridge, Wiltshire, he went to Harrow School, and volunteered for the pre-war Auxiliary Air Force. His body was not recovered.

Symondsbury crash — a Hurricane of 87 Squadron from RAF Exeter successfully crash-landed near the village after attempting to tackle a mass of German aircraft at the peak of the Battle of Britain [15 August 1940].

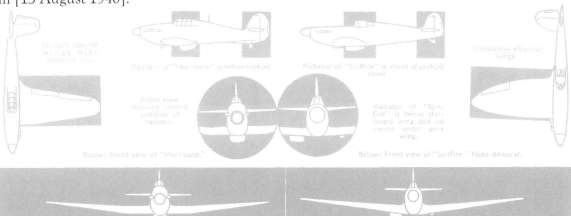

COMPARATIVE PROFILES: "ACHTUNG SPIT UND HURRI," AS THE LUFTWAFFE PILOTS WOULD RADIO TO EACH OTHER (THE HURRICANE IS LEFT AND THE SPITFIRE RIGHT).

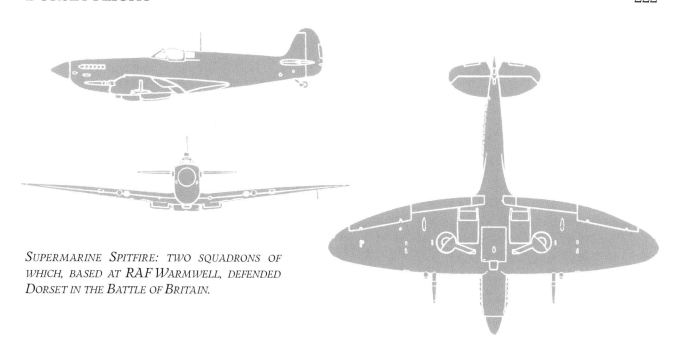

SUPERMARINE SPITFIRE: TWO SQUADRONS OF WHICH, BASED AT RAF WARMWELL, DEFENDED DORSET IN THE BATTLE OF BRITAIN.

THE "STUKA": THIS GERMAN DIVE-BOMBER, THE JUNKERS JU.87, WAS THE SCOURGE OF ALLIED SHIPPING OFF DORSET DUE TO THE PROXIMITY OF ITS BASES ON THE CHERBOURG PENINSULA.

Wings slope down to undercarriage struts. Dive-brakes under wings.

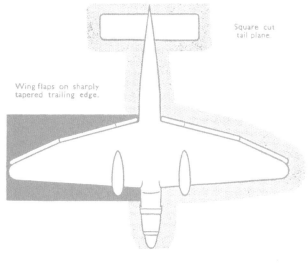

Wheel spats

Fixed wheel. Large square cut fin and rudders.

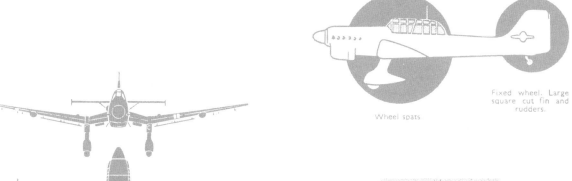

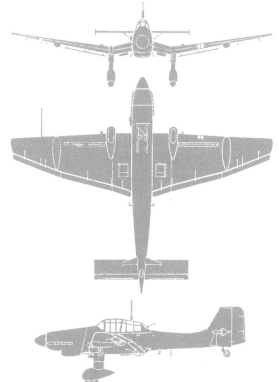

Square cut tail plane

Wing flaps on sharply tapered trailing edge.

T

T serial numbers of RAF aircraft:

T2439 Blenheim — see entry for Frampton crash.

T2565 Wellington — see entry for Telecommunications Research Establishment.

T4299 Whitley — see entry for Manston crash.

T9111 Sunderland — see entry for Poole Harbour crashes.

Talbot Village Aerodrome — now covered by the buildings of Bournemouth University and actually in the north-eastern extremity of the Borough of Poole (Ordnance Survey map reference SZ 075 936). Coming into being as Wallis Down Aerodrome [1909-10], by the time of the Great War it was known as Talbot Village Aerodrome, having become a training airfield, operated by the Bournemouth Aviation Company, as the Royal Flying Corps issued its call for thousands of new pilots [1915]. Some came to grief, including Second-Lieutenant Edward Rebbeck, from a mayoral estate-agency family, who crashed near the aerodrome [24 April 1916].

Organised flying then moved to the new Ensbury Park Racecourse [1917] but the old field resumed its flying traditions, intermittently, after Ensbury Park went under housing estates. Its final famous visitor was British aviatrix Amy Johnson, after her record-breaking return flight to Cape Town [1932].

Tarrant Gunville crash — at Bussey Stool Farm, of a Messerschmitt Bf.110 (S9+JH) killing veteran Luftwaffe pilot 27-year-old Martin Lutz, who had flown with the Condor Legion in the Spanish Civil War. The fighter-bomber, belonging to Erprobungsgruppe 210, an experimental unit from Cherbourg, gradually lost height until it hit trees and ploughed into the ground [27 September 1940]. Lutz had been leading an abortive raid on the Parnall Aircraft Company, at Yate, near Chipping Sodbury. Radio operator Anton Schon was also killed.

Tarrant Rushton Aerodrome — constructed by the Air Ministry [1942-43], on chalk downland between the Tarrant valley and Badbury Rings, four miles east of Blandford (Ordnance Survey map reference ST 950 060). Elevation 301 feet above sea level. Its north-south runway was 2,000 yards; the north-west to south-east 1,500 yards; and the south-west to north-east also 1,500 yards.

Though initial control was passed to No.10 Group, RAF Fighter Command [1 June 1943], the aerodrome's main user was No.38 Wing, Army Co-Operation Command, which was reformed as No.38 Group, Airborne Forces [11 October 1943].

Control of Tarrant Rushton and its 38 Group operators was passed to the Allied Expeditionary Air Force [1 February 1944] in preparation for the invasion of Europe. Its Commander-in -Chief, Air Chief Marshal Sir Trafford Leigh-Mallory visited the station [12 February 1944] and returned with General Dwight D. Eisenhower, the Supreme Commander of Allied Forces in Western Europe [22 April 1944], to see the readiness of the British 6th Air Landing Brigade and its associated 6th Airborne Division.

Exercises, at first at day and then at night, coupled with paratroop drops on Cranborne Chase, were soon to turn to reality. As the preparations for the opening of the Second Front became continuous, geography would give Tarrant Rushton the key position in the unfolding drama, in that it and the overspill field at nearby RAF Hurn lay closer to the selected drop-zones in Normandy than any other major airfields.

Tarrant Rushton would have the distinction of landing the first Allied soldiers to arrive in France on D-Day, with the arrival of Major John Howard and "D" Company of the 2nd Battalion, Oxford

NOSE LOADERS: HAMILCARS (SEEN FROM THE FUSELAGE AND TAIL OF A HORSA GLIDER) WERE THE BIGGEST OF THE WARTIME BRITISH GLIDERS, CARRYING EQUIPMENT UP TO THE SIZE OF LIGHT TANKS, AND ARE SEEN MASSED IN DOUBLE ROWS ON THE NORTH-SOUTH RUNWAY AT TARRANT RUSHTON ON THE MORNING OF 5 JUNE 1944 (LOOKING SOUTH, WITH HALIFAX TUG-PLANES ON THE GRASS EITHER SIDE).

TOWING PROCESS: THE FOUR-ENGINED HALIFAX TUG-PLANE (BOTTOM) TOWING A TROOP-CARRYING HORSA GLIDER, FROM RAF TARRANT RUSHTON, IN AN EXERCISE OVER THE ROLLING CHALKLANDS OF CRANBORNE CHASE.

GERMANY NEXT: VIA SUFFOLK, WITH HORSA GLIDERS AND THEIR HALIFAX TUG-PLANES PREPARING TO LEAVE RAF TARRANT RUSHTON IN NOVEMBER 1944, IN A VIEW EAST-NORTH-EASTWARDS ALONG THE WSW-ENE RUNWAY WITH A BIG MAINTENANCE HANGAR TO THE NORTH (TOP LEFT).

and Buckinghamshire Light Infantry. They emerged from their Horsa glider, the first of six in Operation Coup de Main, to seize and to hold the Orne canal bridge [01.30 hours, 6 June 1944] which would henceforth be known as Pegasus Bridge — from the men's flying-horse emblem.

The station then played its part in the two great setbacks of 1944. First the Halifax tug-planes and 96 gliders took the British 1st Airborne Division to Arnhem and its "Bridge too far" [17 September 1944]. This reversal in the tide of war was followed by a second disaster in the bleak midwinter.

Casualties streamed into Dorset, via Tarrant Rushton, as the Germans flung their armour into a final counter-offensive through the snowy forests of the Ardennes [Christmas 1944]. Up to 500 wounded Americans were flown into Tarrant Rushton by C-47 Dakotas in a single night and taken to the 22nd General Hospital of the United States Army, at Blandford Camp.

Sixty Halifax tug-planes and their Hamilcar and Horsa gliders would leave Tarrant Rushton [21 March 1945] for Operation Varsity, in which the British 6th Airborne Division was dropped beyond the Rhine, into Germany [24 March 1945]. Fifty-two of the Tarrant Rushton gliders landed successfully in daytime landings that had to be mounted from an East Anglian airfield within flying range. RAF Woodbridge, Suffolk, was chosen, and with this final airborne offensive of the Second World War Tarrant Rushton ceased to be a front-line air base.

As the war approached its fiftieth anniversaries, though shortly before the collapse of communism, I penned the following tribute to what was being remembered as "the Pegasus Aerodrome" for *Dorset County Magazine*:

Major John Howard [1912-99] had to win the Battle of Pegasus Bridge twice over. The first time he dropped in, after an uneventful flight from Tarrant Rushton Aerodrome in Dorset, with the 1st

PEGASUS PRELUDE: INVASION-NIGHT HALIFAX TUG-PLANES WITH TWO HORSA GLIDERS AND THE MASSED RANKS OF 30 HAMILCARS ALONG THE MAIN NORTH-SOUTH RUNWAY AT RAF TARRANT RUSHTON (FACING NORTH, BEING SEEN FROM NORTH-WEST) WITH TWO HORSA GLIDERS IN FRONT OF 30 HAMILCARS, ON THE MORNING OF 5 JUNE 1944, IN A DOWNLAND SETTING WITH BADBURY RINGS FORMING THE SKYLINE TO THE SOUTH-EAST (LEFT). ABBEYCROFT DOWN, INSIDE THE AERODROME PERIMETER, COMPRISES THE MIDDLE DISTANCE WITH JUBILEE WOOD AND TARGET WOOD BEING SOUTHWARDS BEHIND IT. THE LEAD HALIFAXES ON THE GRASS (RIGHT) CARRY THE 8A MARKINGS OF 298 SQUADRON AND 9U OF 644 SQUADRON (SEEN IN CLOSER DETAIL OVER THE PAGE). ALL AIRCRAFT CARRY THE INVASION STRIPES.

Platoon of "D" Company of the 2nd Battalion of the Oxfordshire and Buckinghamshire Light Infantry. Minutes into 6 June 1944 they stepped out of their Horsa gliders and opened the Second Front in Normandy. They were pipped at the post by RAF Harwell which would consign the 22nd Independent Parachute Company to enter history as the first Allied soldiers to arrive in France on D-Day.

John Howard's second battle at the bridge over the Orne canal was to save the building he had brought to fame, the Pegasus Cafe, when in 1987 the French threatened it with demolition for a road scheme to improve the approaches to Caen for port traffic.

The Dorset field from which his Halifax bomber tug-plane lumbered into the air at 22.56 hours on the night of 5 June 1944 has fared worse. Far from being a focal point for emotional controversy it has languished into obscurity. Though many will probably approve. For it is a modern day example of swords into ploughshares, the great long runway having been transformed into a prairie of wheat and barley that alternates with an immense cabbage patch. Some hangars survive, partially utilised as barns, but the sky was lifeless and the surroundings silent as I tried to visualise these empty uplands between Badbury Rings and the Tarrant valley as centre-stage for a turning-point in world history.

Only a few square yards cherish the memory. The byway from Tarrant Rushton to Witchampton makes a sudden detour to avoid the airfield which had been constructed across its path. It is a ninety degree bend (Ordnance Survey map reference ST 950 061) beside a hangar, and here is a stone war memorial to the flyers and soldiers they carried to war.

The last time I had been at the spot it had been a little more exciting. A little earlier in the day, in the hot summer of 1959, I had persuaded my father to drive us in his Standard Eight up the narrow lane that ascends the hillside directly above Tarrant Rushton church. It used to be the old road to Witchampton but was cut by the construction of the aerodrome during the war and was physically stopped-up by a gate that should have been locked. That day it was not only open but swung back out of sight; the road suddenly became a runway as it emerged from its hedged confinement into a space that was literally a mile wide.

We drove beside a Valiant, an ex-V bomber converted into a tanker by Flight Refuelling Limited, before turning the little car and seeking out our insignificant hole in the boundary fence. Now however, there is nothing to convey the sheer scale of the operation which was not only to tow the British 6th Airborne Division and unleash it over France but had then to go straight into a repeat the following evening.

Then the two squadrons of Halifax tow-planes from Tarrant Rushton had to be back over Normandy and pulling a convoy of thirty of the heavier, mainly Hamilcar type, gliders of the 6th Air Landing Brigade. These contained the Division's real hardware, with equipment such as Tetrarch tanks, Bren-gun carriers, 25-pounder field guns, scout cars and Bailey bridge pontoons, as well as crates of ammunition and stores.

That success would lead to the euphoria that brought about a defeat. General Dwight D. Eisenhower, the Supreme Commander of Allied Forces in Western Europe, had visited Tarrant Rushton on 22 April 1944. He was totally won over to the concept of airborne landings and would feel D-Day had proved that gliders and paratroops could be used on a far greater scale. The great sequel was Operation Market Garden. "I not only approved Market Garden, I insisted on it," Eisenhower admitted in 1966.

Nearly a hundred Hamilcar gliders, towed by their Halifax tug-planes, lifted off from Tarrant Rushton Aerodrome on the morning of Sunday 17 September 1944 to carry the British 1st Airborne Division to a bridge on the Lower Rhine at Arnhem. In all there were three hundred gliders and paratroop carrying aircraft. Eight thousand men were about to find themselves dropping in on the crack 9th and 10th SS Panzer Divisions under the command of General Field Marshal Walther Model.

That 2,400 of them would, by 26 September be extricated from the "Bridge too far" was largely due to the efforts of 250 men of 4th Battalion of the Dorsetshire Regiment. They maintained a shuttle

PRECISION DROP: THREE HORSA GLIDERS FROM RAF TARRANT RUSHTON, CARRIED TROOPS OF THE 2ND BATTALION, OXFORDSHIRE AND BUCKINGHAMSHIRE LIGHT INFANTRY, TO WITHIN YARDS OF THEIR TARGET BRIDGE (TOP LEFT) OVER THE CAEN CANAL AT 00.16 HOURS ON THE MORNING OF D-DAY. THE GLIDERS ARE NO. 91 (FLOWN BY STAFF SERGEANT JAMES WALLWORK OF THE GLIDER PILOT REGIMENT, CLOSEST TO BRIDGE, INTACT), NO. 93 (STAFF SERGEANT GEOFFREY BARKWAY, CENTRE AIRFRAME, SMASHED), AND NO. 92 (STAFF SERGEANT OLIVER BOLAND, BOTTOM RIGHT, DAMAGED NOSE).

service of assault boats, under withering enemy fire, crossing and re-crossing the Lower Rhine to bring weary paratroopers back from the Arnhem bridgehead. As it became light at 6 o'clock on the morning of the 26th the German fire assumed pinpoint accuracy and further rescues were impossible.

Despite the setback the war was moving away from Dorset. On 21 March 1945, the sixty Halifax tug-planes and their Hamilcar and Horsa gliders left Tarrant Rushton for Woodbridge in Suffolk. They were en route to their final landings of the war. This was Operation Varsity which began at 9.45 in the morning of 24 March and lasted three hours. Fifty-two of the Tarrant Rushton gliders landed successfully on the far side of the Rhine and delivered the British 6th Airborne Division on to German soil. They took Hamminkeln and the bridge over the River Issel.

The war closed before the next operation could get into the sky — it would have been Operation Doomsday to capture Oslo airfield — and hereon the Halifax tug-planes were seconded to conventional transport duties.

That might have been the end of the story, bringing the curtain down on a sheep-down that had been converted into one of Europe's major airfields over the winter of 1942, except that it became the main base for Sir Alan Cobham's Flight Refuelling Limited. Their bulk fuel tankers would be requisitioned for the peak moment of "Cold War" tension, in fact in the year when United States presidential adviser Bernard Baruch coined the phrase. Soviet forces in East Germany cut the highway and rail links between West Germany and Berlin on 24 July 1948.

The following day the first of fourteen Lancastrian and Lancaster tankers that would be committed to the operation from Tarrant Rushton was heading towards Gatow. In all they would carry 26,000 tons of fuel in Operation Plainfare — hastily changed from Operation Carter Paterson to avoid the "Removals" theme — and the flights had to be kept up daily until 30 September 1949.

Forty Tarrant Rushton air crew were involved and five of them would be killed when a Flight Refuelling Lancastrian plunged into the Hampshire Downs near Andover. In vain? Not to the two million people of West Berlin nor perhaps in a wider sense. For the determination to break

CANAL LANDING: JUST YARDS FROM THEIR PEGASUS BRIDGE OBJECTIVE (RIGHT, NAMED FOR THE EMBLEM OF THE GLIDER PILOT REGIMENT) AFTER HORSA GLIDERS FROM RAF TARRANT RUSHTON CAME TO REST BELOW WATERSIDE TREES ONLY MINUTES INTO D-DAY.

the Berlin blockade established for both sides, present Allies and Red Army alike, the inviolability of the boundaries that had been drawn across Europe at the end of the war. What they lacked in cartographical neatness would be compensated for in terms of lasting mutual respect.

For Flight Refuelling there came the excitement on 7 August 1949 of enabling a Meteor jet to set an international endurance record — Pat Hornidge kept it in the air for more than twelve hours. In-flight refuelling was on its way to application and acceptability in all the world's major air forces. It would in 1982 enable a Vulcan bomber to fly from Ascension Island a third of the way across the globe to make the first dramatic gesture against the Argentinians holding Port Stanley airfield. Flight Refuelling Limited continues, from a factory on the Stour riverside at Wimborne, but by the early 1970s it no longer needed its own air force or a square mile of Dorset chalkland.

There was just a little token pleasure flying from Tarrant Rushton — in the lightweight one-man descendants of those wartime troop-carrying gliders — and then in 1980 the bulldozers crunched the hardcore and concrete of the runways. From hereon it is just another cornfield that has had a history. It is quite some cornfield. And one hell of a legend.

Tarrant Rushton crashes — remarkably few, in view of its night and day wartime operations, though several gliders were damaged or written-off in mishaps.

As an Advanced Flying School it suffered a wrecked airframe, of a Vampire, following an aborted take-off [June 1953].

Taylor — sole pilot to be killed in an air crash in the history of Flight Refuelling Limited, **Captain Cyril "Pop" Taylor DFC** [1914-48] went off course and flew Lancaster tanker G-AHJW into the Hampshire Downs. Six of his crew were also killed. They were returning empty to their base at Tarrant Rushton, from Berlin.

He and three others are buried in St Mary's churchyard, Andover, beneath this inscription: "Four of the gallant crew of seven who gave their lives for the cause of humanity during the Berlin Airlift operation in an accident at Conholt Park on November 22nd 1948".

Telecommunications Flying Unit — Air Ministry Flight formed at the new Hurn Aerodrome [13 August 1941]. Its Development Section was a regrouping of the former Fighter Establishment from RAF Middle Wallop. Then it absorbed, as its Research Section, the Special Duty Flight which was previously at Christchurch Aerodrome [10 November 1941]. This provided aerial test-beds and laboratories for the pioneering Telecommunications Research Establishment at Worth Matravers and Langton Matravers, on the Purbeck coast.

The Telecommunications Flying Unit, with its collection of some fifty assorted aircraft, left for Defford, near Worcester, when its parent Telecommunications Research Establishment was evacuated to Malvern [25 May 1942].

Telecommunications Research Establishment — moved from Dundee to a new hutted base between Worth Matravers village and Renscombe Farm (Ordnance Survey map reference SY 966 776), with young radio research scientists Alan Hodgkin and Bernard Lovell being among the advance party [26 February 1940]. They would be joined by Dr Robert Cockburn and the establishment would be fully evacuated to Worth by the spring [5 May 1940].

Later in the year it requisitioned Leeson House and Durnford School in the neighbouring village of Langton Matravers. The scientists at Worth and Langton were soon to be deeply involved in the "Battle of the Beams" as the Luftwaffe targeted inland English objectives by an intersection of radio pulses — one of synchronised dots and the other of dashes — transmitted from Kleve, in Germany near the Dutch border south-east of Arnhem, and from Stolberg near the Danish border.

Dr Cockburn developed a Radio Counter Measure codenamed "Aspirin" which duplicated the continuous Morse dashes, transmitted on a frequency of 30 to 31.5 megacycles per second, which disorientated the German pilots by widening their direction beam [September 1940]. As these asynchronous signals were having their desired effect, the more sophisticated forms of interference — such as an attempt to "bend" the beam — were not necessary.

They would be the recipients of revelations from priceless prizes beached at West Bay, Bridport, in the form of radio equipment on a pathfinding Heinkel He.111 bomber [6 November 1940].

Scientists at the Royal Aircraft Establishment, Farnborough, reassembled its apparatus which comprised three vertical aerials and an intact X-Gerat radio receiver — also known as Wotan I — which enabled the aircraft, from Kampfgruppe 100, to follow a radio direction beam. What surprised the Air Ministry boffins was that the apparatus was tuned to 2000 cycles per second (approximating to the "C" which is two octaves above standard-pitch middle "C") whereas British jamming countermeasures had assumed a note of 1500 cycles (approximating to the "G" below this upper "C").

The discovery came too late to prevent the Coventry raid but it would ensure that radio countermeasures were perfected in time to save the vital Rolls-Royce aero engine plant at Derby. In moonlit conditions similar to those of the Coventry raid, Derby's bombs fell on Nottingham — and those intended for Nottingham fell into open fields [8 May 1941]. As part of the Battle of the Beams, Dr Robert Cockburn commandeered the BBC's pre-war television transmitter at Alexandra Palace, Muswell Hill, on what turned out to be the very night that the Luftwaffe changed to a frequency of 42.5 megacycles per second. This was jammed by Cockburn in countermeasure "Domino" — in which the German signal was re-radiated back to the attacking aircraft, from Alexandra Palace, at 46.9 megacycles per second.

A second transmitting station, constructed on Beacon Hill, near Salisbury, extended Cockburn's jamming across the whole of southern England.

Other suspicious signals were seeping out of France.

Derek Gerrard, an Air Ministry scientist seconded to the Telecommunications Research Establishment, drove to St Alban's Head with a VHF radio set and found himself picking up transmissions from the Cherbourg peninsula on the 2.5 metre wavelength [24 February 1941]. The bearings suggested a source in the area of Ayderville, where Flight Officer W.K. Manifould had coincidentally photographed a "Freya" square-mesh turntable aerial only two days before.

Intercepted German radio traffic had credited this device with the sinking, off Portland, of the destroyer HMS *Delight*. As a result of Gerrard's discovery, Air Marshal Sir Philip Joubert called a meeting with just one item on the agenda: "To discuss the existence of German radar".

The Purbeck scientists also developed British radar innovations, devising the Type 15 ground-to-air antenna which would be built by the Air Defence Experimental Establishment at Somerford, Christchurch, and put into the field at Sopley where it enabled combat guidance, given to 604 Squadron at RAF Middle Wallop, to achieve their first radar-controlled kill [4 March 1941].

The Special Duty Flight, attached to the Telecommunications Research Establishment and based at Christchurch Aerodrome, became the first user of the newly opened RAF Hurn [1 August 1941].

Wellington T2565, being used by the Telecommunications Research Establishment on a signals probe, was lost over France after engine failure [6 November 1941]. Six of the seven crew were taken prisoner of war but the seventh, Sergeant N.W. MacKenzie, was able to avoid capture and escaped to return eventually to Britain.

Meanwhile, the Special Duty Flight had been renamed the Research Section of the Telecommunications Flying Unit, and continued to be based at RAF Hurn [10 November 1941].

It would now make its most remarkable series of flights, which would enable Air Marshal Sir Arthur Harris, Commander-in-Chief Bomber Command, to mount the massive night raids against German cities. Using an AI (Airborne Interception) Mark VII radar set, installed in a Blenheim bomber but with its centimetric beam tilted towards the ground, scientists found themselves mapping Bournemouth and could distinguish streets and houses from the surrounding landscape of heather and pines.

Professor Philip Dee and his assistant Bernard Lovell presented the results of the initial BN (Blind Navigation) tests to the Secretary of State for Air, Sir Archibald Sinclair, who ordered six more test flights to "determine whether signals obtained ... could be definitely associated with ground objects" [23 December 1941].

Scientists at Worth were to receive their greatest prize courtesy "C" Company of the Second Battalion, the Parachute Regiment, who mounted a commando raid at Bruneval, on the French coast between Le Havre and Fecamp, to capture a German Wurzburg radar apparatus [27 February 1942]. This comprised a parabolic aerial, receiver and cathode-ray tube. On this side of the Channel, TRE's Telecommunications Flying Unit received one of the first Halifax bombers, V9977, fitted with a perspex cupola in the space which would normally have housed the nose gun-turret [22 March 1942]. Here the Purbeck scientists would install the magnetron section of a Mark VII AI (Airborne Interception) radar, adapted into the first prototype of a version codenamed H2S which was being developed for ground-mapping. These signals would enable the team to spot Bournemouth, from a distance of six miles at at height of 8,000 feet, and to distinguish it from the outlines and land-forms of the adjoining towns of Poole and Christchurch [17 April 1942]. A repeat performance that night would have proved the system in operational conditions — in the dark and through the clouds — except that the operator failed to find a concealed switch and the radar was not turned on.

Tested by Air Commander Donald "Pathfinder" Bennett, it was put into production, at a factory in West Howe, Bournemouth. H2S was coined after Professor Frederick Lindemann had exclaimed on being given some excuses: "It stinks that it wasn't thought of before." Used operationally to find Hamburg [30-31 January 1943] and henceforth enabled night-bombing of the correct cities for the rest of the war.

The Telecommunications Research Establishment would be evacuated from Worth Matravers and Langton Matravers to Malvern College, Worcestershire [25 May 1942], because of fears that the Germans might attempt their own Bruneval-style raid.

Many ideas and projects from Dorset days would be brought into service later in the war, such as the radar-reflective "Window" which created a smoke-screen effect upon enemy radar sets, when dropped in the form of millions of thin strips of aluminium-backed paper. This made its operational debut before a big raid on Hamburg [24-25 July 1943]. That night it reduced losses among the 791 participating bombers from an estimated 48, based on normal casualty rates, to only 12.

Only a couple of the northern huts survive and the rest of the extensive site has been returned to farmland. Aerials remained for an RAF Gee station, to direct Cold War bombers, until the 1970s.

TH — squadron code of 418 (RCAF City of Edmonton) Squadron, flying Mosquito night-fighters from RAF Hurn [14-29 July 1944].

Thomas — champion boxer **Flight-Lieutenant Frederick Mytton Thomas** [born 1915] commanded the B-Flight Spitfires of 152 Squadron at RAF Warmwell throughout the Battle of Britain. He had joined the RAF on a pre-war short service commission [1935] and joined 29 Squadron at North Weald [1936] followed by 73 Squadron at Digby [1937], during which time he was the Officers RAF Featherweight Boxing Champion [1936, 1938 and 1939] and then the Imperial Service Champion [1939].

From Warmwell he was posted to RAF Middle Wallop, as Sector Controller, on being promoted Squadron Leader [November 1940]. Later in the war he advised the Royal Canadian Air Force on the setting-up of their air defence system [1942] and resumed operational flying at Palma, India [1944]. Post-war he was Wing Commander Night Ops at Headquarters, 12 Group, and retired with that rank [1958].

Thornford crash — Tiger Moth N6648, belonging to 2 Elementary Flying Training School of the RAF, made a forced-landing [9 November 1945].

Tibbets — atom bomb pilot **Major Paul Tibbets** who famously took B-29 *Enola Gay* (named for his mother) to Hiroshima, ferried VIPs from RAF Hurn earlier in the Second World War. He took Lieutenant-General Dwight D. Eisenhower, then Commander of Allied Forces North-West Africa, to Gibraltar [3 November 1942] for the conference that would put the finishing touches to the invasion of French North Africa.

Tillard — Fleet Air Arm pilot **Lieutenant-Commander Claude Tillard** [1909-41] was born in Wimborne. A torpedo-bomber on the aircraft carrier HMS *Furious* [1935], he became a training officer, and was re-called by the Royal Navy on the outbreak of war. He was given command of 808 Naval Air Squadron, equipped with Fulmars, in dockyard defence at Wick [July 1940] and then took the squadron to sea, aboard HMS *Ark Royal* [October 1940]. He was credited with five kills but was then shot down himself, into the Mediterranean [3 April 1941]. He is buried in the War Cemetery at Enfidaville, Tunisia.

TK — pundit code of RAF Tarrant Rushton, displayed on large letters on the ground and broadcast at night in Morse code, from a mobile beacon.

TM — squadron code of 504 (County of Nottingham) Squadron, flying Spitfires on bomber escort duties from RAF Hurn [10-14 July 1943].

Tobin — American volunteer **Pilot Officer Eugene Quimby "Red" Tobin** [1917-41], a messenger from the MGM Studios in Hollywood, went to fight in Finland and retreated to l'Armee de l'Air in Paris, escaping from the Fall of France to become a Spitfire pilot with 609 Squadron at RAF Warmwell. During the Battle of Britain he claimed half the kills of a Messerschmitt Bf.110 over Chaldon Herring [25 August 1940] and a Dornier Do.17 bomber [15 September 1940].

Unlucky on leaving Dorset, he was shot down on 71 Squadron's first sweep over France, from RAF Church Fenton [7 September 1941]. He is buried in the Eastern Cemetery at Boulogne.

Toller Admiralty Airship Station — situated a mile and a half west of the village of Toller Porcorum, in the wooded hills north-west of Gray's Farm, actually in the parish of Powerstock (Ordnance Survey map reference SY 540 980).

Operated as part of No.9 Group, being a satellite station to Mullion, Cornwall, for patrols against German U-boats between Start Point and Portland Bill [spring 1918-November 1918]. Closed within a month of the end of the Great War.

TP — squadron code of 198 Squadron, flying rocket-firing Typhoons on cross-Channel missions from RAF Hurn [22 June-1 July 1944].

Trots — series of water runways, marked out by buoys and car tyres, for flying-boats landing and taking off from Poole Harbour [1939-48].

No. 1 Trot was off the lake area of Hamworthy; No. 2 Trot was off Lower Hamworthy; No. 3 Trot was off Parkstone Bay and Lilliput; No. 4 Trot was between Brownsea Island and Sandbanks.

The four runways joined to form a continuous taxiing route up the Main Channel and then into Wareham Channel, to the hards at Poole Flying Boat Base, Hamworthy.

Turner — veteran balloonist **Hatton Turner** [born 1840] retired to Bournemouth and went up for a ride in a Bleriot monoplane with French aviator Henri Salmet [1913]. The flight ended in a hedge, with the machine "somewhat severely damaged", after Salmet misjudged the landing and flew into the blinding sun — out of which the flyer walked away with a cut, and Turner without any injury.

Turner — early aviator **Lewis W. F. Turner** of Sturminster Newton learnt to fly at Grahame-White's school at Hendon and became an instructor in his own right. He was the chief pilot of the Kennedy Aviation School, St Petersburg, in Russia, and returned to Hendon to be its leading exhibition pilot for summertime displays [1911]. Commuted by air to Dorset — landing at Race Down, Blandford — in a flimsy biplane of wood and wire-braced fabric, powered by a 50-hp engine and an 8.5-feet propeller.

21 — squadron code of 443 Squadron, flying Mark IXb Spitfires from RAF Warmwell [18 December 1944-3 January 1945].

Tyneham crashes — on Povington Heath of Messerschmitt Bf.110 (2N+EP), in a forced-landing, with the first German flyers to be taken prisoner in the Battle of Britain [11 July 1940]. They were Oberleutnant Gerhard Kadow, pilot, and Gefreiter Helmut Scholz, gunner, of the 9th Staffel, Zerstörergeschwader 76, from Laval. The kill was claimed by Spitfires of 609 Squadron from RAF Warmwell.

Less fortunate were the crew of another Bf.110, almost certainly Hans Carschel and Unteroffizier Klose in 3U+BD of Zerstörergeschwader 26, who crashed at Egliston, between Tyneham and Kimmeridge [27 September 1940]. Their Geschwader was named Horst Wessel after the Nazi hero of a militant anti-Semitic song which became a national anthem. They had been taking part in an abortive raid on the Parnall Aircraft Company at Yate, near Chipping Sodbury.

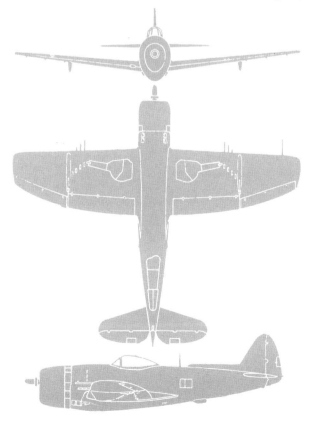

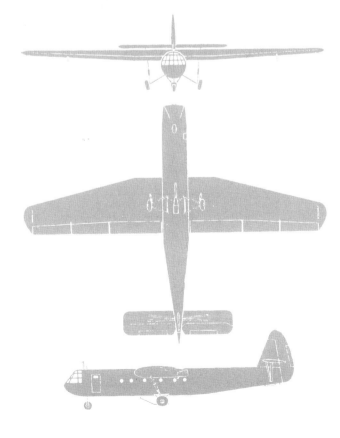

THUNDERBOLT FIGHTER: OPERATED BY THE UNITED STATES ARMY AIR FORCE ON CROSS-CHANNEL MISSIONS FROM CHRISTCHURCH AERODROME.

HORSA GLIDER: MADE AT CHRISTCHURCH AND OPERATED BY AIRBORNE FORCES FROM RAF TARRANT RUSHTON.

BRITISH EUROPEAN AIRWAYS "ELIZABETHAN" CLASS AEROPLANE.

FLY BEA IN EUROPE'S FINEST AIR FLEET

VICKERS VISCOUNT: HURN-MADE (BOTTOM) FOR AIRLINES ACROSS THE GLOBE FROM HOME-BASED BEA TO QANTAS IN AUSTRALIA.

U

UM — code letters of 152 (Hyderabad) Squadron, flying Spitfires from RAF Warmwell [1940-41].

United States Army Air Force — the 31st Fighter Group detachment flew British-made Spitfires, from RAF Warmwell [July 1942].

The 9th USAAF had a number of Dorset bases for the run-up to D-Day and through the Battle of Normandy, with three squadrons each of Republic P-47 Thunderbolts at RAF Christchurch [7 March-11 July 1944], Lockheed P-38 Lightnings at RAF Warmwell [12 March-5 August 1944], and Martin B-26 Marauders at RAF Hurn [3 August-20 August 1944]. The operating formations were the 405th Fighter Bomber Group at Christchurch; the 474th Fighter Group at Warmwell; and the 97th Bombardment Group at Hurn.

Daylight raids over Germany were conducted from further north and east, by the 8th USAAF — comprising the VIIIth Bomber Command, VIIIth Fighter Command and VIIIth Air Service Command. As with British Bomber Command "strays", damaged, disorientated, and out-of-fuel American Flying Fortress and Liberator bombers frequently made emergency landings on Dorset aerodromes.

Upton Admiralty Airship Station — in heathland pines to the west of Poole, operated as a satellite base to Polegate, Sussex, for patrols against German U-boats between Portland Bill and St Catherine's Point, Isle of Wight [1917-18].

ZERO AIRSHIP: ZERO ANTI-SUBMARINE FLIGHT CONCEALED ON ITS MOORING AMID PINES AT UPTON, NEAR POOLE, IN 1918.

Uruguay — an ex-BOAC Mark V Sunderland flying-boat from Poole, converted into a Sandringham-2 for carrying 45 passengers and sold to the Argentine airline Dodero [November 1945].

UT — code letters of 461 (Royal Australian Air Force) Squadron, flying Sunderland flying-boats from RAF Hamworthy [1942-43].

VICKERS VARSITY: HURN PLANEMAKERS BESIDE AND ON TOP OF ITS HUNDREDTH AIRFRAME, IN MARCH 1953.

V

V serial numbers of RAF aircraft:

V6758 Hurricane — see entries for Doe and Warmwell crashes.

V6777 Hurricane — see entries for Covington and Winterborne Houghton crashes.

V6792 Hurricane — see entries for Considine and Shapwick crash.

V6960 Hurricane — see entry for Manston.

V7231 Hurricane — see entry for Jeff.

V7233 Hurricane — see entry for Cock.

V7250 Hurricane — see entry for Wakeling.

VA — squadron code of 125 (Newfoundland) Squadron, flying Mosquito night-fighters from RAF Hurn [25 March-31 July 1944].

Vampire — the familiar shape in Bournemouth's and east Dorset skies through the 1950s when the twin-boom fighter, which was the second of the RAF's first generation jets to come into squadron service, was manufactured by the de Havilland Aircraft Company at its factory in Somerford, Christchurch.

This was the third tier out-station of the firm. Its main base was at Hatfield, Hertfordshire, and the secondary works at Hawarden, on the outskirts of Chester. Production of the Vampire NF.10 night-fighter had been transferred from Hatfield to Hawarden and the first aircraft, WM659, was flown to Christchurch Aerodrome for its trials [December 1951].

VAMPIRE FIGHTER: TAKING OFF FROM CHRISTCHURCH AERODROME IN NOVEMBER 1950.

Meanwhile, the first prototype of a two-seater training variant, Vampire T.11 [G-5-7 construction number 15000, later designated WW456] had been made at Somerford and given its first flight, of 35 minutes, by test pilot John Wilson, from the adjacent Christchurch Aerodrome to Hurn [15 November 1950].

Two pre-production Vampire T.11s were built at Somerford, with both WW458 and WW461 being delivered to the Royal Navy [21 January and 22 May 1952] for Fleet Air Arm appraisal.

Orders followed. The first production Vampire T.11, WZ414, flew from Christchurch [January 1952] and was later transferred to the Aeroplane and Armament Evaluation Establishment at Boscombe Down [July 1954] before eventually being sold to the Mexican Air Force [1962].

The second production aircraft, WZ415, joined WW458 at Boscombe Down [March 1952] with WZ417 following [April 1952]. A total of 123 Vampire T.11s were manufactured at Christchurch for the Royal Air Force and delivered between 1 March 1952 and 11 March 1955.

At the same time the Somerford production line was also turning out Sea Vampire T.22, the naval version used on aircraft carriers, with a total of 73 being produced. Many of them were sent to the Royal Navy via Tarrant Rushton, the former wartime aerodrome near Blandford, for Flight Refuelling modifications.

A further 43 Vampire T.55 trainers were made at Christchurch for overseas sales [29 April 1952 to 2 July 1953]. The purchasing nations were Iraq, Lebanon, New Zealand, Norway, Portugal, South Africa, Switzerland and Venezuela. Also see the entry for de Havilland Aircraft Company Limited.

Varsity landings — the final operation for RAF Tarrant Rushton, carrying the British 6th Airborne Division to Hamminkein and the bridges over the River Issel, on the German side of the Rhine [24 March 1945]. Though 60 Halifax tug-planes and their Hamilcar and Horsa gliders took part from Dorset, of which 52 gliders were to land successfully, they did so by leaving Tarrant Rushton three days earlier and went via a staging-post in East Anglia.

This aerodrome, in range of the German objectives, was RAF Woodbridge, in Suffolk.

Vega — Catalina flying-boat, formerly British Overseas Airways FL, which left Poole Harbour for Trincomalee, Ceylon [17 April 1943] where she was handed over to RAF South-East Asia Command.

Venom — jet fighter, produced by the de Havilland factory at Somerford, Christchurch [1950s]. See entry for de Havilland Aircraft Company Limited.

Ventry — airship-maker **Arthur Frederick Daubeney Olav Eveleigh-de-Moleyns**, 7th Baron Ventry [1898-1987], lived at Lindsay Hall, Lindsay Road, Bournemouth. An accident on the ground ended the career of his airship *Bournemouth* at Cardington, Bedfordshire [1951] and with it the post-war fortunes of dirigible flight. The nation had not forgotten that the R101 became a fireball at Beauvais, France, on her maiden voyage to Australia [1930].

Vickers Armstrongs (Aircraft) Limited — one of the premier British aircraft production companies, came to Hurn Aerodrome to flight-test the first V-bomber [June 1951]. The first prototype of the Vickers Valiant flew burning over Bournemouth and crashed at Harrow Farm, Bransgore, on the edge of the New Forest [12 January 1952]. Ultimately it would be premature metal fatigue that would take the Valiants out of RAF service.

Meanwhile, Vickers set up a factory to manufacture their new passenger plane, the Vickers Viscount, with work being shared between Weybridge and Hurn, where the airframes were completed.

Villae de Poole — Spitfire donated by the people of Poole to the newly formed 411 (Royal Canadian Air Force) Squadron [22 June 1941]. It crashed at Chester during a blizzard, killing Sergeant Pilot S.W. Bradshaw [7 December 1941].

Viscount — made by Vickers Armstrongs (Aircraft) Limited, with production being shared between their main works at Weybridge, Surrey, and the factory at Bournemouth (Hurn) Airport [1950s]. Hurn would produce a total of 200.

von Dalwigk — "Stuka" leader **Hauptmann Friedrich-Karl Freiherr von Dalwigk zu Lichtenfels**, the 33-year-old Staffelkapitan of I Gruppe, Stukageschwader 77, was shot down in his Junkers Ju.87 and killed over the sea off Portland [9 July 1940]. The kill was claimed by Pilot Officer David Moore Crook, flying a Spitfire from RAF Warmwell. Von Dalwigk, who had joined the Luftwaffe in 1933, would be posthumously awarded the Knight's Cross [21 July 1940].

V1 flying bombs — eight "Ski-site" concrete ramps, intended for the launch of flying-bombs into and over Dorset, were destroyed on the Cherbourg peninsula by bombers protected by escort fighters that took off or landed back at RAF Hurn [December 1943].

These launch sites never became operational, being overrun by the Allies during the Battle of Normandy, but two strays from firings to the east are said to have landed in or near the county. One apparently exploded at Ferndown, in the vicinity of Church Road and Victoria Road, and another fell in Bolde churchyard in the New Forest.

Mark VI Mosquito night-fighters from RAF Hurn, flown by Canadians of 125 (Newfoundland) Squadron and 604 (City of Edmonton) Squadron flew Anti-Diver sorties against Doodlebug launch

CAPITAL FLEET: ALL 60 VICKERS VISCOUNTS ORDERED BY CAPITAL AIRLINES OF WASHINGTON DC WERE BUILT AT HURN, WITH THE FIRST BEING DELIVERED IN MARCH 1957.

sites, [summer 1944]. It was also a busy time for 418 Squadron — operating with Mosquito Mark VI night-fighters from RAF Hurn, Holmsley South, and Middle Wallop — across the outer triangle of the weapon's western arc of fire. They would claim a total of 80 scores, in their V1 interceptions, with most having been shot down over the sea. The method of scoring encouraged this. When a flying bomb was put into the sea it counted as one enemy aircraft destroyed. Once it was over land its destruction rated as being equal to only half an aircraft.

V2 rockets — watched on launching from the Hook of Holland by men of the 1st Battalion of the Dorsetshire Regiment, who were holding what they called "The Island" at Bemmel, virtually surrounded by German forces [October 1944]. The terror weapon went straight up to a height of about three kilometres before curving into a 45 degree trajectory, towards London.

After the war scientists from Christchurch, led by Colonel Raby, would test-fire four German V2s which they reconstructed from captured parts. They were flown northwards along the North Sea coast, from Cuxhaven, near Bremerhaven, and fell into the sea off Denmark [3 October 1945]. This was a test carried out by the Signals Research and Development Establishment based at Christchurch Aerodrome and Steamer Point, Highcliffe. What would be dubbed "the first firing of a captured V2", for the benefit of the world's press [4 October 1945], was in fact the second.

Colonel Raby was the director of SRDE, the Signals Research and Development Establishment, which was developing the first British guided weapons.

V3 Hochdruckpumpe long-range gun — emplaced in massive concrete footings at Mimoyecques, near Calais. Bombed by Mosquito night-fighters of 125 Squadron and 604 Squadron, from RAF Hurn [July 1944]. The science of this vengeance weapon had not been perfected, with its shells liable to topple erratically at speeds in excess of 3,300 feet per second, and before this was corrected the site would be overrun by the Second Canadian Corps [26 September 1944].

VZ — squadron code of 412 (Royal Canadian Air Force) Squadron, flying Mark Vb Spitfires from RAF Hurn [1-6 March 1943].

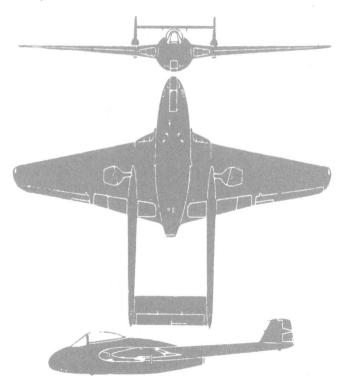

VAMPIRE FIGHTER: THE FIRST JET TO BE MADE AT CHRISTCHURCH.

W

W serial number of RAF aircraft:

W3649 Spitfire — see entry for Shepley.

Waite — Halifax pilot **Ronald Waite** [born 1912], of Weymouth, brought his crippled bomber home from Holland against all odds [31 July 1942]. His gunners shot down a Junkers Ju.88 and damaged a Messerschmitt Bf.110 when the already damaged bomber was intercepted over Poortugaal, near Rotterdam. The Halifax suffered complete instrument failure and one of its gunners was killed.

Despite these multiple handicaps, the bomber managed to limp home, and the story went into the newspapers, though some doubts were later expressed about the men's account. Half a century later this would be confirmed by the discovery of the wreckage of the Junkers during the building of an office block [1994].

Ronald Waite commented: "We were a bit fed up that the RAF wouldn't believe our story, especially after they had given it to the papers. It's been on my mind for the last 52 years. The fact that the wreck has now been discovered is a vindication."

Wakeling — Hurricane flyer **Sergeant Pilot Sidney Richard Ernest Wakeling** [1919-40] of 87 Squadron, from RAF Exeter, was killed when his fighter was shot down in flames over Bradford Peverell [25 August 1940]. He was aged 21 and is buried in the RAF plot at Warmwell churchyard.

Walch — Australian Hurricane pilot **Flight-Lieutenant Stuart Crosby Walch** [1917-40] was shot down and killed off the Dorset coast, east of Portland between White Nothe and Lulworth Cove, in R4097 of 238 Squadron from RAF Middle Wallop [10.45 hours, 11 August 1940]. Born in Hobart, Tasmania, he joined the Royal Australian Air Force in 1936, and transferred to the RAF in 1937.

Wallis Down Aerodrome — has the distinction of having been Dorset's first airfield [1909-10], on a pasture beside the High Road, opposite what is now the suburb of Wallisdown, that then being a hamlet in the Dorset parish of Kinson, prior to being absorbed into Bournemouth. The actual location, however, was on flat pastureland to the east of Vine's Farm, beneath the campus of what is now Bournemouth University, administratively in the Branksome district of Poole.

Holdenhurst Road car dealer William Edward McArdle made the arrangements through local dairyman Charles Vine Groves for a couple of flying friends, whom he had met in France, to test out the site in 1909. By the following Whitsun [May 1910] there was a huge marquee acting as the hangar for four Bleriot monoplanes. One was owned by McArdle and another by his partner, J. Armstrong Drexel, from the family of American banking millionaires who had founded and funded the Drexel Institute in Philadelphia [1892].

By the time of the Great War it had become known as Talbot Village Aerodrome [1914].

Wareham crashes — a Spitfire of 152 Squadron from RAF Warmwell plunged into the ground at Bestwall, east of the town, following a Battle of Britain dog-fight [8 August 1940]. The fuselage of K9894 ended up standing vertically, its propeller embedded in a meadow, and Sergeant-Pilot Denis Robinson had a lucky escape, jumping down on the grass.

Messerschmitt Bf.109s brought down Hurricane P3421 of 56 Squadron from RAF Boscombe Down, killing Czechoslovakian Sergeant Pilot Jaroslav Hlavac, at Manor Farm, Worgret, to the west of the town [10 October 1940].

WAREHAM CRASH: SPITFIRE K9894 OF 152 SQUADRON FROM RAF WARMWELL, SHOT DOWN OVER SWANAGE ON 8 AUGUST 1940 AND SUCCESSFULLY FORCE-LANDED IN MEADOWS AT BESTWALL, WHERE SERGEANT-PILOT DENIS ROBINSON WAS ABLE TO WALK AWAY FROM ONE OF THE MOST DRAMATIC CRASHES OF THE WAR.

SPITFIRE TRAILS: WARMWELL'S REASSURING SIGNATURE IN THE SKY, OVER DORCHESTER, PHOTOGRAPHED DURING THE BATTLE OF BRITAIN FROM THE OBSERVER CORPS POST AT POUNDBURY CAMP.

PILOT'S PLOT: THE RAF GRAVES BESIDE WARMWELL PARISH CHURCH, MAINLY FROM THE BATTLE OF BRITAIN, REPRESENT ONLY A FRACTION OF THE STATION'S LOSSES AS MANY BODIES WERE LOST AT SEA AND OTHERS WERE SENT HOME FOR BURIAL.

152 Squadron: pilots, ground staff and Honorary Pilot Officer Pooch (their mascot) in front of a Spitfire at RAF Warmwell in mid-August 1940. Centre row pilots (left to right) are Sergeant Pilot Harold John Akroyd (killed 8 October 1940), Sergeant Pilot Edmund Eric Shepperd (killed 18 October 1940), Pilot Officer Richard Malzard Hogg (killed 25 August 1940), Squadron Intelligence Officer, Pilot Officer Ian Norman Bayles (survived the war), Pilot Officer A. Weston (not traced), Pilot Officer Walter Beaumont (killed 23 September 1940), Pilot Officer Charles Warren (survived war), Pilot Officer Eric Simcox Marrs (killed 24 July 1941), Pilot Officer Frederick Henry Holmes (killed 4 December 1944), Sergeant Pilot John Keeth Barker (killed 4 September 1940), and Sergeant Pilot Leslie Arthur Edwin Reddington (killed 30 September 1940). Front row pilots (left to right) are Sergeant Pilot Jack McBean Christie (killed 26 September 1940), Pilot Officer Timothy Seddon Wildblood (killed 25 August 1940), Squadron Adjutant, Flying Officer Peter Geoffrey St George O'Brien (survived war), Flight-Lieutenant Derek Pierre Aumale Boitel-Gill (killed 18 September 1941), Squadron Leader Peter Kenneth Devitt (survived war), Flight-Lieutenant Frederick Mytton Thomas (survived war), Flying Officer Edward Sidney Hogg (survived war), Squadron Engineer Officer, Pilot Officer Graham James Cox (survived war) and Sergeant Pilot Kenneth Christopher Holland (killed 25 September 1940).

Dispersal point: visiting Hurricane being prepared for take-off beside the trees of Knighton Heath Wood on the western side of Warmwell Aerodrome.

CHANNEL SHIPPING: BLENHEIM BOMBER OVER WHAT WAS PROBABLY A BRITISH LOSS IN MID-1940, RESULTING IN FIGHTER COMMAND ESTABLISHING A FRONT-LINE COASTAL AIRFIELD AT WARMWELL, NEAR DORCHESTER.

Canadian 'Hurribomber': Mark IIb adaptation of the famous fighter, being bombed-up at RAF Warmwell in 1942, for Squadron Leader R. E. Morrow of 402 (Royal Canadian Air Force) Squadron.

Heinkel bombers: massed ranks crossed Dorset in the summer of 1940, generally heading for aviation factories in Bristol and Yeovil.

DIVE BOMBERS: JUNKERS JU.87 "STUKAS" WERE PARTICULARLY EFFECTIVE AGAINST SHIPPING IN PORTLAND HARBOUR AND CAUSED THE ADMIRALTY TO CLOSE THE CHANNEL TO ALLIED CONVOYS.

FORMATION FLYING: SPITFIRES IN THE BATTLE OF BRITAIN, THESE CARRYING THE "DW" LETTERS OF 610 (COUNTY OF CHESTER) SQUADRON.

MAKESHIFT FACILITIES: THE CREW ROOM FOR SPITFIRE PILOTS OF 609 SQUADRON AT RAF WARMWELL IN THE FIRST WEEK OF AUGUST 1940, AT THE HEIGHT OF THE BATTLE OF BRITAIN, WAS A TENT. SQUATTING IN THE FRONT ROW ARE PILOT OFFICER MICHAEL EDMUND STAPLES (KILLED 9 NOVEMBER 1941), PILOT OFFICER DAVID MOORE CROOK (KILLED 18 DECEMBER 1944) AND PILOT OFFICER ROGERS FREEMAN GARLAND MILLER (KILLED 27 SEPTEMBER 1940). STANDING IN THE BACK ROW, ALSO LEFT TO RIGHT, ARE PILOT OFFICER EUGENE QUIMBY TOBIN (KILLED 7 SEPTEMBER 1941), PILOT OFFICER PIOTR OSTASZEWSKI-OSTOJA (SURVIVED THE WAR AS WING COMMANDER PETER RAYMOND), FLYING OFFICER HENRY MACDONALD GOODWIN (KILLED 14 AUGUST 1940), FLYING OFFICER ALEXANDER ROTHWELL EDGE (SURVIVED WAR), PILOT OFFICER MICHAEL JOHN APPLEBY (SURVIVED WAR), FLIGHT-LIEUTENANT FRANK JONATHAN HOWELL (SURVIVED WAR), SQUADRON LEADER "GEORGE" DARLEY (SURVIVED WAR), FLIGHT-LIEUTENANT JAMES HENRY GORDON MCARTHUR (SURVIVED WAR), SERGEANT-PILOT ALAN NORMAN FEARY (KILLED 7 OCTOBER 1940), PILOT OFFICER TADEUSZ NOWIERSKY (SURVIVED WAR), AND PILOT OFFICER CHARLES NEVIL OVERTON (SURVIVED WAR).

FRESH OXYGEN: REPLACEMENT BOTTLE FOR PILOT OFFICER DAVID MOORE CROOK OF 609 SQUADRON AFTER COMBAT ON 9 JULY 1940, AS SPITFIRE P9322 IS REARMED AT DISPERSAL BESIDE WARMWELL AERODROME.

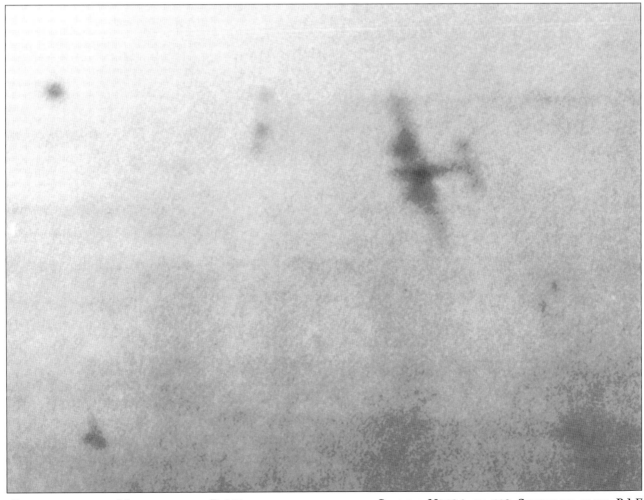

COMBAT CAMERA: MESSERSCHMITT BF.110 IN THE GUN-SIGHT OF SPITFIRE N3024 OF 609 SQUADRON FROM RAF WARMWELL AND ABOUT TO BE DESTROYED BY PILOT OFFICER DAVID MOORE CROOK AT THE HEIGHT OF THE BATTLE OF BRITAIN, ON 12 AUGUST 1940.

HOT SUMMER: DECK-CHAIR DISPERSAL FOR PILOTS OF 609 SQUADRON ON BEING SUMMONED FROM WARMWELL TO RAF NORTHOLT FOR THE AIR DEFENCE OF LONDON, IN WHICH PILOT OFFICER GEOFFREY NORMAN GAUNT (CENTRE) WAS KILLED OVER KENLEY ON 15 SEPTEMBER 1940. PILOT OFFICER VERNON CHARLES KEOUGH, AN AMERICAN VOLUNTEER (LEFT) HAD BEEN A PROFESSIONAL PARACHUTIST AND PILOT OFFICER DAVID MOORE CROOK (RIGHT) WOULD WRITE THEIR STORY IN SPITFIRE PILOT.

A Bf.109 also accounted for Spitfire R6597 which crashed near Wareham [28 November 1940]. Pilot Officer A.R. Watson tore his parachute and it failed to open. His death was immediately avenged by Pilot Officer Eric "Boy" Marrs who sent the culprit Messerschmitt down in flames, into Poole Bay.

Miles Magister N3980 of 302 Squadron crashed whilst low flying near Wareham [6 May 1942].

Warmwell Aerodrome — as RAF Woodsford was renamed [July 1938], lying four miles east-south-east of Dorchester (Ordnance Survey map reference SY 760 888). Airfield pundit code: "XW". Opened and operated by Flying Training Command, its three grass runways would be transferred to 10 Group Fighter Command as a frontline coastal satellite station to RAF Middle Wallop on the Hampshire Downs, when the Battle of Britain gathered pace and intensity [6 July 1940].

The neat rows of uniform headstones to the young men of the British Empire in the RAF section of Warmwell churchyard are part of a wider tragedy. Many other pilots, flying from Dorset in the Battle of Britain, came down in the front line itself — the English Channel — which became a mass grave for the flyers of both sides. Warmwell Aerodrome provided Dorset's air defence in 1940 and the Spitfires of 152 and 609 Squadrons intercepted the bombers crossing the county en route for Bristol.

Radar and decoded German radio traffic provided the scramble warnings so that the defenders' Rolls-Royce Merlin engines were only heard when there was an enemy presence approaching. There was less scope for predicting attacks on the station's other front, the Channel shipping, where the "Stukas" from the Cherbourg peninsula had pickings at will. The situation became so desperate that the Admiralty closed the Channel to Allied convoys.

Four bombs were dropped on the station by a solitary Junkers Ju.88 but there were no casualties and damage was limited to holes in the grass [26 March 1941]. Much worse was the surprise attack by three Heinkel He.111s that slipped low across the Dorset coast from Lyme Bay and followed the railway east from Dorchester [1 April 1941]. Their bombs and bullets killed ten and injured twenty. Among the dead was Sergeant Pilot Fawcett of 152 Squadron.

Warmwell was soon proclaiming itself to be "the most cosmopolitan air station in the world" as the peoples of every European nation (including the odd German connection), plus both land-masses of the Americas, were augmented by representatives from all over the British Empire. They stepped from the train at Moreton Station and were met by a coach in the car-park opposite the Frampton Arms. This would be their closest off-duty hostelry.

The names of many of the operating squadrons proclaim ethnic origins, though with wartime attrition rates they would be reinforced by very British names and faces: Punjab (130 Squadron); Hyderabad (152 Squadron); Argentine-British (164 Squadron); Mauritius (174 Squadron); Madras Presidency (234 Squadron); Northern Rhodesia (245 Squadron); Burma (257 Squadron); Rhodesia (266 Squadron); Poznanski (302 Squadron); Czech, though not named as such (312 Squadron); Royal Canadian Air Force / Ram (401 Squadron); Royal Canadian Air Force / Winnipeg Bear (402 Squadron); Royal Canadian Air Force (403 Squadron); Royal Canadian Air Force (411 Squadron); Royal Canadian Air Force (438 Squadron); Royal Canadian Air Force (439 Squadron); Royal Canadian Air Force (440 Squadron).

By 1944, from March to August it was a very different war as RAF Warmwell doubled as Station 454 of the 474 Fighter Group of the United States Army Air Force. The Lockheed Lightning P-38J fighter-bombers of 428, 429 and 430 Squadrons now flew offensive sorties against invasion objectives and targets of opportunity — the luxury of being able to turn their attention to anything that moved.

Warmwell's 48 Lightnings would suffer severe losses in the D-Day campaign. Two were shot down whilst escorting B-26 Marauders over northern France [7 May 194] but one of the pilots, Lieutenant Thacker, was to surprise his comrades by escaping into Spain and making it back to Warmwell after D-Day. One was lost in an accident, killing Lieutenant Kimball, as it crashed near Cheselbourne [21 May 1944]. Three were lost in low-level attacks on a bridge over the River Seine [5 June 1944] from which several of the surviving aircraft brought back tree boughs wedged in their tails.

Two or three losses per offensive sweep became the regular attrition rate, including the day when the group claimed ten of a formation of 25 Focke-Wulf 190s over north-west France [18 July 1944]. By then, however, the war had moved on, and two of the three pilots were able to bale out, with some prospect of landing behind Allied lines.

Warmwell's Americans were redeployed to a forward airfield in Normandy, as the German front-lines fell back [5 August 1944].

The RAF station at Warmwell effectively disbanded with the departure of the Central Gunnery School for Sutton Bridge, Lincolnshire [June 1945]. Official closure followed [November 1945].

Warmwell's war constantly overlaps my studies of *Dorset at War* and *Battle of Britain Dorset* which have now been expanded into *Wartime Dorset* [2000]. The station would, however, lose the peace. Victory in Europe resulted in closure for the station and its transition to a lunar landscape of gravel pits. Some of its buildings survive west of Crossways. The lane to West Stafford crosses the former Woodsford Heath along the undug northern edge of what was a grass airfield. Embanked dispersal pads survive tucked into the eastern edge of Knighton Heath Wood.

A memorial stone for the base would be unveiled in Mount Skippet Way [11 June 1989].

Warmwell crashes — started when the newly opened aerodrome was known as RAF Woodsford, with the belly-landing of Bristol Blenheim K7056 from the Home Aircraft Depot of the Royal Air Force [26 November 1937].

This was followed by the loss on landing of Hawker Audax K3086 belonging to 2 Flying training School of the RAF [12 April 1938].

There would be a spate of similar mishaps as the "Phoney War" entered its final month and the Wehrmacht prepared for the invasion of the Low Countries.

Boulton-Paul Defiant L6982, operated by the Central Gunnery School which was based at Warmwell, crashed on the airfield [2 April 1940].

The following day Hawker Hind K5544, with 10 Bombing and Gunnery School, crashed on landing at Warmwell [3 April 1940].

Likewise Hind K6839, also of 10 School, had its prang on landing [24 April 1940].

ALL PILOTS NOTE
ENGAGEMENTS A
RESULTS SEEN B
THESE ARE CHECK
REPORT SENT B
BY THE FIGHTE
CONCERN

WHEN A MESSERSCHMITT
THROWS UP THE SPONGE.

A BALE-OUT BY AN OPPONENT
IS NOW TAKEN AS A VICTORY—
A GERMAN PILOT WHEN
VANQUISHED HAS TO TURN
HIS FIGHTER UPSIDE DOWN SO
THAT HE CAN DROP HEAD FIRST
OUT OF THE NARROW COCKPIT.

AN R.A.F. FIGHTER CAN CLAIM
A DEFINITE VICTIM WITHOUT
FURTHER PROOF IF HE SEES
HIS OPPONENT GO DOWN
IN FLAMES.

—OR, FOLLOWING HIS
ANTAGONIST DOWN HE
SEES HIM HIT THE GROUND.

—OR SEES HIM CRASH
INTO THE SEA.

THE TIME AND POSITION OF
ALL CRASHING AIRCRAFT
IS TAKEN BY ANTI-AIRCRAFT
BATTERIES AND REPORTED
TO THEIR H.Q.—

—BY MILITARY POSTS
HOME GUARDS
AND POLICE ON LAND.

—AND SCOUTING NAVAL
PATROLS AND VESSELS
AT SEA.

Reproduced by permission of

HOW THE R.A.F. CHECK THE NUMI

Scrupulous care is taken by the R.A.F. to count and check the number of enemy machines destroyed in daily air battles. Unlike th
Nazis, who issue the most fantastic figures, in some cases while combat is still in actual progress, the R.A.F. demand absolute proo
of destruction before accepting a claim. Attached to each fighter aerodrome is a station Intelligence Office, where all pilots' report

AFTER AN ACTION A FIGHTER PILOT FIRST LANDS AND REPORTS RESULTS TO THE THE LOCAL INTELLIGENCE OFFICER WHO SENDS IN A PRELIMINARY ACCOUNT. AN ENTHUSIASTIC PILOT MAY MAKE SIGNALS OF VICTORY AFTER LANDING, BUT NEVER STUNTS OVER AERODROME AS HIS PLANE MAY BE DAMAGED UNKNOWN TO HIM

TER AN ENGAGEMENT
ERE ARE A GREAT PERCENTAGE
DAMAGED ENEMY PLANES WHICH GET AWAY
NONE OF THESE ARE COUNTED AS A SCORE.

AT THE END OF THE DAY THE PILOT PROCEEDS TO HIS AERODROME WHERE THE OTHER FIGHTERS ASSEMBLE AND POW-WOW WITH THE SQUADRON-LEADER AND INTELLIGENCE OFFICER WHO WORK OUT DETAILED REPORT FOR GROUP H.Q.

FINALLY H.Q. FIGHTER COMMAND RECEIVES THE REPORTS FROM THE VARIOUS GROUPS, WHICH ARE CAREFULLY CHECKED AND VERIFIED WITH THE MESSAGES FROM THE ADMIRALTY AND WAR OFFICE. EVENTUALLY COMPILING THE DAY'S TOTAL BAG. A LENGTHY AND LABORIOUS TASK.

Bryan de Grineau 1940

ENEMY MACHINES DESTROYED
re sorted, checked and counter-checked before being communicated to the Air Ministry. Intelligence officers are men experienced
n the testing of evidence and the establishment of facts. Some of them are barristers and many of their number saw considerable
ervice in the last war. The ebb and flow of constant battle since *blitzkrieg* broke over Britain has kept them fully occupied.

THE SPITFIRES INCREASE THEIR SCORE

Specially drawn for   HUTCHINSON'S PICTORIAL HISTORY OF THE WAR by C. GIBBERD

WRECK OF ANOTHER RAIDER
An artist's impression of a scene familiar to the shores of England. Two Spitfires have chased a Heinkel raider and shot
it down into the sea. The crew climb out of their cockpits and wait for a British boat to pick them up.

RARE SURVIVAL: THIS BLOCKHOUSE IN KNIGHTON HEATH WOOD IS ONE OF THE FEW WARTIME BUILDINGS TO SURVIVE BESIDE WARMWELL AERODROME.

NEW VILLAGE: THE COMMUNITY OF CROSSWAYS HAS BEEN BUILT ACROSS THE EASTERN SIDE OF THE BATTLE OF BRITAIN AERODROME AT WARMWELL.

Lunar landscape: the site of RAF Warmwell ripped apart for sand and gravel, all the way from Crossways to Knighton Heath.

Warmwell dispersal: pads of tarmac beside the aerodrome, with the mossy blast-wall being set into the eastern edge of Knighton Heath Wood.

Tree grafitto: for 152 Squadron, etched in beech bark, at Knighton Heath Wood.

Fatal shot: through the windscreen of Spitfire N3173 into the head of Pilot Officer Kenneth Christopher Holland of 152 Squadron from RAF Warmwell, by return fire from a German bomber as it crashed into the ground on 25 September 1940.

Göring defeated: the Reichmarshal's portrait brought back to Warmwell as a souvenir when the war crossed the Channel to Normandy in 1944.

Propeller blade: of Messerschmitt Bf.110 3U+JP shot down at Kingston Russell on 7 October 1940.

England alone: when everything depended on her airmen, in the Prime Minister's immortal words, in the summer of 1940.

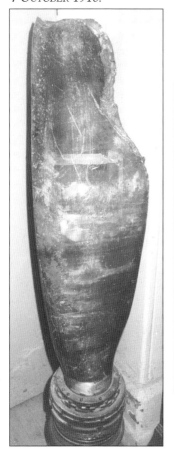

Hendon exhibit: Spitfire X4590 of 609 Squadron from RAF Warmwell, in which Pilot Officer Sidney Jenkyn Hill claimed a half-share of a Junkers Ju.88 bomber shot down on 8 October 1940.

K5425, another Hind belonging to 10 Bombing and Gunnery School, crashed on taking off from Warmwell [27 April 1940].

Warmwell's final "Phoney War" crash, in training at Langton Herring, was of Fairey Seal K3480, also from 10 Bombing and Gunnery School [7 May 1940]. Three days later Hitler made his big move westwards, bringing down the Chamberlain government, and beginning the process that would establish the Luftwaffe in bases on the Cherbourg peninsula, only 70 miles from the Dorset coast.

Hurricane P3598 of 87 Squadron from RAF Exeter crash-landed close to Warmwell Aerodrome after being crippled in a Battle of Britain dog-fight [11 August 1940]. Pilot Officer Andrew McLure survived, as did his fighter.

Hurricanes P3870 and P2910 of 56 Squadron from RAF Boscombe Down force-landed at Warmwell Aerodrome, though without major damage, on the day the Luftwaffe blitzed Sherborne [30 September 1940].

Hurricane V6758 of 238 Squadron from RAF Chilbolton made a forced-landing on a snow-covered Warmwell Aerodrome after icing-up at night over Portland [4 January 1941]. Pilot Officer Bob Doe survived, with eye injuries, but his fighter was ripped apart as it careered into oil-drums.

The next Hurricane in trouble, carrying the "GZ" of 32 Squadron, also attempted a forced-landing but slewed wildly out of control and crashed into the ammunition dump [11 November 1941]. The pilot and two soldiers of the Dorsetshire Regiment, on guard duty, died in the explosion.

There would be a crop of mid-air crashes on and around Warmwell Aerodrome.

Westland Whirlwind P7014 of 263 Squadron crashed while attempting to take-off [8 October 1942].

Hawker Typhoon R8823 of 266 Squadron overshot the runway on landing at Warmwell [27 October 1942].

The following year 263 Squadron experienced a chapter of crashes and other mishaps at and over RAF Warmwell, involving six of its Westland Whirlwinds. P6991 crashed on take-off [9 February 1943]. P7075 crashed on landing [7 May 1943]. P7059 had its emergency when the engine caught fire as it was flying above the base [22 May 1943]. P7110 crashed while attempting a forced-landing near the airfield [13 July 1943]. P6981 crashed on landing at Warmwell [1 August 1943]. P7096 also crashed on landing [10 September 1943].

Tragedy marred Warmwell's welcome for the 474th Fighter Group of the United States Army Air Force, arriving with their P-38 Lightnings, when one of four RAF Typhoons of 263 Squadron spun out of a low roll and crashed half a mile west of the airfield. Pilot Officer Graham Smith was killed as HHS MN129 exploded [15.00 hours, 12 March 1944].

Warnes — commanding one of only two Westland Whirlwind units in Fighter Command, **Squadron Leader Geoff Warnes** also had the distinction of being one of the first pilots in the Royal Air Force to wear contact lenses. His Whirlwinds, of 263 Squadron were based at RAF Warmwell [1941-43].

The lenses may have contributed to his death, after the squadron had re-equipped to Typhoons, on returning from a low-level raid across the English Channel [1944]. After his vision had blurred, one of his pilots made a valiant attempt at leading him home, flying immediately in front and giving directions by radio.

Watercombe crash — of Spitfire N3238 belonging to 609 Squadron from RAF Warmwell, at Watercombe Farm, between Warmwell and Owermoigne, which had been crippled by Messerschmitt Bf.109s over Weymouth [7 October 1940]. Pilot Officer Alan Norman Feary baled out, but at a height that was too low for his parachute to open.

WESTLAND WAPITI: RESEARCH AND DEVELOPMENT MARK IIA MACHINE J9728 AT THE ARMAMENT EXPERIMENTAL ESTABLISHMENT, AMID THE PINES OF MARTLESHAM HEATH, SUFFOLK, AT A TIME WHEN THE EARLIER VERSION WAS IN SQUADRON SERVICE WITH THE RAF IN THE PERSIAN GULF COMMAND AND INDIA.

WESTLAND WALLACE: PROTOTYPE K3488, EFFECTIVELY A REVAMPED WAPITI WITH A 680-HORSEPOWER BRISTOL PEGASUS ENGINE, AT YEOVIL ON 9 MARCH 1934.

WESTLAND LYSANDER: THIS MARK I "LIZZIE" OF AN ARMY CO-OPERATION SQUADRON, L4729, WAS ONE OF THE FIRST PRODUCTION BATCH OF 144 AIRCRAFT IN 1938, BEFORE GAINING LASTING FAME IN COVERT OPERATIONS ACROSS OCCUPIED EUROPE FOR AGENTS, THE RESISTANCE AND RECOVERING ESCAPED PRISONERS.

WESTLAND WHIRLWIND: PROTOTYPE L6845 GOING THROUGH ITS EVALUATION PROCEDURES AT THE AEROPLANE AND ARMAMENT EXPERIMENTAL ESTABLISHMENT AT BOSCOMBE DOWN IN JULY 1940.

WELKIN PROTOTYPE: DG558 FIRST FLEW FROM YEOVIL ON 1 NOVEMBER 1942 AND WAS INTENDED AS A HIGH-ALTITUDE FIGHTER, BUT NEVER ENTERED SQUADRON SERVICE.

EQUIPMENT CARRYING: WESTLAND WESSEX HELICOPTER XT481 OF 845 ROYAL NAVAL AIR SQUADRON ON AN EXERCISE AT RNAS YEOVILTON IN 1975.

WESTLAND WESSEX: THE WORKHORSE OF THE ROYAL NAVY AT THE HEIGHT OF THE COLD WAR, WITH A MARK HU5 HELICOPTER ON THE HARD-STANDING AT RNAS YEOVILTON.

ROYAL PILOT: PRINCE CHARLES TAKING OFF IN WESTLAND WESSEX XT481 OF 845 ROYAL NAVAL AIR SQUADRON IN 1975.

FRONT LINE: WESSEX HU5 HELICOPTER LIFTING AND DROPPING IN AN EXERCISE ON THE DECK OF HMS BULWARK, WITH THE COMMANDO-CARRIER BEING SEEN FROM THE HEAT OF THE MEDITERRANEAN TO MINUS-40 IN THE ARCTIC WHERE ITS HELICOPTERS LANDED ON SKIS AT FORWARD AIR BASE BARDUFOSS.

EXERCISE CLOCKWORK: COMMANDO-CARRIER HMS BULWARK IN THE FJORDS OF NORTHERN NORWAY, AT THE HEIGHT OF COLD WAR IN THE MID-1970S, CONTRASTING WITH MEDITERRANEAN TOURS OF DUTY.

WORLD RECORD: THE WESTLAND LYNX PREPARING FOR ITS FLIGHT THAT BROKE THE 400 KILOMETRES PER HOUR BARRIER FOR A HELICOPTER ON 11 AUGUST 1986.

WINGS APPEAL: THE WARTIME BADGE PROMOTING THE AVIATION SIDE OF WAR WEAPONS WEEK, IN WHICH NATIONAL SAVINGS WERE TARGETED INTO BUYING AIRCRAFT, SHIPS, TANKS AND MUNITIONS.

Watson — Spitfire flyer **Pilot Officer Arthur Roy Watson** [1921-40] of 152 Squadron from RAF Warmwell claimed a Heinkel He.111 bomber when the Dorset fighters were drafted eastwards for the air defence of London [15 September 1940]. He fell to his death near Wareham after engagements with Messerschmitt Bf.109s over Poole Bay [28 November 1940]. He was seen to have "bungled his baling out and tore his parachute" which "streamed out behind him but owing to the tears did not open". Pilot Officer Eric "Boy" Marrs then crept up on the culprit Bf.109, in his blind spot, and avenged Watson's death with "the easiest victory I've had". Watson's body was not recovered.

Welham — RAF fitter **Aircraftman L. W. Welham** [died 15 August 1941], is buried at Langton Herring, in the churchyard extension above Lantern Cottage. He was aged 21.

West Knighton crashes — Typhoon HMS MN129 of 263 Squadron crashed in fields north of the village, half a mile west of Warmwell Aerodrome when it spun out of a low roll that had been staged as part of the RAF's welcome for the 474th Fighter Group of the United States Army Air Force [12 March 1944]. Pilot Officer Graham Smith was killed.

Westland Aircraft — operated as Petters Limited [1910-35] until the Westland Works subsidiary of the oil-engine business, in Yeovil, was reformed in its own name.

Major Laurence Openshaw, the Westland test pilot, was killed when his Westland Widgeon collided with a Blackburn Bluebird in front of the stands at Ensbury Park Racecourse, Bournemouth [6 June 1927].

Westland Aircraft Limited had Sir Ernest Petter as company chairman and a share capital of £250,000 [16 July 1935]. Managing director was Captain Peter Acland. William "Teddy' Petter (the chairman's son) was technical director. Air Vice-Marshal N. D. K. MacEwen was non-administrative director. Stuart Keep was general manager. Harald Penrose was their test pilot.

He would put prototypes through their paces across the Dorset sky. The Purbeck coast was his favourite scenic backdrop, and the then deserted Boscombe Down, in Wiltshire, became the second objective on a 150-mile triangle. Returning home became easier when Yeovil Aerodrome, a narrow grass strip from east to west, was enlarged to 1,200 yards [1936]. That coincided with big extensions to the factory as Britain re-armed.

An attempt to buy out British Marine Aircraft Limited failed by one vote and blocked Sir Ernest Petter's hopes of moving main airframe construction to Hamble, on Southampton Water [1937]. Westland's failure to extend and expand made it vulnerable as one of the Cinderella companies of British aviation at a time when the arms and engineering industries were awash with money and projects.

Coinciding with their launching of the *Queen Elizabeth*, the world's largest liner, Clydebank shipbuilders John Brown and Company announced the acquisition of a controlling interest in Westland Aircraft Limited, from Petters Limited [27 September 1938]. Sir Ernest Petter had sold out, over the heads of managing director Captain Peter Acland and his own son, Teddy Petter.

There were questions in the House of Commons after Browns announced the redundancy of Yeovil's foundry workers, having closed it when Brush Electric bought the engine-making side of the Petter business, and moved metal working to Loughborough [1938]. Westland was on the verge of a strike until re-training was promised for all of them.

Sir Ernest Petter was succeeded as chairman by Charles Melville McLaren [born 1913], who would become 3rd Baron Aberconway on his father's death [1953].

North of the town, Harald Penrose noted the flatness of the plain beyond Yeovilton village, unaware that a Handley Page Harrow had made a successful crash landing there [1937], and the test pilot carried out a forced landing in his Hawker Hector to prove the point. Westland wanted a new aerodrome and the Admiralty and Air Ministry were also searching the maps for suitable locations.

Commander John Heath of the Admiralty Air Division put his finger on Yeovilton's fields which were acquired from the Ecclesiastical Commissioners of the Church of England as Europe slipped back into war. Lieutenant T. W. Harrington, with 758 Fleet Air Arm Squadron at Eastleigh, Hampshire, drove to Somerset to see flood waters around what was becoming the first purpose-built Royal Naval Air Station to be created since the Great War [November 1939]. Its offices were initially in Rag Cottages at Yeovilton. The new aerodrome would be commissioned as HMS Heron [18 June 1940] for No. 1 Naval Air Fighter School.

Soon it would double as Westland's satellite facility. Westland Aircraft Limited was provided with a hangar of 40,000 square feet on the south side of a bend in Pyle Lane, Yeovilton. The building was 400 feet in length with raised offices at the east end looking down on the workshop floor. A concrete apron led to an aircraft park. Gateways across the lane provided access to the airfield on the other side of the road. The works was a "metal-bashing" facility, rebuilding RAF Spitfires and stripping down Yeovil-made Lysanders for shipment overseas, such as to Malta, or adapting them with Harrow long-range fuel tanks for use by the Special Operations Executive on secret missions across occupied Europe. Such machines were painted matt black and carried special radio equipment and a boarding ladder. Combat-damaged Westland Whirlwinds would land for urgent repairs. This Westland out-station was under the control of the wartime Civilian Repair Organisation.

Post-war refurbishment of Spitfires and refitting Gloster Meteor jet fighters with pressurised cockpits kept the Yeovilton works in business until the new Queen's reign [1952]. Military helicopters followed for adaptations, such as the Dragonfly and Whirlwind, and a big contract to refurbish and test-fly 430 swept-wing North American Sabres followed their shipping to Europe for secondment to Nato.

What had become Westland's post-war specialisation in helicopters was consolidated by acquisition of Saunders-Roe Limited [1959] and the Helicopter Division of Bristol Aircraft Limited [1960] after which it had no serious rival in the United Kingdom.

Westland Aircraft Limited acquired Fairey Aviation Limited [1960]. The Westland Hangar at Yeovilton turned out its last aircraft, a Fairey Gannet, when refurbishment operations moved to Locking at Weston-super-Mare [1972]. It was then used for repairs and flight-refuelling adaptations until eventual purchase by the Royal Navy [1985].

The company's helicopter operations became a separate entity with the creation of Westland Helicopters Limited [1 October 1966]. It had interests in the British Hovercraft Corporation and partnered Aerospatiale in France and Agusta in Italy in joint projects. A subsidiary company, Normalair-Garrett, manufactures pressurised and hydraulic equipment.

The Westland name attached to the following aircraft which are listed in chronological order:

Westland N.1B — a float-plane, the company's first aeroplane, was a single-seat biplane to Admiralty specifications for "a fighting scout seaplane" in the second half of the Great War. Designed by Robert Bruce and Arthur Davenport it was powered by a 150-horsepower Bentley BR-1 rotary engine and armed with Vickers and Lewis machine-guns. Prototypes Westland N16 and N17 carried Royal Naval Air Service serial numbers. They were tested on the Isle of Grain, near Rochester, Kent [August 1917], but though this was followed by successful sea trials, the European war would draw to a close before production could start.

Westland Wagtail — a single-seat fighter, designed to Air Board specification A.1(a), for a manoeuvrable biplane capable of 135 mph at 15,000 feet [1917]. Three prototypes were constructed, each carrying two Vickers and a Lewis machine-gun, and again took to the sky as the Great War moved into its final spring [April 1918]. The second prototype was destroyed by fire [29 April 1918]. There were continuing problems with the 170-horsepower ABC Wasp-I seven-cylinder radial engine. This was abandoned [October 1918] and replaced by the 160-horsepower Armstrong-

Siddeley Lynx engine, with two machines being delivered for evaluation to the Royal Aircraft Establishment at Farnborough [1921].

Westland Weasel — two-seater fighter reconnaissance biplane, designed to an Air Board specification for a successor to the Bristol F.2b fighter [April 1918]. It also came to grief with engine trouble. The 320-horsepower ABC Dragonfly nine-cylinder radial engine would be replaced by a 385-horsepower Cosmos Jupiter-II. Meanwhile, as with other projects, the beginning of flight tests coincided with the end of the war [November 1918]. The fourth Weasel, F2913, reached the Royal Aircraft Establishment with its full armament of two forward-firing synchronised Vickers machine-guns and a revolving Lewis gun for the observer. The aircraft never went into production.

Westland Widgeon — this was the aircraft in which Westland test pilot Major Laurence Openshaw met his death, in front of crowded stands, in a collision at Ensbury Park Racecourse, Bournemouth [6 June 1927].

Westland Walrus — a failed attempt at turning the de Havilland DH-9A into a naval airframe, which was abandoned after only a few had been built [1920].

Westland Westbury — twin-engined heavy night-fighter to Air Ministry specification 4/24 for a new generation biplane with wooden wings and steel fuselage [1924]. The Westbury was assembled in direct competition with the Bristol Bagshot which had won the same contract. They both had a pair of uncowled 450-horsepower Bristol Jupiter-VI nine-cylinder radial engines. The Westbury was a three-bay machine with a pilot and two gunners. Flight tests failed to coincide with a time of economic and military possibilities [September 1926]. Another prototype, the Westbury II, had 480-horsepower Bristol Jupiter VIII engines, and a rounded nose, plus tail adaptations.

Westland Racer — single-engine parasol monoplane fighter, being designed as an independent company venture, with the emphasis on speed and performance [spring 1926]. One prototype, powered by a 275-horsepower Rolls-Royce Falcon-III in-line engine, went through flight tests [November 1926]. It was written-off in a crash landing [1927] but the parts were recycled to a revised design that was named the Westland Wizard.

Westland C29 Autogiro — a two-seater derivation of a French machine, at a time when Juan Cierva lectured the Royal Aeronautical Society on refinements to his C30 with an inclined rotor hinge to enable jump starts, having increased revolutions per minute by upwards of 25 per cent [1935]. Following the death of Flying Officer L. W. Oliver in the crash of a French RAF Autogiro at Old Sarum, Wiltshire test pilot Harald Penrose reminded Westland chief designer Arthur Davenport of his "tentative dives with the Autogiro and my certainty that there was a critical speed after which the dive would increase uncontrollably due to blade-twist". George Lepère, its designer, visited Yeovil to discuss the problem with Westland's young technical director, William "Teddy" Petter, who was the son of Westland's chairman, Sir Ernest Petter.

Westland Wapiti Mark II — metal-framed biplane, replacing the wood-built Mark I, it progressively replaced the de Havilland DH-9A and went into RAF service with 5 Squadron and 27 Squadron, and with the Hart in 604 Squadron, until replacement by the Demon [1935]. By then, when the Wapitis were mainly in India and Iraq, spares were being problematic.

Westland Wallace — went into RAF service with the General Reconnaissance Unit. A closed-cockpit version was also put into production [1935].

Westland Wizard — the variant version of the Westland Racer, being a metal single-seater parasol monoplane fighter [autumn 1927]. It was uprated to a 490-horsepower super-charged Rolls-Royce F-XI twelve-cylinder engine which gave a sharp rate of climb to 188 mph cruising speed at 10,000 feet. Two Vickers machine-guns protruded on pylons from either side of the fuselage. It was given an Air Ministry contract for RAF trials on Martlesham Heath, near Ipswich, Suffolk. Performance was good but its fighting usefulness was compromised by poor forward visibility. J9252, with a new cabane and elevated wing, was much improved and given a 500-horsepower super-charged Kestrel-II engine. Its demise was brought about by RAF resistance to monoplanes.

Westland Interceptor — a monoplane fighter with low-slung wings, designed to meet Air Ministry specification F.20/27 [1927]. This called for an air-cooled radial engine and twin Vickers machine-guns firing from the fuselage. It was powered, initially, by a 440-horsepower Bristol Mercury-IIA radial engine, which was superseded by the 480-horsepower Mercury-IIIA, and then replaced by the 420-horsepower Bristol Jupiter VII engine. Modifications were also made to the wing and tail with the latter being enlarged, but performance was disappointing. The speed reached 192 mph at 10,000 feet but the Interceptor lost out to the competition and a biplane from Hawker won the production order.

Westland COW-gun Fighter — another low-wing monoplane, built to Air Ministry specification F.29/27 which was to be armed with an upward-firing 37-mm cannon produced by the Coventry Ordnance Works [1927]. It was fitted with a 485-horsepower Bristol Mercury-IIIA nine-cylinder air-cooled radial engine. Prototype J9565, uprated with a Mercury-IVA engine, was delivered to the Aeroplane and Armament Experimental Establishment at Martlesham Heath [1931] but the RAF saw limited potential in vertical gunnery. J9565 remained in limbo for years [July 1934] and COW-style cannon would be left to the Germans to develop, for attacking Allied bombers towards the end of the Second World War.

Westland Wessex — small feeder airliner, being a monoplane with simple wing-struts [1929]. Two were sold to Imperial Airways for pilot training near Croydon, being operated through a subsidiary, Air Pilots Training Limited [February 1935]. It was also bought by Wilson Airways of Nairobi for services in Central Africa.

Westland F.7/30 — a biplane fighter built to meet the requirements of Air Ministry specifications F.7/30 [1930]. It was powered by a 600-horsepower Goshawk-VIII engine and mounted four Vickers machine-guns around the nose. Evaluation at Martlesham Heath, with prototype K2891, achieved 185 mph at 15,000 feet, but general performance was poor [1934].

Westland PV7 — a private venture 75-feet wing-span monoplane to specification G4/31, which attracted six other contenders by the time the prototypes were being evaluated by the Aeroplane and Armament Experimental Establishment. The RAF test pilots and technical staff recommended the Westland PV7, despite an ill-timed crash [1935], but were over-ruled.

Westland CL20 Autogiro — two-seater successor to the C29, designed by Teddy Petter and George Lepère. It failed rotor tests on the ground and was sent by road to Hanworth. There Henry Alan Marsh took it up for its first flight and found it deficient in lift, being unable to reach 1,000 feet with a passenger aboard [November 1935]. Nonetheless, six metal fuselages were constructed at Yeovil, and machine parts ordered.

Westland-Hill Pterodactyl Mark IA — revolutionary experimental airframe with swept-back wings and no tail [1925].

Westland Pterodactyl Mark V — more sophisticated but still novel and tail-less, this turret-fighter never saw its public debut. Both authorised pilots were grounded by influenza at the time of the RAF Display at Hendon [29 June 1935]. Fate was on their side, given the "torsional flexibility of the wing" which prevented a dive in excess of 200 mph with the stick fully forward. Test pilot Harald Penrose passed on this warning to company technical director Teddy Petter who abandoned the project when its designer, Captain Geoffrey Hill, became a professor at University College, London. Penrose then had a close-call when he attempted taking the prototype to the Royal Aircraft Establishment at Farnborough for investigation: "Within seconds of take-off to the east, over Yeovil, the coolant warning light flashed danger. Height was 100 feet above the houses. I instantly turned down-wind, and the engine seized solid as the machine skimmed the hedge and landed. Inspection revealed that the front wheel of the articulated undercarriage had gone full travel and knocked the radiator cock closed. At Petter's instigation the machine was sent by lorry to Farnborough and never flown again."

Westland Lysander — a general purpose aeroplane to specification A.39/34, for replacement of the Audax in Army Co-Operation Squadrons [1935[. Westland's technical director, Teddy Petter, looked for inspiration to the Pegasus sail-plane and experimented with hollow extrusions for struts, produced by W. C. Devereux at High Duty Alloys. Silver-painted prototype K6127 had its first flight only a year after "Instructions to Proceed". Test pilot Harald Penrose took off on the very same day that bomber specification B.9/32, the Vickers Wellington made its aerial debut with "Mutt" Summers of Spitfire fame [15 June 1936]. Trials took place at a deserted Wiltshire airstrip from the Great War, on Boscombe Down, to which the Aeroplane and Armament Experimental Establishment would be evacuated as the Suffolk coast became uncomfortably close to the renewed prospect of a world at war. Petter's design incorporated Arthur Davenport's enthusiasm for strut-braced high-wing monoplanes, and had a distinctive look that was more French than English, with a hairpin undercarriage. Light alloy extrusions made for an easy climb but Penrose found that the tail trim needed to be much bigger if an ordinary pilot would ever stand a chance of bringing it safely back to earth: "The wind tunnel, as so often, had failed to predict so big a change of downwash, and this necessitated several re-designs of the trimming gear to secure an exceptionally big negative tailplane angle for landing." This successfully turned it into the perfect Army support and special operations airframe "with its ability at slot hanging and take-off and landing in the length of a football pitch". Landing and turning on a postage stamp often had to be done in the dark. During the Second World War it saved hundreds of agents, escapees and downed airmen in flights for the Special Operations Executive across occupied Europe. One such black-painted Lysander, guided only by torch signals, landed near Rouen at night [15 April 1943] to pick up British "White Rabbit" Maquis liaison officer Wing Commander Forest Yeo-Thomas, and a shot-down pilot, Captain Ryan of the United States Army Air Force. The highly manoeuvrable aircraft landed at 60 miles per hour and took off again in just 36 yards. Navigation had been dead reckoning from a fixed point on the French coast. Going home the airframes frequently soaked up punishment — famously the Lysander with 30 bullet holes through its fuselage and the 31st in its pilot's neck.

Westland Whirlwind — evolved from John Digby's drawing for an innovative magnesium-skinned slender fuselage with high-aspect ratio wings, to Air Ministry specification F37/35. This requirement, for a twin-engine fighter mounting four 20-mm cannon, arose from suggestions by Air Marshal Sir Ralph Sorley and Teddy Petter's team were encouraged by Air Vice-Marshal Wilfred Freeman who had been impressed by the Lysander [spring 1936]. They decided upon 885-horsepower Rolls-Royce Peregrine engines. The striking lines of the innovative "cannon fighter" took two years to take to the sky. Having learnt from an earlier bad experience with Yeovil rooftops, test pilot Harald Penrose once again insisted that the prototype was carted by lorry to a still empty Boscombe Down, above Amesbury, Wiltshire, "for first flight above countryside giving better chance of a forced landing". Dark grey L6844 had to be stopped, steaming on the grass, in the calm early afternoon [11 October 1938]. The third attempt, down the grassy slope, lifted with only 100 yards to spare before the perimeter fence. Watchers from Westlands and the RAF continued to hold their breath as Penrose battled with an ineffective rudder, dropping nose, and shuddering turns. The problems would never be totally resolved. The 885-horsepower Rolls-Royce Peregrine I engine failed to meet expectations. Works management at Yeovil barely coped with the progress from development to production as 400 Whirlwind Mark I were ordered for the RAF, in two placements of 200 each [1939]. The first would fly just in time for the Battle of Britain [June 1940] but in the event only 114 were ever delivered. These found their way into just two operational units, 263 Squadron and 137 Squadron, and would be based at West Country airfields, including Dorset's RAF Warmwell. Dennis Edkins at Yeovil, listed specific defects: "Too many technical innovations such as a one-piece high-lift Fowler flap from aileron to aileron which also controlled radiator cooling: ducted radiators of light alloy with horizontal tubes and reverse-flow; plenum chamber inlets; exhaust carried dangerously through the petrol tank; pure magnesium monocoque structure; butt-jointed longitudinal plating; high strength steel castings; torsion taken on the engine cowls; sealed inset balanced nose for controls; offset rudder hinge — all adding up to longer development time than necessary." The hydraulic Exactor controls added to the delays. Then there were operational fears as the "tricky demon of speed" experienced what would later be realised as Mach trouble as it dived to 445 mph and began to go out of control. Mishaps marred its operational life at Warmwell and elsewhere. Not a suitable aeroplane for air show nostalgia. See entries for Warmwell crashes and Whirlwinds at Warmwell.

Westland Whirlwind — derived from the Sikorski S-55, being the principal British helicopter of the 1950s.

Westland Welkin — twin-engined, high-altitude fighter, to specification F.4/40, carrying six 20-mm cannon and authorised for development to prototypes from Westland's project P14 two-seater design [9 January 1941]. Powered by 1,565-horsepower Rolls-Royce Merlin-61 engines the first flew nearly two years later [1 November 1942]. It looked much like the de Havilland Mosquito and went into production with 1,650-horsepower Merlin-72/73 engines, followed by Merlin-76/77, with confirmation of contracts for 100 and then 200 machines. Pressurisation of the cockpits was by Rotol blower from the starboard engine. Tests were carried out by the Aeroplane and Armament Experimental Establishment at Boscombe Down [September 1943]. Manoeuvrability was far from perfect, and the RAF's requirements for high-altitude interceptions were proving less than anticipated, so the Air Ministry cancelled production. A total of 75 had been delivered and another 26 airframes were being completed at Yeovil. The aircraft never proceeded to squadron service.

Westland Welkin II — an attempt at salvaging the abandoned Welkin night-fighter design, modified to specification F.9/43 which incorporated bulbous nose-mounted Airborne Interception radar. Two prototypes were ordered as conversions of existing Welkin airframes [4 February 1943]. They were fitted with Mark VIII radar pods and delivered to Boscombe Down for flight evaluation [23 October 1944]. By this time an order for 60 of the final batch of the earlier Welkin had been reinstated, subject to revision to Welkin II specifications. Cancelled when it became clear that the war was drawing to a close [early 1945].

Westland Wyvern — evolved from company project P10 for a long-range sea-borne day fighter for aircraft-carriers [1944]. It was envisaged that it would need to carry a variety of anti-ship weapons, from one torpedo to eight rockets, and had Naval specification N.11/44 written to meet its capabilities [November 1944]. Six prototypes were ordered, as single-seat fighters of standard contemporary design, carrying four 20-mm Hispano Mark V cannon. A 3,500-horsepower Rolls-Royce Eagle engine was selected for the first production order of 20 machines [August 1946]. The first prototype, TS371, would be flown by test pilot Harald Penrose [16 December 1946] and had its photo-call over Swanage and the Isle of Purbeck. Meantime, technology was moving on, and

WESTLAND WYVERN: TEST FLIGHT OF TS371 BY HARALD PENROSE, WESTWARDS ACROSS DURLSTON BAY WITH PEVERIL POINT BEHIND THE PILOT ON 16 DECEMBER 1946, AND THE CHALK CLIFFS OF BALLARD DOWN BEYOND SWANAGE BAY.

provision had been made for conversion to Rolls-Royce Clyde turboprop engines. However, the Armstrong Siddeley Python was then specified, and heavier munitions needed to be carried. Though 456 mph had been achieved, with a range of 1,186 miles with external fuel tanks, the design was sent back to the drawing board.

Westland Dragonfly — the American Sikorski S-51 helicopter, as produced under licence by Westland Aircraft Limited [1947]. A total of 133 were produced and the success of the Sikorski venture persuaded the Yeovil management that their future would be in helicopters.

Westland Wyvern TF Mk II — adapted to meet naval specification N.12/45, this became Britain's first turboprop-powered shipboard fighter. Prototypes compared the performance of the Armstrong Siddeley Python with the 4,500-horsepower Rolls-Royce Clyde. The former went into the production version which was otherwise much like the original Wyvern. Its empty weight of 15,600 pounds could be increased to 24,500 pounds when fully armed. Maximum speed was 383 mph and the range, with external tanks, 910 miles. It was first flown by test pilot Harald Penrose [16 February 1950] and would be the first turboprop aircraft to land and take-off at sea, from the aircraft-carrier HMS *Illustrious* [June 1950].

Westland Wyvern S Mk IV — modifications of the Wyvern for operational orders developed into the strike S Mk IV variant, powered by a Python-3 of 3,670 super-horsepower plus 1,180 pounds residual thrust. The first deliveries, from an order for 87 aircraft, went into Fleet Air Arm service with 813 Royal Naval Air Squadron [1953]. Three more front-line squadrons would receive the S Mk IV. It would become the first British turboprop aircraft to see combat use, off Egypt during the Suez campaign [1956], and continued in squadron service until later in the decade [March 1958].

Westland Wasp — the first Small Ship Flight of this sea-based anti-submarine helicopter was established by the Fleet Air Arm [11 November 1963], with platforms being built for this light-weight machine on frigates and other smaller warships.

Westland Westminster — a "sky-crane" helicopter, which never progressed beyond two prototypes [1968].

Westland Sea King — heavy naval transport helicopter developed under licence from the airframe and rotor of the Sikorsky SH-3D [1959]. To meet Royal Navy requirements it was fitted with Rolls-Royce Bristol Gnome H-1400 engines. XV642, the first production Sea King HAS Mark I, flew from Yeovil [7 May 1969] and another five followed to 700S Intensive Flying Trials Squadron at RNAS Culdrose. HMS *Blake* was converted into a command helicopter cruiser and allocated a squadron of Sea Kings. It was always intended by the Royal Navy for hunter-killer operations but has also triumphed in a Search and Rescue role, notably when 22 passengers and crew were winched from the blazing wreck of the Swedish freighter Finneagle and taken to Kirkwall in the Orkney Islands [2 October 1980].

Westland WG-13 Lynx — came into being through the Anglo-French helicopter agreement [1967-68] and co-operation with Aerospatiale. The prototype of this general-purpose military helicopter made its first flight from Yeovil [21 March 1971]. It was powered by Rolls-Royce BS.360 engines and was flown with skid-landing gear to British Army specifications. The first Royal Navy deck-landing took place on the Royal Fleet Auxiliary Engadine [29 June 1973].

Westland Wessex — the first twin-engined helicopter to enter service with the Royal Air Force. It carried up to 16 troops and was also versatile in rescue and medical support modes. In the latter role it could carry eight stretchers. Its HU-5 version had Royal Navy trials with 846 Royal Naval Air Squadron at RNAS Yeovilton [May 1972]. Commando helicopter pilots were also trained in the Wessex HU-5, with 707 Royal Naval Air Squadron at Yeovilton, including the Prince of Wales [autumn 1974].

Westland Commando — fixed-gear adaptation of the Sea King for an Egyptian troop-carrying order, the prototype of which first flew from Yeovil [12 September 1973]. Built for long-range land use it dispensed with amphibious capability.

Westland Lynx — went into Royal Navy use with 702 Royal Naval Air Squadron, commissioned at RNAS Yeovilton [26 January 1978].

Westland WG-30 — transport version of the Lynx helicopter offering more space for civilian and military operators, with the production version G-BGHF carrying the name "Westland 30" and landing in London heliports [1980].

Westland Lynx 3 — combat version, the prototype of which first flew from Yeovil [11 August 1984]. The demonstrator model, registered as G-LYNX, took the world speed record for a helicopter, from the Soviet Mil Mi-24 gunship, by breaking through the 400 kilometres per hour barrier [11 August 1986]. The average speed over a 15/25 kilometre course was 249.09 mph. Flown by Trevor Egginton, it had been fitted with British Experimental Rotor Programme BERP-III main rotor blades — promising improved efficiency approaching 40 per cent — and had a water-methanol injection system and tuned jet-pipes added to the standard Gem-60 turboshaft engines. The gearbox was uprated, new tail surfaces installed, and the airframe cleaned for maximum streamlining.

Though the military Lynx 3 was 27 per cent heavier than the standard model, it operated with the same dynamics, and offered greater firepower capacity and more advanced avionics.

Westland Lynx AH-9 — popularly known as the Battlefield Lynx, this featured wheeled landing gear and noticeable infra-red exhaust suppressers, to reduce its vulnerability to heat-seeking missiles [1989].

Westland-Aerospatiale SA-330 Puma — air-transportable logistic helicopter for the RAF and French Armed Forces, developed as a result of the partnership agreement [1968]. Those for British use had French-built components which were assembled by Westland's Hayes Division in Middlesex.

Westland-Aerospatiale SA-341 Gazelle — light-weight military helicopter for the RAF and French Forces also developed under partnership agreement. Production took place at Westland's Weston Division, in the Oldmixon Works, near Weston-super-Mare.

Weston — Spitfire flyer **Pilot Officer Weston** from RAF Warmwell claimed a third share of 152 Squadron's kill of a Heinkel He.111 off Portland [15 September 1940]. He delivered the coup de grace which sent it blazing into the sea. The bomber probably belonged to Kampfgruppe 55 from Chartres.

Weymouth crashes — Hurricane P2950 of 238 Squadron from RAF Middle Wallop crashed at South Down, above Chalbury Lodge, Preston, after a Battle of Britain dog-fight [13 July 1940]. The pilot, Flight Lieutenant John Connelly Kennedy, was killed.

Next, into the countryside, was a German Dornier Do.17 bomber shot down by Spitfires of 152 Squadron from RAF Warmwell [25 July 1940].

The first RAF fighter to be lost offshore was Spitfire N3023 of 609 Squadron from RAF Warmwell [27 July 1940].

Hurricane P3222 of 238 Squadron from RAF Middle Wallop was shot down off Weymouth by a Messerschmitt Bf.109, killing Pilot Officer Frederick Norman Cawse [11 August 1940]. He was aged 22.

A Messerschmitt Bf.109 escort fighter was put into the sea during the Luftwaffe's Adlertag (Eagle Day) attack [13 August 1940]. The kill was claimed by Pilot Officer Tadeusz Nowierski in a Spitfire of 609 Squadron. The German pilot, Leutnant Heinz Pfannschmidt, was rescued and taken prisoner.

As a result of the next series of engagements a crippled Hurricane crash-landed at Field Barn Farm, beside Chafeys Lake, Radipole [15 August 1940]. R2687 belonged to 87 Squadron from RAF Exeter. It was a total write-off but Pilot Officer Dudley Jay was able to walk away from the wreckage.

Spitfire N3061 of 234 Squadron fell into Weymouth Bay [6 September 1940], followed by Hurricane P3414 of 504 Squadron [30 September 1940]. Both were shot down in Battle of Britain dog-fights.

Hawker Hurricane Z4993, an adapted airframe being tested by the Aeroplane and Armament Experimental Establishment, flew into the side of Ridgeway Hill, above Upwey, when it was shrouded in hill-fog [25 October 1941].

Whirlwinds at Warmwell — the Westland Whirlwind, a wartime rarity in squadron service, evolved during its time at RAF Warmwell with 263 Squadron. The fitting of bomb-racks was suggested by Squadron Leader T. Pugh in 1941.

Modifications were made so that a single 250-lb or 500-lb bomb could be carried under each wing and the trial operation took place from Warmwell when two sections of Whirlwinds, escorted by Spitfires, crossed the Channel to attack four armed trawlers steaming westwards from Cap de la Hague, towards Alderney [9 September 1942].

Two were sunk. No bomb-sight was used and the Whirlwinds generally dropped their loads from 50 feet or less, utilising delayed action fuses. "Working on the railway," they also used the aircraft's four 20-mm Hispano cannon to attack trains in northern France.

Named Whirlwind P7094 "Bellows" was a war weapons donation from the Bellows Fellowship of 70,000 wealthy British expatriates in South America. Others followed — P7116 being "Bellows Argentina" and P7121 "Bellows Uraguay No.1".

Whitcombe crash — near Whitcombe Barn, of Hurricane P2987 belonging to 504 Squadron from RAF Filton [17.00 hours, 30 September 1940]. Damaged in the dog-fights following the Luftwaffe's blitz of Sherborne, Pilot Officer Edward Murray Frisby also found himself running out of fuel, only four miles from Warmwell Aerodrome. He was able to make a successful forced-landing on rolling chalk downland.

Wick — Luftwaffe ace **Hauptmann Helmut Wick** [1918-40], holder of the Iron Cross First Class, who had 57 white kill-bars painted on the rudder of his Messerschmitt Bf.109E, was shot down over the sea by Flight-Lieutenant John Dundas of 609 Squadron from RAF Warmwell [28 November 1940]. "I've finished an Me.109 — whoopee" were the last words heard from Dundas as he then disappeared into radio silence, off the Isle of Wight. Neither body was recovered.

Wight — Hurricane pilot **Flight-Lieutenant Ronald Derek Gordon Wight** [1918-40] was shot down and killed off Portland, in N2650 of 213 Squadron of RAF Exeter [10.23 hours, 11 August 1940]. His body would be washed ashore in France and he is buried in Cayeux-sur-Mer Communal Cemetery. Born at Skelmorlie, Ayrshire, he had entered the RAF in his teens [1934], and flown to Merville to support the British Expeditionary Force during the fall of France.

Wigley — Navy flyer **Captain Anthony Wigley** was killed when his Wessex Mark V helicopter crashed on one of the breakwaters of Portland Harbour [3 December 1984].

Wildblood — Spitfire flyer **Pilot Officer Timothy Seddon Wildblood** [1920-40] claimed a Messerschmitt Bf.109 [11 August 1940], followed by a Bf.110 [12 August 1940], then a Junkers Ju.87 and half a share in another Ju.87 the same day [18 August 1940].

He was reported "Missing in Action" after being lost over the sea in R6994 during a day of fierce Battle of Britain dog-fights [25 August 1940]. His body was not recovered.

Williams — Spitfire flyer **Pilot Officer William Dudley Williams** [1915-76] served with 152 Squadron at RAF Warmwell and claimed a total of five enemy aircraft during the Battle of Britain. He was awarded the Distinguished Flying Cross [7 January 1941].

He would become an instructor and then returned to combat in the Far East, commanding 615 Squadron from Feni, India [1943]. Though he died in Sussex he had maintained his love of Dorset and is buried at West Knighton, only a mile from the former Warmwell Aerodrome.

"ONE OF THE FEW", his gravestone reads.

Wills — glider pilot **Philip Wills** was towed by an ancient Avro 504 biplane into the middle of the English Channel, and released in a German Minimos glider to drift back to the Purbeck cliffs at St Alban's Head, Worth Matravers [23 June 1940]. The object of the exercise, which was successfully accomplished on behalf of the Telecommunications Research Establishment, was to ensure that current radar technology would pick up signals from the wooden gliders of any German invasion force.

Window — codename for radar-reflective foil, deployed from the air in the form of millions of strips of aluminium foil, developed by the Telecommunications Research Establishment at Worth Matravers. Perfected in Dorset by radar pioneer Robert Watson-Watt [winter 1941-42] it was devised to create a smoke-screen effect upon enemy radar sets at the onset of mass bombing raids. Fighter Command blocked its operational use, however, fearing that it might give the Germans the idea at a time when they were still able to carry out major air attacks against Britain.

"Let us open the window," Prime Minister Winston Churchill eventually decided, and it was first used in an air raid on Hamburg [24-25 July 1943] by 791 British bombers. Forty tons were dropped — a total of 92 million strips — and all but twelve of the aircraft returned. Normally the losses from such a raid would have been about 48, so the use of Window had saved 36 aeroplanes and their crews.

Winfrith Heath Decoy Aerodrome — rigged with flares and moving lights to draw air attack from RAF Warmwell, being three miles south-east from the actual airfield. It added a Junkers Ju.88, apparently brought down by anti-aircraft fire, to its collection of bomb craters [4 May 1941]. The crew were able to bale out safely.

Winfrith Newburgh crashes — having clashed with Messerschmitt Bf.109 and Bf.110 fighters over Bournemouth, Pilot Officer Kenneth Marston of 56 Squadron from RAF Boscombe Down managed to bring damaged Hurricane P2866 down at Longcutts East, East Knighton, in a crash-landing [11.30 hours, 30 September 1940]. It was the day that the Luftwaffe blitzed Sherborne. Marston survived, with shrapnel wounds and minor cuts, but would lose his life at the end of the year when a fighter overshot the grass runway at RAF Middle Wallop and sliced through his tail [12 December 1940].

A Junkers Ju.88, apparently hit by anti-aircraft fire, crashed on the decoy-airfield that had been established on Winfrith Heath to draw the Luftwaffe from RAF Warmwell [4 May 1941]. The crew were able to bale out safely.

Spitfire P8656 of 234 Squadron crashed at West Knighton [14 July 1941].

Wings over Dorset — book title of the county's first gloriously illustrated flying history, compiled by Poole glider pilot Leslie Dawson [1983]. It is subtitled "Aviation's story in the South" and the present author contributed several sections and the captions. I also produced the book for him, through Dorset Publishing Company.

The revised edition would have even more pictures [1989].

Winkton Advanced Landing Ground — in the Avon valley, extending from Winkton in the parish of Burton and north to Ripley, near Christchurch (Ordnance Survey map reference SZ 169 971). Elevation 40 feet above sea level. Hedges were grubbed out and two runways were laid as sheets of steel mesh directly on to the grass [July 1943].

Four blister hangars were erected. Officially opened in March 1944 and handed over to the United States Army Air Force, though nominally under 11 Group RAF Fighter Command. One runway ran north-south from east of Parsonage Farm to west of Clockhouse Farm, and the other east-west from the Ripley road to within a third of a mile of cottages at Bransgore. Used as a satellite airfield to Christchurch, principally for cross-Channel ground attack missions. Closed when the war began to move into Germany [January 1945]. Pundit code "XT".

Winterborne Houghton crashes — on Great Hill, the downland above Heath Bottom, of Hurricane V6777 belonging to 238 Squadron from RAF Chilbolton [16.00 hours, 7 October 1940]. It was gunned down by Messerschmitt Bf.109s which had been escorting bombers attacking the Westland Aircraft Company at Yeovil.

Pilot Officer Aubrey Richard Covington baled out over Dorset for the second time in a week — apparently the first occasion was near Sherborne after accounting for two Messerschmitt Bf.110s [1 October 1940]. The second time he was not quite unscathed, being taken to Blandford Cottage Hospital for treatment of minor injuries.

Gloster Meteor Mark T7, WL350, operated by the Fleet Requirements Unit provided by Airwork Services Ltd from Hurn Aerodrome, was returning there on a training flight from Yeovilton Royal Naval Air Station [12.30 hours, 13 February 1969], when it spun into the northern side of North Houghton Down (Ordnance Survey map reference ST 808 063). It was being flown by Robert Edward Martin "Bob" Woolley, aged 26, of Lacy Drive, Wimborne, and Flight-Lieutenant Robert Valen Pratchett, 31, from the Central Flying School at RAF Little Rissington, Gloucestershire.

Bob Woolley's son, Mark, writes that the cause of the accident "was never officially established but a combination of a flat spin, a relatively low altitude, and the absence of ejector seats were all contributory factors". Witnesses in the area of Okeford Hill and Turnworth said they heard "a loud surging noise" followed by "its engine alternating between roaring and stopping" after which the jet was seen "spinning in level flight before descending out of sight". No one saw it crash, on a shallow hillside in remote farmland two kilometres west of Hedge End, but local farmers Don Browning and John Tory soon arrived on the scene and made a brave attempt to remove the aircrew from the burning wreckage.

Both had been killed on impact. Though no distress call had been received from the aircraft, at 12.30 Yeovilton radio recorded a burst of heavy breathing, sighs, and the word "Christ" in a transmission that was assumed to have come from the Meteor.

Withall — Australian Spitfire pilot **Flight-Lieutenant Latham Carr Withall** [1911-40], in P9456 of 152 Squadron from RAF Warmwell, was shot down and killed by the gunners of Junkers Ju.88 bombers, within sight of the Isle of Wight [12 August 1940].

Wolton — Spitfire flyer **Pilot Officer Ralph "Bob" Wolton** [born 1914] claimed the first two kills for 152 Squadron from RAF Warmwell [25 July 1940]. One was a Dornier and the other a Junkers Ju.87 "Stuka". The gunner of another "Stuka" would shoot down Wolton's Spitfire, into Lyme Bay, three weeks later [15 August 1940]. He managed to swim to one of the offshore marked buoys of the Chesil Beach Bombing Range, from which he was rescued by an RAF launch from Lyme Regis.

He nearly plunged to his death after losing control in a dive [7 September 1940]. Though he baled out of the Spitfire at 13,000 feet above Dorchester, he did not manage to sort out the cords and activate the chute until only a thousand feet from the ground.

Wolton picked off one of the Junkers Ju.88 that wrecked the Vickers Supermarine Works at Woolston, Southampton — the main centre for Spitfire production — with 70 tons of bombs [26 September 1940]. The kill fell into the sea off the Isle of Wight.

Following the Battle of Britain he was posted to the Central Flying School, Upavon, to become an instructor. Then taught Polish pilots, at Newton, and was later attached to 417 Squadron of the United States Army Air Force, training them to fly British Beaufighter night-fighters.

He survived the war and retired from the RAF as Flight Lieutenant [1948].

Woodsford Aerodrome — RAF Woodsford, a grass airfield of three runways at 207-feet above sea level on a gravel plain four miles east-south-east of Dorchester (Ordnance Survey map reference SY 760 885) was established by Flying Training Command for its School of Air Firing [May 1937]. It was renamed RAF Warmwell, in which parish it also lies, because unlike Woodsford that has an identifiable and findable village [July 1938].

Wool crash — Brigadier D.V.L. Allott, the Commandant of the Royal Armoured Corps Centre, was killed in a helicopter crash at Bovington Camp [14 May 1969].

Woolley — former Naval pilot **Lieutenant Robert Edward Martin "Bob" Woolley** [1942-69] left the Fleet Air Arm [1968] to fly with the Fleet Requirements Unit operated by Airwork Services Ltd from Hurn Aerodrome. He would be killed, when flying a Gloster Meteor, returning from a training flight at RNAS Yeovilton. It crashed into a hillside north of Winterborne Houghton [13 February 1969]. His home was at Lacy Drive, Wimborne.

In his career with the Royal Navy [1961-68] he had flown a variety of aircraft, including Sea Vixens with 893 Squadron on HMS *Victorious*, during its commission to the Far East [1963-64]. He also qualified as a flying instructor for the Hawker Hunter.

Wootton Fitzpaine crash — north of the road to Monkton Wyld, of Hurricane N2434 of 56 Squadron from RAF Boscombe Down, during dog-fights following the Luftwaffe attack on Sherborne [16.30 hours, 30 September 1940]. Though wounded in his right knee, Sergeant Pilot Peter Hutton Fox was able to bale out successfully.

Worth Aerodrome — known as Swanage Aerodrome, opened with a flying display [16 August 1928] and was located on The Plain between Worth Matravers village and St Alban's Head. Inspired and maintained by veteran flyer Lieutenant-Colonel Louis Strange who lived at Worth.

Worth Matravers — **RAF Worth Matravers** [1942-70] came into being in buildings vacated by the Telecommunications Research Establishment, as a link in the Gee Chain navigation system. Its ten national transmitting stations, operating in pairs, provided accurately timed radio pulses. Differences in arrival time between the signals enabled the aircraft's position to be determined by its navigator intersecting hyperbolic lines on a pre-printed Gee lattice chart.

The system "revolutionised the effectiveness of RAF bombing raids" with "targets being found and bombed as never before". By the late 1960s, however, the Ministry of Defence announced that other ground-based navigation aids and airborne systems had effectively replaced Gee, leading to the standing down of the system and demolition of its tall aerials.

No.407 Signals Unit operated from the Purbeck station.

Worth Matravers crashes — Miles Magister P6362 of 32 Maintenance Unit of the Royal Air Force dived into the top of the Purbeck cliffs half a mile south-west of the Telecommunications Research Establishment, in a field on the north side of Emmetts Hill [14 September 1940].

A Messerschmitt Bf.109 belonging to Lehrgeschwader 2, a unit testing improvised aircraft under operational conditions, came down following engine failure whilst on a weather reconnaissance flight [30 November 1940]. Unteroffizier Paul Wacker belly-landed at Woodyhyde Farm. The tail section of his machine survives, having been used to repair the captured test-flown Bf.109 that is now in the Royal Air Force Museum, at Hendon.

Wellington X9677 of 218 Squadron from RAF Marham, Norfolk, crashed into the sea off St Alban's Head whilst on a bombing mission to Bordeaux [10-11 October 1941]. Three members of the crew were picked up by lifeboat but the other three drowned.

Hit by anti-aircraft fire from an escort vessel, Luftwaffe ace Oberleutnant Werner Machold, Staffelkapitan of the 7th Gruppe of Jagdgeschwader 2 Richthofen, turned his Messerschmitt Bf.109E landwards and successfully crash-landed among the stone workings at Worth Matravers [6 June 1941]. He was taken into captivity as was his fighter, for inspection by the Royal Aircraft Establishment, Farnborough, on account of its improved Zusatz-gear mechanism which fed nitrous oxide to boost the engine power.

WX — squadron code of 302 (Poznanski) Squadron, flying Mark IIb Hurricanes [5 September-11 October 1941] and then Mark Vb Spitfires [27 April-1 May 1942], from RAF Warmwell.

Wynford Eagle crash — at Shatcombe Farm, of Spitfire N3039 from RAF Warmwell, which had been crippled by enemy fighters following the Luftwaffe attack on the Westland Aircraft Factory at Yeovil [16.30 hours, 7 October 1940]. It burst into flames on impact and though he was pulled from the wreckage Pilot Officer Harold John Akroyd of 152 Squadron, based at RAF Warmwell, died the following day from burns.

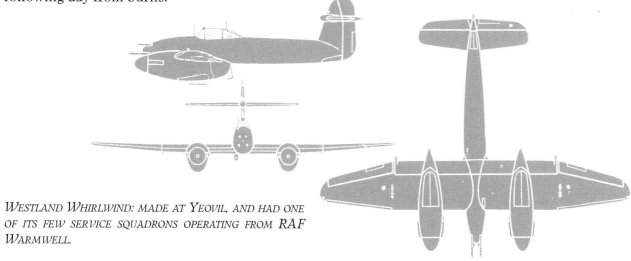

WESTLAND WHIRLWIND: MADE AT YEOVIL, AND HAD ONE OF ITS FEW SERVICE SQUADRONS OPERATING FROM RAF WARMWELL.

X

X serial numbers of RAF aircraft:

X4107 Spitfire — see entries for Cheselbourne crashes and Miller.

X4472 Spitfire — see entry for Sutton Waldron crash.

X4586 Spitfire — see entry for Dundas.

X9677 Wellington — see entry for Worth Matravers crashes.

X9785 Wellington — see entry for Powerstock crash.

XC — pundit code for RAF Christchurch, on ten feet high white letters at the airfield and flashed at night in red light Morse code, from a Pundit mobile beacon some miles from the station.

X-Gerat — known also as Wotan I, being the German radio direction beam used by pathfinders of Kampfgruppe 100 [1940-41], against which countermeasures were successfully developed by the Telecommunications Research Establishment, Worth Matravers, in time to foil a raid that would have devastated the crucial Rolls-Royce aero engine works at Derby [8 May 1942].

XM — squadron code of 182 Squadron, flying rocket-firing Typhoons on cross-Channel missions from RAF Hurn [1 April-20 June 1944].

XP — squadron code of 174 (Mauritius) Squadron, flying Mark IIb Hurricane "Hurri-bombers" from RAF Warmwell [1-21 September 1942].

XT — pundit code, in letters on the ground and in Morse code lights at night, of RAF/USAAF Advance Landing Ground Winkton, near Christchurch.

XW — pundit code for RAF Warmwell, on ten feet high white letters at the airfield and flashed at night in red light Morse code, from a Pundit mobile beacon some miles from the station.

FIRST ARRIVAL: WITHOUT KNOWING IT, THE PILOT OF THIS HANDLEY PAGE HARROW BOMBER IN DIFFICULTIES IN 1937 MADE HIS SUCCESSFUL FORCED LANDING, BESIDE THE A303 ROAD, IN PASTURES THAT WOULD BE REQUISITIONED IN 1939 FOR YEOVILTON ROYAL NAVAL AIR STATION WHICH BECAME OPERATIONAL IN JUNE 1940.

"FLY NAVY": THE MOTTO OF THE FLEET AIR ARM ON THE ROOF OF THE REFURBISHED CONTROL TOWER AT RNAS YEOVILTON IN 1985. ITS TYPE 965 RADAR SCANNER HAD BEEN REMOVED FOLLOW THE INSTALLATION OF PRECISION APPROACH RADAR. THE "T" ON THE SIGNAL SQUARE INDICATES THE ACTIVE RUNWAY.

Y

Yeovilton Royal Naval Air Station — the oldest air station of the Royal Navy which has remained fully operational, since being commissioned as shore base HMS Heron just before the Battle of Britain [June 1940]. Its presence on the edge of the Somerset Levels only four miles north-west of the Dorset village of Trent (Ordnance Survey map reference ST 545 235) has dominated post-war military aviation across much of both counties. Not only were night interceptor fighters based there after the Second World War but it went on to become the principal training base for helicopter crews and the "working-up" of squadrons for secondment to aircraft-carriers, including those which went to war at Suez [1956], the Falkland Islands [1982], and in the Gulf [1991]. Most of their comings and goings have been across west Dorset and Lyme Bay. A succession of older aircraft also cross Dorset, en route to air shows and commemorative events, from the Royal Navy Historic Flight. This was established [1972] as a separate entity to the Fleet Air Arm Museum which was established by Rear-Admiral Percy Gick and Commander Robin Foster, being formally opened by the Duke of Edinburgh [29 May 1964].

The development and expansion of the base, modernising its runways, was for the Christchurch-built Sea Venom and is described here under the entry for de Havilland.

Y-Gerat — also known as Wotan II, being the German radio direction target finding system deployed across Dorset by the pathfinding 3rd Gruppe of Kampfgeschwader 26, whose aircraft carried the cross on the rear fuselage [1940-42]. It transmitted from the Hague peninsula, north-west of Cherbourg, on 42.4 megacycles.

YO — squadron code of 401 (RCAF Ram) Squadron, briefly flying Mark IXb Spitfires from RAF Warmwell [24 October-4 November 1944].

PRESERVED SWORDFISH: W5984 ARMED WITH A TORPEDO AT THE FLEET AIR ARM MUSEUM, YEOVILTON, WHICH WAS A FAMILIAR SIGHT OVER POOLE HARBOUR WHERE ROYAL NAVY PILOTS TRAINED FROM SANDBANKS.

PRINCE CHARLES: THE "RED DRAGON FLIGHT" OF TWO WESSEX HU5 HELICOPTERS WAS FORMED WITHIN 707 ROYAL NAVAL AIR SQUADRON AT RNAS YEOVILTON IN 1974 FOR THE PURPOSE OF TRAINING LIEUTENANT HIS ROYAL HIGHNESS THE PRINCE OF WALES WHO THEN JOINED 845 SQUADRON WHERE HE IS SEEN WITH XT481.

ROYAL FLYPAST: DIAMOND FORMATION OF WESSEX HELICOPTERS OF 707 ROYAL NAVAL AIR SQUADRON, LED BY PRINCE CHARLES OVER RNAS YEOVILTON IN DECEMBER 1974, WITH THE TWO MACHINES OF "RED DRAGON FLIGHT" STREAMING THE ROYAL STANDARD (RIGHT) AND THE WHITE ENSIGN (CENTRE).

WESTLAND WESSEX: RESCUING AN IMMOBILISED HUGHES OH1 HELICOPTER IN AN EXERCISE AT BOVINGTON.

Z

Z serial numbers of RAF aircraft:

Z1312 Wellington — see entry for Fifehead Magdalen crash.

Z3349 Hurricane — see entry for Corfe Castle crashes.

Z4993 Hurricane — see entry for Weymouth crashes.

Zeals Aerodrome — just over the Wiltshire border, a mile north-east of Bourton which is Dorset's most northerly parish (Ordnance Survey map reference ST 780 330). Provided by the Air Ministry for 10 Group Fighter Command [May 1942] and then handed over to the United States Army Air Force [August 1943].

British night-fighters continued to operate from it and were active above Dorset, with coverage being provided by the Mark XIII Mosquitoes of 488 (New Zealand) Squadron [12 May-29 July 1944], 410 Squadron [18 June-28 July 1944] and 604 Squadron [25-28 July 1944].

William Rumbold, in retirement at Wincanton, recalled his arrival at RAF Zeals [24 May 1944], just five days after his daughter, Carol, had been born in a dilapidated cottage at Yarlington, Somerset:

"I had driven a load of aircraft spares up from Romney Marshes and they turned out to be the wrong sort. They were for Tempest aircraft instead of for Mosquitoes. After a day or so I had taken them back to Dimchurch. A week went by and I got posted to Zeals, and joined 488 Squadron. I joined up with the rest of the MT section. There were seven LACs and a Corporal.

"The MT section had to supply drivers on 24-hour shifts which meant that they had to drive the flight wagon, take the CO wherever he wanted to go, to fill up the aircraft from the tanker from the petrol bowsers. We were in two teams.

"At the end of my 24 hours I would get on my bike and cycle down to Gambles the builders in Bourton where I had worked before I was called up. Harry Cross was a Gambles' driver. He would give me a lift to Wincanton and I would then cycle on to Yarlington. I had to be back by 7.30 the following day to take over. Sometimes, Ernie Welder, my mate who was on the opposite shift to me, would drive the flight wagon to Yarlington to pick me up. We would have been up the creek without a paddle if we had ever been found out but fortunately we never were.

"The ground crew at Zeals consisted of New Zealanders, Canadians, Scots, Welsh and English. The air crew were mostly New Zealanders. All the ones I met were gentlemen. We were all treated as equals. The engineering officer Flight-Lieutenant Norman was a clever man. We all got the impression that he was a friend of Geoffrey de Havilland, the maker of the Mosquito.

"In the time that we were at Zeals the squadron downed thirteen German aircraft. We left Zeals for Colerne, where the squadron was supplied with a more updated Mosquito which was fitted with four 20-mm cannon. We thought we were the best squadron in the Royal Air Force! We knew we were.

"I enjoyed my stay with 488 Squadron and finished up in Holland when I got sent to a unit in Brussels, a base radar and repair unit, which I didn't like very much because I didn't think they had been anywhere. I came out of the RAF in 1945 and returned to Yarlington where my wife and I did up an old thatched house. We did it up and stayed there for about 18 months, almost rent free as it was derelict when we went in. When Miss Wright-Rogers let it again it was for £5 a week, which was a lot of money back then."

After the departure of the Mosquitoes, with the European war moving eastwards, the new priority became the training of aircraft-carrier flight crews for the Japanese conflict. The base passed to the Fleet Air Arm and was named HMS Humming Bird [April 1945]. It closed as soon as the last ships returned from the Pacific [January 1946]. Pundit code "ZL".

RAF ZEALS: THE PERIMETER TAXI-WAY PASSING INTO HISTORY IN THE 1970S, WHEN GRAHAM SWANSON OF NEARBY SEARCH FARM AT STOURTON REGARDED THIS AS A COMMENDABLE EXAMPLE OF "SWORDS TO PLOUGH-SHARES".

Zero — 112-feet SSZ type of Admiralty airship, based in Dorset during the latter part of the Great War, [1917-18], with mooring stations at Upton, in the parish of Lytchett Minster, at Moreton in the Frome valley, and on the hills above Powerstock. Though only armed with a Lewis gun its presence could prove deadly to U-boat commanders as the gunner also doubled as wireless operator. His prime role was to call and direct surface warships. Each flight could remain airborne for ten hours and their observations effectively kept enemy submarines underwater where they were no longer a threat to Allied shipping. Being weightless, they were tricky to manoeuvre and moor on the ground, with the result that each mooring point was provided with a pit — 30 feet wide and of similar depth — for the gondola and engine, to minimise wind resistance by bringing the supporting envelope to ground level.

ZH — squadron code of 266 (Rhodesia) Squadron, flying rocket-firing Typhoons on cross-Channel missions from RAF Hurn [13-20 July 1944].

ZL — pundit code of RAF Zeals, in large white letters on the airfield and flashed in red light Morse code at night.

Zuraskowski — Spitfire pilot **Pilot Officer Janusz Zurakowski** [born 1914] transferred from 234 Squadron to 609 Squadron at RAF Middle Wallop [4 October 1940] and was then stationed at RAF Warmwell. He survived the war, leaving the service as Squadron Leader, and became a test pilot for Gloster Aircraft [1950] and then chief test pilot for Avro's Canadian division [1952] where he settled.

ZY — squadron code of 247 (China-British) Squadron, flying rocket-firing Typhoons on cross-Channel missions from RAF Hurn [24 April-20 June 1944].